Crisis
Communications

Also by Steven Fink

Nonfiction

Crisis Management: Planning for the Inevitable

Sticky Fingers: Managing the Global Risk of Economic Espionage

Fiction

The Hailing Sign

Crisis
Communications

THE
DEFINITIVE GUIDE
TO MANAGING
THE MESSAGE

STEVEN FINK

NEW YORK   CHICAGO   SAN FRANCISCO
LISBON   LONDON   MADRID   MEXICO CITY   MILAN
NEW DELHI   SAN JUAN   SEOUL   SINGAPORE
SYDNEY   TORONTO

1 2 3 4 5 6 7 8 9 10   DOC/DOC   1 8 7 6 5 4 3

ISBN 9781265849696

MHID   1265849692

eISBN 978-0-07-179922-5
eMHID   0-07-179922-2

Library of Congress Cataloging-in-Publication Data
Fink, Steven.
   Crisis communications : the definitive guide to managing the message / by Steven Fink. — 1 Edition.
      pages cm
      ISBN 978-0-07-179921-8 — ISBN 0-07-179921-4
1. Crisis management.   2. Public relations—Management.   I. Title
   HD49.F5596 2013
   658.4'056—dc23

                                                                          2013002324

McGraw-Hill books are available at special quantity discounts to use as premiums and sales promotions, or for use in corporate training programs. To contact a representative please e-mail us at bulksales@mcgraw-hill.com.

"What we've got here is failure to communicate."

—from *Cool Hand Luke*

Contents

■   ■   ■

Preface

"Fortune Favors the Bold"

■　■　■

Some years ago, I wrote *Crisis Management: Planning for the Inevitable*, the first book ever written on the subject. It took the position, as the subtitle boldly asserts, that today, a crisis in business is as inevitable as death and taxes; it is not a question of *if*, but rather *when*. The passing years have only reinforced that ironclad belief, and I daresay the universe—bolstered by sad history lessons and a veritable graveyard littered with companies and managers that have fallen victim to all manner of crises—agrees with me.

In that book, and at that time, I believed that I had included everything that needed to be said about crisis communications. In fact, I devoted two full chapters to the subject, one subtitled "Controlling the Message" and the other "Handling a Hostile Press." At the time, that was sufficient.

But that was before the Internet explosion and the advent of never-ending 24/7 news cycles, cell phone videos, the runaway profusion of still emerging social media, ever-lurking-in-the-bushes paparazzi, blogs and websites devoted to "gotcha" journalism, and electronic mob-mentality consumerism/activism. There was a time when a client of mine could make a verbal gaffe to a reporter in the morning and I had time to "correct" the statement and "rehabilitate" the client before the afternoon news cycle began and the client's ill-chosen words got out in print or made the evening news. Those halcyon days are long gone, never to return.

The truth is, even the phrase "24/7" sounds antiquated today. We're really talking about an instantaneous, live news stream; you can't use the word *cycle*, since that implies a beginning, an end, and a restart. And woe to any company whose crisis communications strategy is not prepared for that phenomenon, especially since in this current paradigm, where risks have magnified exponentially and where news and pseudonews break in the blinking of an eye, the risk of inaccuracies and resulting damage to businesses and reputations—real or imagined—is huge.

Also, there seems to be a new generation of business leaders (and politicians and celebrities, too) who think that they're above the strict laws of crisis communications or think that they're smarter than a horde of ravenous, take-no-prisoners reporters and cell phone videographers. They think their verbal gymnastics skills can extricate them from any trouble they find themselves in, especially trouble of their own making. Or worse, they clam up, adopt a bunker mentality, and refuse to talk to the media or to their constituencies when that is exactly what they *should* be doing. What these so-called leaders and newsmakers fail to realize is that reporters are smarter than they are—and they *always* have the last word. Even if you believe that's not true, it's more prudent to act as though it were. As some wise wag once quipped, "Never pick a fight with anyone who buys ink by the barrel."

Today, that old saw could be updated to, "Never pick a fight with anyone who buys bandwidth by the geobyte."[1]

Benchmarks in crisis management and its important counterpart, crisis communications, have been well established and long recognized as essential corporate business disciplines since 1979, the year of the infamous Three Mile Island nuclear accident. According to the *New York Times*, it was during that then-unprecedented disaster and near catastrophe that modern-day corporate crisis management was born. It was then that the world first saw a side-by-side comparison of both good and bad crisis management and crisis communications in the form of the management and communication skills of the Office of the Governor of the Commonwealth of Pennsylvania (the former) and the Metropolitan Edison utility company, the nuclear plant operator (the latter). In fact, the utility company's crisis communications pronouncements were so problematic, so misleading, and so frightening to the public at large that the White House took the unprecedented step of gagging the company by ordering it to stop issuing *any* public statements on anything to do with the accident or the crisis response that was underway.

While the utility company *may* have been able to manage the crisis in time, its abysmal crisis communications were so badly flawed that utility company management made a bad situation worse, made a frightening situation horrific, and needlessly scared the hell out of millions of people within and outside of Pennsylvania. The company's statements, especially those that the news media immediately proved to be false or less than accurate in failed attempts to placate raw and legitimate terror, only served to further panic and inflame the population of the state and surrounding regions and overshadowed anything positive that the utility may have been able to do to deal with the crisis. Met-Ed's abject failure in the art of crisis communications robbed it of any shred of credibility that it had once had, and essentially neutered the utility giant and sent the nuclear industry back to the Stone Age.

Shortly thereafter, the Nuclear Regulatory Commission stripped the company of its operating license and refused to allow it to restart a perfectly good undamaged reactor (which had been in a cold shutdown for routine maintenance at the time of the accident) sitting alongside the damaged reactor. Why? Essentially because the company had so badly misled the public with its feeble and misleading attempts at crisis communications that all confidence in the company's ability to manage the undamaged reactor with competence and integrity had been lost. It didn't help that postaccident investigations revealed that some plant personnel had cheated on their tests to become licensed operators of a nuclear power plant.

Since that time, crisis management and crisis communications pioneers have carved well-traveled paths with many clearly marked signposts along the way to guide companies safely through the deadly minefields that almost any crisis offers. So today, when a company stumbles badly in dealing with a crisis, the public and the media are quick to criticize or praise, as appropriate, because they have a long history of past crises with which to compare and contrast the company's response. Thus, it is easy for the public (including shareholders) and the media to keep score of how a company acquits itself (or fails to do so) when trouble brews, and the public is a tough grader.

Famed former New York City mayor Ed Koch used to greet voters with the catchphrase, "How'm I doing?" and Big Apple denizens would tell him, usually without hesitation and with much gusto. When a company falls victim to a crisis, it may not go around channeling Mayor Koch, but stakeholders are answering the unasked question just the same.

And more than ever, the accepted method by which companies are graded is by their crisis communications skills.

That is why it is so critical for managers and executives at all levels, "average" businesspeople and business owners, educators, anyone who invests in the stock market, and even the media to dis-

sect, understand, study, and learn from crisis communications successes and failures, especially the failures.[2]

Most of us are not CEOs of Fortune firms, so why is it essential for
us to analyze the lamentable utterances of a crisis-riddled company like BP during its epically ill-fated Gulf of Mexico oil spill, for
instance? How relevant are those examples for the rest of us? After all, how likely is it that any of us might one day find ourselves
in a similar position?

Actually, if history is any indicator, the odds are quite high, and
we don't have to be in the oil business; we just have to be *in business*.
And we don't even have to be a CEO; we just need to have "constituents" (customers, shareholders, lenders, elected officials, government regulators, investors, employees, subordinates, colleagues,
and so on). The SIC codes and types of industries may vary from
company to company, as may the size of the business, but the common denominators are universal, just like crises. The point is clear:
at some time, *every* company—large or small, publicly traded or privately held—will find itself mired in a crisis of *some* kind and have
some communicating to do. It's only a matter of time and of degree.

And how that crisis is managed—*and how the management of that
crisis is communicated*—often spells the difference between the life
and death of the company, the rise and fall of its stock price, and the
hero or goat label attached to management. Crisis communications
defines a company, for better or worse, and for many years to come.

Make no mistake, the ripple effects of poor crisis communications are far-reaching and can disrupt lives, livelihoods, stock
prices, shareholder value, employees, employee morale, the company's image, management's reputation, the firm's ability to conduct
business, its ability to obtain credit, and on and on; it can also lead to
loss of jobs or loss of business, as well as triggering media exposés,
litigation, hostile takeover battles, government oversight and investigations, labor woes, legislative hearings, and so much more. All
this can happen in a heartbeat, all with the slip of a tongue.

And if a poorly handled and communicated crisis at a publicly traded company can drive down stock prices, it is no exaggeration to say that in a crisis, a skilled crisis communicator can stabilize, if not boost, stock prices.

In short, regardless of the different types of business that you and they may be in, the crisis communications missteps of leaders that we will discuss in this book demonstrate that in a crisis, every word and every action counts—for you or against you.

In particular, managers at all levels (especially those who aspire to rise on the corporate ladder) need knowledge that will give them an edge in business and an edge over their company rivals. Crises produce many phenomena: fear, panic, analysis paralysis, acute stress, uncertainty, insecurity, and a host of other angst-filled hallmarks. A crisis also needs people to serve on crisis management and crisis communications teams, either formalized or ad hoc, and CEOs look for managers who can keep their wits about them and help the company's leaders make vigilant decisions during chaotic times. It is my hope that these lessons will prove an important arrow in your management quiver.

Good crisis communications can stave off crises or manage the perception of a crisis effectively when one occurs. Moreover, a company that handles its crises well typically emerges a better, stronger, and more respected company and management team than it was before. And it's crisis communications that seals the deal.

The stakes in a crisis today are higher than ever, and stakeholders are holding company management's feet to the proverbial fire for poor performance in a crisis, especially when crisis communications missteps cause a plunge in shareholder value or loss of company prestige. Heads have rolled for poor management performance and worse communications in a crisis.

Consequently, if a company or a management team's crisis communications skills are dull or, worse, nonexistent, this book may head off disaster. From my unique vantage point, I can see that the mistakes made by companies today are easily correctable and downright preventable. Together, we'll examine some glaring examples, and I will provide concrete instructions on what *should* have been done and said in those cases.

The seemingly nonstop media outpourings on so many crisis events are a clarion call for the need for a definitive book devoted exclusively to this subject. It is long overdue. Ultimately, remember, some day it will be *your* ass on the firing line. You will be the one who will have to face a bank of microphones while the flop sweat from your hairline trickles icily into your shoes. Do you think you are ready? Every time you see a fellow business executive do a face-plant in a public crisis communications setting, ask yourself how *you'd* have performed. Better? Worse? How do you know?

I first became intrigued with crisis management and crisis communications during and soon after my involvement in the aforementioned, highly acclaimed Three Mile Island crisis management team in the administration of then–Pennsylvania governor (and later U.S. attorney general) Dick Thornburgh. Why, I wondered, were we able to succeed when the utility company that owned the nuclear reactor had failed so miserably in its handling of the very same crisis? Perhaps it was as simple as different agendas and different mindsets. And perhaps it was more than that.

My subsequent research led to my first book on crisis management, and to my contention that both proactive and reactive crisis management can be taught, as long as companies have their sails set correctly before and during the ensuing storm. It is the companies that lack a moral compass or that allow themselves to be tossed about on the stormy seas of a crisis, when a firm and sure hand on the tiller is needed, that suffer the most.

It's not a fair game out there, and the odds are stacked against you from the start. There is so much riding on the outcome of almost any crisis these days, and the crisis-induced stress levels are so stratospheric, that otherwise coolheaded managers are afraid that *any* move they make may be a wrong one. When that occurs, analysis paralysis sets in, and the company suffers from inertia, which only compounds the problem. This offering is designed to help level the playing field, if not tilt it in your favor.

Crisis communications has become a blood sport. It is not for the faint of heart. Play at your own risk; ignore the advice that follows at your own peril. And when it is your turn to don the armor (and your turn *will* come; it is inevitable), keep uppermost in your mind Virgil's sage advice: *"Fortune favors the bold."*

—*Steven Fink*

You Can't Make This Stuff Up

■ ■ ■

"I 'd like my life back."

With those five whiny words at the height of one of the planet's worst environmental crises, one of the world's most successful CEOs cracked publicly under the strain of crisis-induced stress. That pathetic plaint forever sealed his reputation as a seemingly unfeeling, gaffe-prone dunderhead whose glamorous, jet-setting lifestyle was inconvenienced by the tragic loss of 11 lives during a massive oil rig explosion, the resulting runaway oil spill in the Gulf of Mexico, and the heartbreaking loss of livelihoods for countless thousands of area families—all caused by his company, his minions, and their combined sins. That one ill-chosen utterance, in full view of the world's media,[1] at once thrust former BP head Tony Hayward into the pantheon of such other insensitive, kindred luminaries as Marie ("Let them eat cake") Antoinette and Emperor ("Hand me my fiddle") Nero. Did Hayward fiddle as the Gulf of Mexico was engulfed in oil and flames? In a manner of speaking: he went sailing on his luxury yacht half a world away, while the ashes of his self-immolated image were blown out to sea.

What kind of crisis communications message was Hayward intending to convey to the world? How does such a successful and accomplished executive crumble so completely on the world stage of a megacrisis? Was it ineptitude, fear, or lack of crisis communications training that allowed him to turn a worldwide crisis into a "What about *me*?" moment?

But Hayward—a complete novice in the art of crisis communications—was on a roll and was only just getting started. In fact, it was nearly impossible to stop him. He later "guesstimated" publicly that the spill was averaging a mere 5,000 barrels a day ("A guesstimate is a guesstimate,"[2] he truculently sniveled in the face of demands for more accurate numbers) when the actual number was closer to 60,000 barrels a day, and he further pooh-poohed the environmental impact of the soon to be millions of barrels of oil awash in the Gulf as "very, very modest."[3] He also predicted that the spill would be "tiny" compared to the size of the ocean,[4] conveniently overlooking the fact that prevailing winds and unrelenting tides were driving the oil toward previously pristine shores, once-rich fishing areas, family-oriented recreational beaches, fragile marine and bird sanctuaries, and delicately balanced ecosystems. When the well was capped for good in August 2010 and the flow was permanently stemmed—more than three full and agonizing months after the drilling rig explosion—official government figures put the total spill at nearly five million barrels, or some 200 million gallons, making it the worst offshore oil disaster in U.S. history[5] and completely dwarfing the previous record holder, the *Exxon Valdez*, which struck a reef in Prince William Sound, Alaska.

"Very, very modest," indeed.

Meanwhile, testifying on live television before a congressional investigative committee, Hayward responded petulantly to a U.S.

representative who wanted to know what happened at the explosion of the deepwater oil-drilling platform, saying, "I don't know; I wasn't there."[6]

In response to direct congressional questions seeking more information and less obfuscation, his testimony included such cover-your-ass gems as, "I'm not a drilling engineer" or "actually qualified" in these matters, "I'm not a cement engineer," and "I'm not an oceanographic scientist."[7] It was becoming all too clear that Hayward was not a lot of things, including a competent crisis communicator. For someone who had served for years as head of oil exploration and production at BP before ultimately becoming CEO, Hayward went out of his way to portray himself as ignorant of any aspect of drilling operations. He even testified before a disbelieving Congress that he had "no prior knowledge of the drilling of this well, none whatsoever."[8]

But an angry Representative Henry Waxman, chairman of the House Energy and Commerce Committee, accused Hayward of blatant "stonewalling" and charged, "You have consistently ducked and evaded our questions."[9]

But even feigned ignorance is no excuse. If you're the CEO, you're paid to know. And in Hayward's case, he was paid plenty.

As a contributory consequence of all of the foregoing missteps, the stock value of BP, then the world's fourth-largest company, soon plummeted into an abyss deeper than its *Deepwater Horizon* oil-drilling rig. The beleaguered company lost $17 billion just in the second *quarter* of 2010, on top of the more than $32 billion it was forced to set aside for spill-related costs. At one point, BP's market value declined 40 percent and the company was forced to sell off valuable assets to help pay its mounting costs.

The passage of time hasn't helped the oil giant recover: in the second quarter of 2012, BP reported an additional loss of $1.4 billion.[10] A drop in the oil-slick ocean to a deep-pocket company like BP, maybe, but a disturbing trend indicating perhaps a deeper crisis.

But the silver lining for Mr. Hayward was that his fervent wish ultimately was granted: he got his life back. His board of directors removed him from office . . . although he was exiled to Russia.

Seriously.

The only relevant question was: what took them so long?

Even as he was exiting the oil-slick stage, the unrepentant Hayward still didn't know when to shut up, publicly bellyaching in a farewell interview with the *Wall Street Journal*, "I became a villain for doing the right thing."[11]

Shortly thereafter, upon the completion of the company's own internal investigation, he led an official corporate chorus of finger-pointing at other companies involved in the construction and maintenance of the rig. BP, by now the consummate poster child for failed crisis communications, fared little better in its corporate doublespeak, calling the accident "a complex and interlinked series of mechanical failures, human judgments, engineering design, operational implementation and team interfaces."[12]

But not our fault.

Then, in a sweeping settlement agreement with the U.S. government toward the end of 2012, BP agreed to pay a $4.5 billion fine, pleaded guilty to 11 felony counts related to the deaths of the workers on the oil rig, and pleaded guilty to one additional count of obstruction of Congress.[13]

Let's be clear: effective crisis communications would not have stemmed the flow of oil or cash, but it *would* have saved the company's image, its stock value, and its CEO and helped it survive this crisis with its reputation intact. Poor crisis management and even worse crisis communications have left the company reviled around the world and facing a mountain of litigation and cleanup costs that will take years and years and billions and billions of dollars to overcome.

Rehabilitating its badly tarnished image will take much longer.

The long, sorrowful travails of BP (formerly British Petroleum) are by now well known throughout the world. What is neither

well known nor well understood is how such a successful company could have self-imploded on such a grand and public scale.
No, I am not referring to the company's oil-rig disaster; I am talking about its total meltdown in its woeful crisis communications
efforts. An army of skilled surgeons would not have been able to
cure its epidemic outbreak of nonstop foot-in-mouth disease, led
by its feckless leader. It is permissible to ask without sounding
snarky: seriously, *what* was he thinking, and why didn't anyone
stop him?

Is this critique an unfair and undeserved "bashing" of a hapless
business leader? Not at all. In today's instant, 24/7 news media
paradigm, it is indefensible and inexcusable that BP unleashed on
the world such a loose and woefully unprepared cannon as Tony
Hayward. Businesses and the men and women who run them have
a fiduciary responsibility to be well versed and well trained in crisis management and crisis communications (see Chapter 32, "The
Failure of Business Schools," for more on this), especially since
public images and stock prices rise and fall on such utterances
and the perceptions they engender. It is almost inconceivable that
Hayward had received no instruction in crisis communications
during his corporate climb to the top of BP's ladder, which makes
his unfortunate display all the more puzzling. At a minimum, had
he learned nothing from watching scores of other companies in
crises over the years? A scorecard was needed to tell which was
gushing more, the well or his mouth.

Which begs the ultimate question: is Tony Hayward the sort of
unfeeling, uncaring, pompous, arrogant jerk he appeared to be on
any number of occasions? Going out on a limb here, I'd say: probably not. How is it possible, then, that this previously proven leader
of such a successful behemoth of a company could misspeak so
often and so publicly, and in ways that would heap shame, ridicule,
and public scorn on himself and the company he once led, result-

ing in a significant loss in personal and company prestige, credibility, and market value? Leaders like Hayward spend a lifetime in stressful business situations. What is it about sudden, unexpected, and *public* stress—such as that which is almost always associated with a crisis—that causes the wheels to fall off many companies' communications wagon? Do they choke, and if so, why?

Moreover, what are the critical lessons that managers today need to know in order to survive the ever-taxing gantlet of crisis communications challenges? Every time a company undergoes a public crisis that is widely reported in the media, prudent company managers and executives should put themselves in the picture and ask: How would *I* do in a similar situation? How would *our* company respond? Would *we* have done better? More pointedly, if a guy like Hayward and a company with the resources of BP can screw up *their* crisis communications so badly, what chance do *I* have?

The lessons in this book are designed to give you an excellent chance.

When you see some business leader making questionable—if not moronic—public pronouncements under the very real stress of a crisis, ask yourself what he's doing wrong and how *you* would handle it differently. This book will tell you, by word and by example, how crisis communications *should* be handled in order to survive all manner of crises, but it's a good learning exercise to second-guess the decisions and the public pronouncements of those in the crucible while safely ensconced at home in your den. After all, when it's *your* crisis, others will be judging you just as harshly.

In Chapter 3, we'll explore what Tony Hayward *should* have said—an important alternative for you to keep in mind when it's your crisis.

Defining Our Terms

■ ■ ■

First, though, let's define our terms.

People used to say that all the time; sadly, most don't these days, and we as a community are the poorer for it. A lack of up-front agreement on what a given discussion is about leads to ambiguities, confusion, and, at times, dissension—all of which I hope to avoid in this book, and you most assuredly want to avoid in dealing with a crisis.

For example, crisis management is *not* synonymous with crisis communications, and vice versa, even though far too many people use the terms interchangeably, sometimes with tragic results. There is a distinct and important difference between the two, and knowing that difference can be a lifesaver. More on this later.

So, let's define our terms:

> A *crisis* is a fluid and dynamic state of affairs containing equal parts danger and opportunity. It is a turning point, for better or worse. The Chinese have a word for this: *wei-ji*.[1]

Crisis management deals with the *reality* of the crisis. It is the actual *management* of the precarious situation that is rapidly unfolding. It is making swift and vigilant decisions, gathering resources, marshaling troops, and so on, sometimes under great stress and enormous time constraints, to resolve a pressing problem. It is (hopefully) gaining the upper hand over an event that could potentially cause great or greater harm to a company, its various publics, its employees, its stakeholders, and its bottom line. It is preventing the situation from escalating. It is, in short, the *reality* of what's going on—the actual management of the drama—often behind the scenes and far from public view. It is the steps taken by the crisis management team that will determine the ultimate outcome of the crisis.

Crisis communications is managing the *perception* of that same reality. It is telling the public what is going on (or what you want the public to know about what is going on). It is shaping public opinion.

Thus, crisis management deals with managing *reality*; crisis communications deals with shaping *perception*.

While this book will address both crisis management and crisis communications, its focus will be on the latter—shaping critical perceptions and opinions during a crisis. If a crisis is being managed well, the goal of effective crisis communications is to form the public's perception to match the reality. If the crisis is not being managed well, different strategies are required, which will be discussed.

It's the difference between being a thermostat and a thermometer. As Princeton's Cornel West once put it, "A thermostat shapes the climate of opinion; a thermometer just reflects it."[2] The thermostat of crisis communications, when done right, is transformative.

Ironically, after the BP well finally was capped, retired U.S. Coast Guard Admiral Thad Allen, who belatedly was put in charge of overseeing the crisis in the Gulf, summed up BP's efforts this way: "At the wellhead, I think they've done very well. What they are not good at . . . is one-on-one transactions with individual citizens. And I think that's where the biggest gap in performance has been and where the most improvement needs to take place."[3]

In short, even though BP, in Admiral Allen's professional assessment, may have been doing everything that was technologically possible to stem the oil flow and manage the reality of the crisis, the company failed miserably at its lame attempts at crisis communications, and that cost the company dearly. Because as essential as good crisis *management* is, in the end, crisis *communications*—or the lack thereof—is all the public remembers.

It is an immutable law that in the pitched battle between perception and reality, perception *always* wins.

THE ROLE OF PERCEPTION IN CRISIS PLANNING

The majority of our discussion is about using effective crisis communications strategies to generate positive perceptions of your company when it is in a crisis. But it is worth noting that some have examined the role that senior management's perception of the crisis plays in how the actual crisis is managed.

"The perception of crises may ultimately affect crisis outcomes,"[4] writes business communications professor John M. Penrose of San Diego State University. He believes that if the likely outcome of a crisis is positive and more controllable, the company is likely to include more team members in the resolution process, which will generate an increased of number of ideas and viable alternative options.

"On the other hand, the perceiving of a crisis as a threat will cause managers to limit the amount of information they consider," he writes. "Thus, perception has the potential to influence the extent to which an organization is willing to engage in crisis management activities."[5]

This seems to fit the classic definition of a self-fulfilling prophecy, and Penrose admits that more study is needed.

The fact remains that virtually any crisis, as stated earlier, may turn out either positive or negative. But since you don't know at the outset which it will be, it is incumbent upon prudent managers to devote all appropriate resources and consider all possible alternatives early so that a positive outcome is given a fair chance of prevailing.

Also, Penrose is in agreement with our overarching theme, "Crises can destroy a company's reputation in a concentrated time frame."[6]

Just ask BP.

3

What BP *Should* Have Said

■   ■   ■

Poor crisis communications actually has the power to make a crisis worse.

In BP's case, such demeaning, condescending, and anger-invoking phrases from the CEO as "I don't know; I wasn't there," and such smoke-screen attempts as "I'm not a drilling engineer or technically qualified engineer in these matters," "I'm not a cement engineer," and "I'm not an oceanographic scientist" heaped scorn and ridicule upon a once-admired company. Whom did Hayward think he was fooling? Those frustrating, anger-provoking, lawyer-like, admit-nothing responses were an insult to BP's public, its shareholders, the government, and, most especially, everyone who was affected by the spill. People had every reason to be infuriated with a company they viewed as either incompetent or dishonest.

So, what *should* Hayward have said?

That's really the essential question, and the one I get asked often by reporters during interviews and by audience members when I make speeches on crisis management and crisis communications. It is, after all, easy to sit on the sidelines and take cheap potshots at some clueless, deer-in-the-headlights executive, but in this book I intend to walk readers through what crisis-stricken companies and their CEOs *should* have said or done—and what readers *should* say or do—in actual crisis situations in order to gain control and help bring perception and reality into sync.

It's probably a good time to also ask: why do smart people (like Hayward) say such stupid things in crisis situations? Sometimes it's because they just choke or they're in uncharted waters and they're scared, or sometimes it's because they're actually stupid. But in my experience, it's often because of overly cautious lawyers.

I don't want to be accused of "lawyer-bashing," especially because I do so much work with lawyers on shared clients, but here's the situation: lawyers generally have the very important and often very difficult mission of keeping a company out of trouble. And, when a company gets into trouble, lawyers instinctively and by training try to keep the trouble from escalating. In a BP type of situation, that often means reducing liability or minimizing exposure to additional liability—no mean feat, I assure you. And any lawyer will tell you (correctly, by the way) that the less you say, the less chance there is that you will utter something that may haunt you later on, that may be hard to defend down the road, or that may increase a company's exposure to liability. So, lawyers try to keep their clients from saying anything that can be used against them or the company in court, in a deposition, or in the media.

But while that advice may be prudent in court, it's not always the best policy for the overall good of the company. It's the quintessential definition of a Pyrrhic victory: winning the battle (read: the litigation), but losing the war (read: public support, shareholder value, perceived credibility—the company).

The public is not stupid and can see right through a ruse of obfuscation, and when we're working with a client in a crisis, we sometimes have to ask ourselves, which does more *overall* harm— saying *nothing*, which makes it look as if we're hiding something, or saying *something*, which shows that we have compassion and are willing to communicate?

Remember that earlier quote from BP's internal investigation, in which the company called the accident "a complex and interlinked series of mechanical failures, human judgments, engineering design, operational implementation and team interfaces "? The underlying message—"It wasn't our fault"—was designed to spread the blame to try to reduce the company's liability. How many lawyers do you think had a heavy hand in crafting that tortuous statement? What do you think was the public's perception after having that line forced down their throats?

What the public wants to see in a crisis—especially a crisis that affects lives or public health and safety—is a knowledgeable leader or a skilled management team that is firmly in command of the rapidly unfolding events, not a milquetoast puppet of a manager whose every utterance looks for all the world as if he is being manipulated by an unseen hand. The former builds confidence and enhances the perception of a company that is in control of its actions and its fate, whereas the latter raises suspicion and depresses a company's stock value, employee morale, and overall reputation.

Look no further than former New York City Mayor Rudy Giuliani's crisis communications tour de force during the 9/11 terrorist attacks. New Yorkers with long enough memories will tell you that prior to the attacks, Giuliani was a lame duck mayor with abysmally low approval ratings who the voters were glad was on his way out. But on that fateful September morning and in the days and weeks that followed, Giuliani appeared to all the world as a take-charge mayor and a skilled crisis manager. His tough-guy/former federal prosecutor communications skills came to the fore, and his crisis communications prowess helped calm a panicked city and nation. Did Giuliani thwart the terrorists? Did he prevent another attack? No, of course not, but he presented the face of a tough leader who was in charge (you almost felt he wanted to challenge Osama bin Laden to a *West Side Story* knife fight in a dark New York City alley), and he helped create the much-needed *perception* that everything was going to be all right. People may still have been frightened, but they felt some degree of confidence from the perception that a leader was in charge.

Conversely, every time Hayward purported self-imposed ignorance (for example, "I'm not a drilling engineer"), he drilled himself and his company into a deeper hole. You could almost hear a lawyer whispering into his ear, "Don't admit to anything that could be used against us." But a guiding tenet of crisis communications, apparently lost on BP or suppressed by its lawyers, is this: when you're in a hole, *stop digging!*

Despite his self-professed lack of knowledge about drilling, Hayward actually graduated with honors in geology from Aston University in Birmingham, England, and then went on to earn a PhD in the same field from the prestigious University of Edinburgh. Ironically, his first job with BP in 1982 was as a rig geologist. He rose quickly and in 1990 became one of the then-CEO's assistants in the Exploration and Production Division, a division in which he was elevated to CEO in 2003. When he became CEO of the entire company in 2007, he had had 17 years of solid experience in all phases of the company's oil exploration and production operations, and nearly 25 years of experience with the company as a geologist in general. That sure sounds like the perfect guy to run an oil company, and the sort of person you'd want to have in charge of an oil-spill crisis.

So coming up with remarks that portrayed him as unknowledgeable about key drilling operations of the oil business was a ludicrous insult to our collective intelligence and painted him as either a fool, a liar, a lawyer's puppet, or all three. I understand why lawyers might have advised him to take that unenlightened path, but sometimes you have to look at the bigger picture and do the right thing for the benefit of your customers and your company.

While crisis communications is not an exact science and a public statement can always be tweaked here and there, Hayward would have been much better served by saying the polar opposite of the sum of his remarks, and saying it *early*. Something along these lines would have been a welcome balm for those suffering the most, as well as the rest of the world that was watching:

> I spent 17 years running various oil exploration and production operations for BP all over the world, and I was head of that global department for four years, just before being named CEO of the company three years ago. As you would expect, I know quite a bit about oil exploration, including deep-sea drilling procedures. Nevertheless, I cannot at this time tell you with certainty what caused this tragedy, and I'd rather not speculate while the investigation is underway. But you can rest assured that we will spare no expense in bringing to bear whatever specialists and resources are necessary to cap this well, clean up the spilled oil, and make whole those whose lives and livelihoods have been disrupted by this unfortunate accident. Moreover, I personally will oversee a thorough investigation to find out exactly what happened, why it happened, and what we can do to ensure that it doesn't happen again. If inadvertent mistakes were made or equipment failed, we will issue a full report and take corrective measures—not just because it is our legal obligation to do so, but also because it is our moral responsibility to do so. We also want other members of our industry—our competitors—to learn from any mistakes we or our subcontractors may have made so that this sort of tragedy is not repeated anywhere in the world. Moreover, we are not above asking our competitors for assistance if we feel that will be beneficial in resolving this crisis. This is not a time for finger-pointing, it is a time for action, and BP is up to the task, regardless of how long it takes. In the days, weeks, and months ahead, I ask you to judge us by our actions in ultimately making this right—for the environment in general, and for the good people of the Gulf Coast in particular.

Now, BP might still be in the mess it's in right now in terms of containment, cleanup, and costs, plus massive litigation, but at least the public's *perception*—and the company's stock price—would be loftier than it is now. And Tony Hayward might still be running the company.

Lawyers (especially BP's legal team) might try to poke some holes in my suggested statement, and I understand why: everyone likes to tinker. But in looking at the truly bigger picture, one can see that the issues here go far beyond mere litigation. The goal of crisis communications is to save the company, its employees, its management, its reputation, and its stock value. There will always be litigation, no matter what you do; count on it.

However, let's parse my suggested Hayward statement and see if there is anything in there that would make lawyers or anyone else unduly nervous.

The first few sentences merely cite Hayward's bona fides, which are public knowledge anyway, and then explain that it's still too early in the crisis to speculate on causes. In my version, he says:

> I spent 17 years running various oil exploration and production operations for BP all over the world, and I was head of that global department for four years, just before being named CEO of the company three years ago. As you would expect, I know quite a bit about oil exploration, including deep-sea drilling procedures. Nevertheless, I cannot at this time tell you with certainty what caused this tragedy, and I'd rather not speculate while the investigation is underway.

There's nothing there for lawyers to get too nervous about; it's a recitation of publicly known facts. Just because he knows "quite a bit about oil exploration" doesn't mean that he was the guy in charge of the *Deepwater Horizon* drilling operation in the Gulf. People want to see a knowledgeable leader who's in command of the situation; the alternative—a leader who knows nothing about his own business and professes ignorance—is risky and downright frightening.

Then I have him saying:

> But you can rest assured that we will spare no expense in bringing to bear whatever specialists and resources are necessary to cap this well, clean up the spilled oil, and make whole those whose lives and livelihoods have been disrupted by this unfortunate accident.

Isn't that what BP was doing anyway—trying to cap the well? Of course. This statement just makes the point more forcefully and proactively, illustrating that the company knows what it is doing and boosting the public's confidence in its ability to get the job done. The same is true of the line about making people "whole." BP and its insurance companies were always going to have to pony up big bucks—that was a given; everyone knew it—but saying it early, proactively, and in this context makes it seem as if it was BP's idea, rather than the U.S. government forcing the company to set aside $20 billion for cleanup costs and reimbursement to affected businesses in the Gulf. Had Hayward stated this early, it would have appeared more magnanimous on the company's part, rather than its doing it after the government had put a gun to BP's head, and the people of the entire Gulf region might have been more supportive of the company that was going to make them "whole." The way it actually played out, the government came off looking like the hero, and BP like the heavy. Given the general public's disdain for any form of government today, you've really got to screw up big time to have the government wear the white hat instead of you.

Then:

> Moreover, I personally will oversee a thorough investigation to find out exactly what happened, why it happened, and what we can do to ensure that it doesn't happen again. If

inadvertent mistakes were made or equipment failed, we will issue a full report and take corrective measures—not just because it is our legal obligation to do so, but also because it is our moral responsibility to do so. We also want other members of our industry—our competitors—to learn from any mistakes we or our subcontractors may have made so that this sort of tragedy is not repeated anywhere in the world. Moreover, we are not above asking our competitors for assistance if we feel that will be beneficial in resolving this crisis.

Again, there is nothing here that BP wouldn't be doing anyway. With a crisis this large, wouldn't the CEO be the guy who would oversee an investigation of this magnitude? Even if you, the CEO, don't do the actual heavy lifting, aren't your subordinates going to report to you? Certainly they are. So saying that you will oversee the investigation could be viewed by a cynic as merely stating the obvious, but if it were so obvious, why didn't Hayward take the initiative and say it himself first? The same can be said of the "If inadvertent mistakes were made or equipment failed, we will issue a full report and take corrective measures" phrase. Again, you're going to have to do this anyway, so why not get credit for your early resolve to do the right thing?

Now I can possibly foresee some lawyerly concern over the use of the word *mistakes*, even *inadvertent mistakes*, but I would point out that the phrase as written is conditional—"*if* inadvertent mistakes were made"—which is not the same as saying, "we made mistakes" or "we are responsible." But let's be realistic: there *will* be an investigation, and *if* mistakes were made or equipment failed, these things *will* be reported. Having Hayward say it early makes it a proactive company strategy and changes the perception from the negatively charged "government-ordered investigation." You always want to be perceived as being proactive, not reactive, in your statements and your actions.

And finally:

> This is not a time for finger-pointing, it is a time for action,
> and BP is up to the task, regardless of how long it takes. In the
> days, weeks, and months ahead, I ask you to judge us by our
> actions in ultimately making this right—for the environment in
> general, and for the good people of the Gulf Coast in particular.

After all, wouldn't you want the people in the Gulf to think this anyway, and to give you a chance to make things right, rather than rush to judgment? So why not boldly say it up front? Face it, no matter *what* you do or *what* you say, you're going to be judged. Proactive crisis communications can set the ground rules for that judgment: "Don't judge us until we've had some time to fix things." It's not an unreasonable request, and in the absence of such a request to buy some time, people will judge you—and harshly—from the outset. The way I've framed it, you might get some much-needed breathing room to figure out what happened and how to fix it before all the doomsayers emerge from the woodwork.

Of course, if you ask for and receive some breathing room, don't squander it; get busy so that you can report back to your constituents on your progress in a timely manner.

When you get right down to it, there really are only two plausible explanations for Hayward's many obfuscating statements: either he was muzzled by the lawyers or other advisors, or he really is that arrogant. I've already stated that I don't think Hayward was or is an unfeeling, arrogant dunderhead. That leaves only one possible alternative, and that can be a big problem in dealing with a crisis that has as one of its core components a loss of confidence in the company or the company's management.

One of the primary goals of any crisis communications strategy is to maintain or restore confidence in the company and its leadership. Anything or anyone that interferes with that key policy is doing you a disservice.

To be fair, Hayward eventually did make some of the comments I just outlined, but it took him two full months to do so, and it happened only when he was forced to testify before Congress. In fact, almost all of his comments were perceived as his having been dragged to the microphones by his ear, like a misbehaving boy being forced to apologize to his elders.

When you are faced with a situation in which people are verbally attacking you from all sides and saying things that you know or believe are not true, you owe it to your company and all its many stakeholders to publicly defend yourself and your company—and to do so fast! In a crisis, time is always of the essence. If you do not *properly* communicate in the early hours of a crisis, thus allowing others to set the agenda and put you on the defensive, the public's perception of you is going to start to stick and will drag you, your company, and your stock price down.

Being coy with your public, "lawyering up," and playing fast and loose with carefully and legally parsed comments will fly about as well as President Clinton's saying, "I did not have sex with that woman." The public does not like being taken for fools and has no patience for slick nuance.

Keep that in mind when we talk about attitude adjustments in the next chapter. Remember, the public *wants* to be on your side, it *wants* you to succeed when you're dealing with a dangerous crisis, it *wants* to believe your story, and it *wants* to believe that the situation is being handled properly, especially in threatening situations.

Try not to go out of your way to give the public a reason to dislike and distrust you.

4

Attitude Adjustments

■　■　■

S o, taken in its entirety, is my suggested statement for BP "snake oil"? Is it "spin"? Is it misrepresentation? Is it misdirection? Is it inaccurate? Is it false?

No.

It is simply and strategically making perception match reality. Remember, Admiral Allen himself—the federal government's designated on-scene expert—admitted that BP was doing a good job at the wellhead; my suggested statement just packages what was taking place already, or was about to take place, and presents it in a more positive and proactive light for BP. Thus, it makes perception come as close to reality as possible.

This is the essence of good crisis communications, and if you have trouble accepting this premise, it may be time for an attitude adjustment.

There are many elements at work in any given crisis, and chaos and confusion generally reign supreme, especially in a crisis of confidence. If a company is not struck dumb with fear, there may be bedlam, with different camps voicing opposing views of the best way to proceed. In Chapter 6, I will discuss some proven strategies designed to help companies separate the wheat from the chaff so that they can quickly focus on the most important aspects of a crisis and locate what I call the keystone crisis. And in Chapter 10, we will discuss what to do about sometimes misguided advice from the lawyers, who always seem to speak from a bully pulpit. But for now, in a crisis, whose advice will you follow when it comes to speaking out or remaining silent?

There is comfort and security in saying nothing; I know that.

Clients often make that argument to me, trying to persuade me that their desire to avoid the public limelight might be a prudent crisis communications strategy. It seems safe. If you say nothing, you can't be accused of saying the wrong thing or being tripped up by a sly reporter. Remaining mute, it might seem, keeps you from making matters worse. Staying silent prevents you from saying something today that you will regret tomorrow, especially when the inevitable litigation ensues. And perhaps most important to those who feel the very real effects of stress during a crisis, if you stay in the bunker, you won't have to face an angry mob of customers or shareholders or the media shouting questions at you.

This is wrong.

In a crisis, tongues will wag, ink will flow, bandwidth will be bustling, blogs will be bloated, online chat rooms will be swamped, tweets will follow and comment on your every move—no matter what you do or don't do. And all the talk will be focused on you, your company, and your crisis. Count on it.

But, will these discussions be accurate or inaccurate, favorable or unfavorable? In a vacuum, with nothing to counteract it, my money is on speculative, inaccurate, and unfavorable discussions.

Now, what is the likelihood that a litany of wild, heavily biased, and inaccurate stories will be good for your company, your employees, company morale, your stakeholders, or your company's stock value? Your 401(k)? Hmmm? Okay, those were loaded questions.

One more rhetorical question, though: if you subscribe to the theory that accurate, rather than inaccurate, information will be better for your company in a crisis, especially if it helps bring perception and reality together and demonstrates that competent people are managing the crisis competently, how will that accurate information get out to your constituencies if your company doesn't handle the task itself?

Moreover, if you* are a visible and recognizable source of solid information, the media and your other constituencies will have a place to turn for updates concerning wild, unconfirmed, and damaging rumors. You can actually position yourself to stem the flow of rumors and inaccurate stories *before* they get out.

This is *not* to suggest that you should shoot from the hip; you should be well and properly trained in dealing with the media in a crisis, you should have a short and targeted list of key message points that you want to convey, you should stick to those message points, and, if time allows, you should rehearse before "going public" in whatever form that takes. Don't wing it, and don't allow yourself to be ambushed. Get on the stage, speak your prepared lines, and have a viable exit strategy for leaving that stage—until you return with a further update on a fast-breaking crisis. We'll talk about what to say and how to say it later, but for now, merely adjust your attitude to the fact that as painful and as frightening as it might seem, *communicating in a crisis is the right thing to do if you want to survive.*

But wait . . . !

What if what you have to say is (gulp) *bad* news? Surely, you may ask, I don't mean to suggest that you actually go out there and tell people something *negative*, do you?

Yes.

---

* The use of *you* throughout this book means both you the reader and you the CEO or company manager, who may designate a competent spokesperson to be the person who speaks for the company. Exactly who that spokesperson should be will be covered later.

Reporting accurate and reliable information quickly and regularly is your best hope for long-term redemption, *especially* if the news is negative. If, for example, your constituents view you as a good company that had the misfortune to suffer an explosion, and you are openly and candidly reporting factual information, whether good or bad, the public's estimation of you will grow, not diminish.

Of course, there is a right way and a wrong way to present bad news, which we will discuss, but the fact remains that the alternatives are to lie, to say "no comment," to cover up, or to play dumb, and any of these strategies will come home to roost eventually. If bad news is going to come out—*and it will!*—I'd rather it come from me (or my clients), at a time and place of my choosing, and in the manner in which I want to present it. Remember, if someone else leaks the negative story and you are asked to comment on it, you are automatically on the defensive right from the start.

In a crisis, it is always better to play offense than defense.

Additionally, if there are equal parts danger and opportunity in a crisis, this is one place where the opportunity can emerge. Owning up to your or your company's missteps—especially if you announce corrective remedies at the same time—creates the perception of a stronger company. And sometimes that even means a financially stronger company.

It also helps demonstrate that the company is in control of its own destiny, and during a crisis that can lead to enhanced confidence in management.

Some years ago, for example, a unique joint study[1] by researchers at the graduate business schools of the University of Michigan and Stanford University looked at a stock price analysis of 14 companies over a 20-year period. Their illuminating findings showed that the shares of those companies that accepted most of the blame for their own negative outcomes outperformed the shares of those companies that placed most of the blame on external factors by between 14 and 19 percent, as reported at the time in the *Personality and Social Psychology Bulletin.*

The researchers found, for example, that when public companies took the blame for their own missteps and internalized it rather than trying to shift the blame externally, shareholders had more confidence that the company had within itself the ability to turn things around. Laying blame outside of the organization had the same effect as if the company said, *This event was out of our control . . . and therefore, since we are powerless to control it, it might happen again.*

"When being in control is conducive to positive outcomes, external attributions can be disserving," the authors write. "We suggest that making external attributions for negative events could be disserving for business organizations."[2]

In other words, mea culpas are good for the soul and sometimes even better for the bottom line, and finger-pointing during a crisis is a zero-sum game. If you or one of your advisors is advocating a "no comment" strategy, think again. It is hard any time to say you were wrong, and even more so when your actions could be quite costly to your company's bottom line. But if you are in this for the long haul, the short-term hit you may take may pay bigger dividends down the road if you have the public's trust on your side. So be sure to couple your mea culpa with a sound and well-articulated strategy for fixing the problem and the steps you will implement to ensure that it doesn't happen again.

In short, *never go "radio silent" in a crisis.*

5

Toyota: On a Slippery Crisis Communications Slope with No Brakes

■   ■   ■

Despite the many years that I've been managing crises for clients or consulting with companies that are going through crises, it still never fails to amaze me how many companies consider themselves immune to crises, or believe that whatever happens, they can handle it. Many of those companies, or the executives who once ran them, can be spotted along the side of the highway, labeled "roadkill."

The fact is, no company—no matter how well managed or highly regarded it is, and no matter how loyal its customers are— is immune to a crisis, which means that all companies need a solid crisis communications playbook. Just ask Toyota.

Question: how did Toyota—along with its luxury Lexus subsidiary—free-fall from grace so rapidly? Answer: nonexistent crisis communications helped speed the company's slide into late-night punch line lore.

The company spent decades and hundreds of millions of advertising dollars to burnish its reputation as the gold standard for automotive safety, reliability, value, and value retention, topping or placing near the top of the J.D. Power annual customer satisfaction surveys for years. Its competitors—and maybe even the company itself—began to believe that it could do no wrong. In fact, the *New York Times* once described Toyota, the largest automobile manufacturer in the world, as "engineering cars so utterly reliable that they seemed boring."[1]

That is, until reports began to surface that many of the company's cars had a glitch that caused unintended acceleration and a nagging inability to stop, even though the brake pedal had been firmly depressed. Numerous reports of car crashes, injuries, deaths, and property damage ensued, as did massive litigation, government investigations, congressional hearings, and media exposés. In 2010, Toyota plummeted to a lowly twenty-first position in the J.D. Power Initial Quality Study, a category it had previously dominated.

That would have been bad enough, but the company compounded the problem by playing fast and loose with the public and the truth. Company executives actively tried to minimize the severity of the crisis and—horrors!—ultimately blamed the company's customers for the problems. The last significant case of unintended acceleration happened to the long-departed Audi 5000 in the late 1980s, and that automaker saw its sales plummet by two-thirds, largely because of poor crisis communications with its customers, its potential customers, the government, the public at large, the media—hell, *everyone!* Audi also had publicly blamed its affluent, well-educated customers for confusing the brake pedal with the gas pedal, most devastatingly in a now classic *60 Minutes* interview with the late Ed Bradley. One problem with that interview, which mirrored the company's overall crisis communications messages, was that the car manufacturer assigned two highly analytical automotive engineers to the interview, rather than including someone from management who might offer a kind word of empathy for its customers' travails. Audi's argument was that its cars were safe, and therefore, only human error could account for the mishaps. But reality and perception were far apart.

A disturbing pattern quickly emerged in the Toyota crisis: every time the company issued one crisis communications statement or claimed to have fixed one particular problem, a new difficulty would pop up with another of its models. It seemed that the wheels had completely fallen off the company's crisis communications vehicle, pun intended.

The unintended acceleration problem was not new, as Toyota tried to spin the story initially. In fact, it was soon revealed that its customers had reported the problem as far back as three years earlier. But it seemed that with each passing day, Toyota reported a new and "ultimate" fix, from replacing sticking floor mats to shortening too large accelerator pedals to inserting a needed brake "shim" fix to updating faulty software for the cars' highly advanced—but highly complicated—electronics.

As sales of Toyota and Lexus vehicles nosedived, competing car companies—especially the Big Three Detroit carmakers—increased their own market shares by capitalizing on the Japanese automaker's misery, while savoring the sweet taste of schadenfreude and the onslaught of nonstop negative news aimed at the once-invincible Japanese carmaker. Toyota and Lexus were recalling cars by the millions (nearly four million at last count) and even stopped production on some models altogether. Worse, a lawsuit in August 2010 revealed that Toyota first knew of reports of sudden acceleration in its vehicles as early as 2003, *even though the company did not issue any recall notices for six years*. Profits in the relevant quarter were down some 39 percent.

And then "suddenly" there was a problem with the electronic braking system on Toyota's hybrid car, the Prius, leading to a worldwide recall of *that* once highly regarded brand.

And yet another new problem arose: in July 2010, the company recalled nearly 450,000 Toyota Avalons and Lexus LS 470 SUVs because of steering defects. More troubling, besides the obvious, is the fact that the models involved were from 2000 and 2003, respectively, once again begging the question: how long had the company known about and failed to address—or covered up, as it was accused of doing—safety problems? This was a legitimate crisis communications issue and one that the company never got its arms around. Instead, it tap-danced as more problems emerged.

Just one month later, Toyota recalled more than one million Corollas and Matrix cars after revealing that defective electronic engine control units could cause the car to stall while underway.

Was all this coincidence, or a massive breakdown in quality control? It is not credible to believe that these problems had just come to Toyota's attention, as the company publicly claimed in its pitifully inept crisis communications attempts. People— including those pesky congressional investigative committees that quickly got involved and levied record fines against the company— demanded to know how long the company had been aware of the ever-growing mountain of problems. In addition, the congressional committee summoned the head of the company, Akio Toyoda, to come from Japan to testify amidst the crucible of public outrage. Company spokespersons said one thing, but embarrassing documents leaked by anonymous insiders contradicted them.

"Clearly, Toyota has endured a difficult year,"[2] understated David Sargent, vice president of global vehicle research at J.D. Power and Associates, in trying to explain the auto manufacturer's unprecedented fall from grace and its bottom-scraping rankings.

Crises do not occur in a vacuum; they come in thundering herds. Toyota was quickly being trampled by a stampede of its own making, and the company's failed crisis communications strategies only increased the speed of the onslaught. In an ironic twist, it was most assuredly a case of unintended acceleration.

It is telling to note that the record fines levied against Toyota were paid without a whimper by the company, perhaps in tacit acknowledgment that it knew it had done wrong; at least, that was the perception of the message that was conveyed when the company paid a whopping $15 million fine without protest. Appealing the fine would only have served to further enflame the passions of its angry customers.

Remember that in a crisis, perception *always* trumps reality; in Toyota's case, the perception was bad, and it appeared that the reality was worse.

It was a fair question to pose: how many lives had Toyota knowingly risked by leaving its flawed cars on the road and failing to warn its customers that their lives could be in jeopardy?

And more to the point, how could a paragon of success and safety like Toyota have wound up in this perfect storm of a crisis? Was it a predicament of its own making (did Toyota knowingly put profit ahead of public safety?), or was the automotive behemoth merely a hapless victim of the often capricious winds of crisis gales? As with most crises, the answer is complex, but poor crisis communications lies at the heart of it; good crisis communications would have provided some much-needed salvation.

At no time did Toyota ever get a firm handle on its ever-growing crises and communicate with the world in a proactive way that conveyed that it was in charge. It was all reactionary, and the company was playing defense deep in its own end zone from the get-go.

With virtually every new wrinkle in its long-drawn-out crisis drama, it appeared that the company had again gotten caught in an attempt to cover up dangerous and damaging facts that it had known for years. Whether or not that was true is beside the point; that was the *perception*, and when perception and reality don't neatly mesh, perception is what people remember. Perception is what makes the lasting impression.

Then, a Transportation Department report in late summer 2010 seemed to exonerate the company somewhat. A government investigation that examined data from so-called black box record-ers from 58 Toyotas involved in reported cases of sudden accelera-tion showed that the brakes were never applied in 35 of the cases, and that the cars essentially had no safety defects that would cause sudden acceleration. Translation: the cars accelerated because drivers were stomping not on the brake pedals, but on the gas ped-als. In other words, *driver error.*

But wait! In mid-September came the news that Toyota's black boxes were not reliable—according to Toyota's own testimony in accident cases going back several years.

It is not at all unusual to find government regulators on oppo-site sides of an issue with a company they regulate, but now a new dilemma for the beleaguered car company was born with a bizarre twist: who should the public now believe—the government, which said that the black boxes indicated that the cars were in fact safe, or the company, which had earlier said that the boxes were unreliable?

The public is generally forgiving and willing to give a good com-pany a second chance, or more—provided the unspoken pact of honesty and trust between manufacturer and customer is not abro-gated. That is at the core of good crisis communications: the peo-ple with whom you're communicating must believe you or believe you are trying, or all bets are off. If facts are hard to come by and customers are demanding answers, your posture concerning the lack of facts is important. Do people think you are working hard to ferret out the problem? Toyota had previously been considered a great—not just good—company, but its abject failure to adequately communicate to any of its numerous constituents in a candid and believable way during the height of the crisis was hugely detri-mental to the company, and no one can say for sure whether Lexus will ever regain its prestige and the right to claim its "pursuit of excellence" slogan without people laughing.

However, one thing is certain: the only thing that got Toyota out of the media's crosshairs was the BP oil spill.

But for companies that can't rely on the capriciousness of another company's crisis to trump their own and provide much-needed cover, it's time to learn and practice the art of survival: crisis communications.

"Toyota's communication coordinators say the company never ducked problems, even as they wish they had been quicker to deploy top executives. 'We made lots of mistakes,' says Jim Wiseman, a communications executive at Toyota Motors North America. 'We could have been out there even more. We should have been. We're trying to take various actions to learn from this.'"[3]

Often, one of the biggest problems facing companies is getting them to own up to their own blunders. The reasons why are myriad, but at the heart of the problem is the gut-wrenching fear engendered by the huge stakes involved. Taking the charitable view, let's assume that businesses *want* to do "the right thing," but are afraid to do so because of the possible consequences: perhaps actual hard dollar costs or stock devaluation or negative media coverage or layoffs or even loss of one's own job—all legitimate concerns, to be sure.

This fear of loss is usually the leading cause of companies finding themselves behind the proverbial eight ball when a long-festering crisis is exposed. But some businesses may have been sweeping known problems or product defects under the carpet for so long that those obfuscation instincts are now so well ingrained that the company doesn't know *how* to "come clean."

It's harsh to call an otherwise good company an outright liar, but in a crisis, and realizing what's on the line, too many companies fall victim to what Winston Churchill once famously labeled as "terminological inexactitude."

And the longer it persists, the more terminal—literally and figuratively—this inexactitude becomes.

Toyota made numerous gaffes once it found itself on the slippery crisis slope, but in this global village, one key mistake was sending as its primary spokesperson a man who studied English as a second language (if that), just because he was the company CEO. Akio Toyoda's communications in general, to say nothing of his crisis communications skills, were AWOL.

While designating the CEO as the spokesperson in any crisis involving the loss of life, severe threat of same, or massive property damage (see Chapter 8 on spokespersons) is usually the right course of action, sometimes a foreign accent can be an impenetrable brick wall that keeps the speaker and his audience separated and at odds—especially in a contentious situation—simply because it underscores an unassailable fact: he's just not one of us. Toyota had a more than qualified head of U.S. operations here who could walk the walk and talk the talk. This crisis communications error can and should easily be avoided.

Toyota seemed to be forever playing defense. It was never able to (1) pinpoint the source of the problems or (2) offer remedies. And you may as well know now that there are crises for which there are no quick panaceas, but your customers and the government are demanding just that. In such instances, you need to take the public into your confidence and report on the tests you've conducted, all of which have so far failed to reach a conclusion. Explain what you are trying so as to at least give the public a fighting chance to get on your side by showing people how diligently you're working to *try* to solve the problem. If the public has the impression that you're trying to help, that's half the battle. In Toyota's case, the perception was that whatever the source of the troubles, the company had known for some years that it had a series of major problems—and never reported them. To anyone.

In short, the takeaway of Toyota's crisis communications messages was that not only wasn't it "one of us," but it didn't even care about us or our safety.

It just kept selling cars and burnishing that preeminent J.D. Power ranking.

Then, in the summer of 2010, another omission was brought to light: problems with steering wheel relay rods, causing the *New York*

Times to editorialize: "Toyota Still Doesn't Get It."[4] Even though the company recalled some 330,000 cars in Japan that suffered this steering problem, it never reported this to its American car customers because it had had no similar complaints from its U.S. customers. Nevertheless, the following year, Toyota notified the National Highway Transportation Safety Administration and quietly issued a voluntary recall of more than one million of its U.S. cars.

In fairness to Toyota, it must be noted that two years later its image problems seemed to have dissipated, even though at the end of 2012 the company paid more than $1 billion to settle the class action suit dealing with the sudden acceleration matter—the crisis that started Toyota's spiral. The same year, Toyota was once again the top performer in a J.D. Power survey of vehicle dependability and had overtaken General Motors to once again become the world's top automobile seller, demonstrating that there is life after crisis. And that is a lesson not to be forgotten.

But better crisis management and crisis communications could have avoided most of the drama and the damage to its reputation.

Understanding *Your* Crisis

■ ■ ■

Before you can even begin to think about communicating during a crisis, there are three absolute imperatives that must be undertaken in any crisis situation:

- Identify *your* crisis.
- Isolate *your* crisis.
- Manage *your* crisis.

IDENTIFY

How hard can it be to identify a crisis when it's happening to you or your company? Actually, it's harder than you might think. Or, if not hard, then perhaps tricky is a better descriptor of the trouble managers often encounter. But note the emphasis on the pronoun *your*; that's significant.

Sometimes it's just denial (*"This can't be happening to us!"*) and sometimes it's the whirlpool of events, but in any crisis situation, there generally are multiple chaotic events all taking place simultaneously. It's very easy to get sidetracked and pulled in multiple and conflicting directions over which you have no control. *Focus!* Focus on identifying *your* crisis—the one with which you have to deal, the one over which you have some measure of control. Try to avoid distracting scenarios, of which there will be many.

For example, a few years ago, Wendy's, the fast-food chain, badly bungled a rather simple crisis, although it got off to a relatively good start: a patron in one of its restaurants claimed to have found a severed finger in her lunchtime bowl of Wendy's chili. Pretty ghastly stuff.

But was it true, or was it a nefarious scheme to try to extort money from the company?

In as little as 24 hours, and probably much less, Wendy's had ample proof that *if* there had been a finger in that woman's chili, it did not come from any of the restaurant's workers or from any of the chain's food suppliers during cooking or food preparation. How did the company know? Easy; since no one at the restaurant was missing any digits, the outside suppliers had been cleared, and there was no connection between the alleged victim and any Wendy's employee or outside vendor, the only logical conclusion was that the finger had to have come from a source outside of the restaurant chain's circle of possibilities.

In other words, it was in all likelihood planted by an outsider, and the patron was the likely culprit.

While the alleged victim was the logical choice, Wendy's had no proof of this at the time. What the company did know very early on was that improper food handling on the part of the restaurant was not the cause, and this was significant knowledge.

Wendy's properly and swiftly reported the incident to law enforcement authorities, who quickly began to investigate. So far, so good. But the company then blundered badly by turning virtually all control of the crisis over to the police; whenever a reporter called for a comment or an update, he was referred to the lead criminal investigator for comment, *and the company failed to manage its own crisis.*

To be clear, the finger in the chili was *not* Wendy's actual crisis, even though Wendy's acted as though it were. No, the police were handling that. But no one was managing the *loss of customer confidence*, which was Wendy's actual crisis . . . and the resulting loss of business continued unchecked and rumors were rampant. As a result, the company's actions were ineffectual and anemic, and its reputation—certainly its reputation as a crisis manager—suffered.

On the subject of Wendy's, as well as other companies whose crises are cited in this book, a few points of clarification are necessary before we proceed further. I am often interviewed by the news media and asked many questions about whatever company is in crisis at that particular time. If it's a company I am not representing, I almost always begin my response with an important disclaimer. I tell the reporter that I am not privy to inside information and can only respond to, and draw my conclusions from, what I've seen or heard reported by the media. And I typically say that there may be things going on behind the scenes that, were I to be informed of them, might change my opinions and alter my response. As many times as I've said that, I've never seen or heard my caveat used in the ultimate story that appears or airs. But since this book is about crisis communications and the importance of perception, if I take a company to task for certain shortcomings in its crisis response, I am reacting to the perception that the company has put out there or allowed to be established by its actions or inactions. And if the perception is faulty, who's to blame if not the company?

In a crisis, especially a crisis with competing interests, the only person who is looking out for your company's reputation is *you.* Do not forget that, and do not think for a moment that anyone else is going to be concerned about your reputation or your loss of customers. This type of misstep is quite common in crises of this type because the company managers are often relieved at not having to face the public or the media; it's easier to foist reporters off onto law enforcement, they erroneously think.

With everything that was going on simultaneously, the *only* thing Wendy's had any degree of control over was the loss of customer confidence. If you think for a minute that Wendy's could not possibly mount a confidence-building campaign for its customers and its franchisees (some 75 percent of the company's outlets are franchisee-owned) until the finger-in-the-chili crisis had been resolved, you are wrong.

And as the police took their sweet time being very cautious and deliberate before making an arrest, that delay did not help Wendy's bottom line, which was *its* crisis.

This is just one example of what is meant by identify *your* crisis. Wendy's failure to properly identify *its* crisis led to its failure to communicate effectively during the crisis, and the company and its image suffered.

Oh, and it turned out the "victim" was in fact the culprit, probably looking to make a fast buck.

ISOLATE

Wendy's should have quickly analyzed the entire situation and said, let the cops do what *they* do best, and let us do what *we* do best. The company's responsibility was clear: cooperate with law enforcement, but take care of its customers, its business, and its bottom line.

There should have been a better and more proactive crisis communications strategy that was designed specifically to restore confidence in the chain, while still allowing the police to conduct their investigation. The crisis should have been isolated in such a way that other aspects of the overall business operations were not compromised or contaminated by the fallout from the finger-in-the-chili accusation.

Other times, there may be a business crisis that is so distracting that it runs the risk of disrupting the rest of the company. Suppose, for example, that you have to recall a popular product because of an alleged safety defect. The news coverage is so extensive that everyone at the company in question seems to be riveted by the news and gossip: it is the prime topic of conversation around the watercooler. Consequently, the rest of the business might suffer because too many people are riveted and distracted by the crisis.

In this instance, isolation might very well mean designating a crisis management team to deal exclusively with the crisis, with its members temporarily delegating their normal duties and responsibilities to others for the duration of the crisis. Ideally, this team would be isolated from the rest of the company and, hopefully, keep quiet about its progress until the appropriate time.

Once the crisis has been identified and properly isolated, the next step is to manage it.

MANAGE

If you've never been through this, you might find the statement that follows hard to fathom, but if you have properly identified and then successfully isolated the crisis, the actual management of the crisis is the easiest part (assuming that you're a good manager to begin with). That's because you now will be laser-focused on the specific task at hand, and once you've cleared away the distracting brush, your mission becomes crystal clear. When that occurs, making vigilant decisions—the epitome of good crisis management—is well within your grasp.

If you attempt to manage a crisis that hasn't been identified and isolated, you may wind up "managing" the wrong issue.

Professional baseball pitchers often describe a tunnel-vision phenomenon when they're on the mound. They are able to completely tune out the extraneous noise of 50,000 shouting people in the stands, thousands of whom are behind the batter, catcher, and home plate umpire in what should be the pitcher's direct line of vision. However, what does a good pitcher see after receiving signs from the catcher? Just the catcher's mitt. The pitcher has isolated his crisis (remember, a crisis is a turning point for better or worse, so, especially in a big game, making that next pitch qualifies as a crisis): putting the ball where the catcher wants it. That pitch is his management of his crisis. He has identified it and isolated it, and if his wicked slider is working tonight, he will manage it right where it needs to go.

THE KEYSTONE CRISIS

When I lecture on these crisis subjects at companies and business schools across the country, I usually spend a few minutes teaching a little simplified lesson on architecture. I often display on a PowerPoint screen a photograph of an archway. I then explain the importance of the keystone—the stone that is directly at the top and center of the arch. It is designed to be load-bearing, and if it were to be removed, the entire arch and all that it supports would collapse in on itself. In short, everything depends upon this one keystone.

Then, I ask the class to imagine a crisis as being in the form of an arch, and I explain that in virtually every crisis, there is one aspect that is more important than all the others—more important because it is the one component of the crisis that must be tended to immediately.

I call that the *keystone crisis*, and its importance cannot be overstated because it is the most critical of the load-bearing occurrences in the overall crisis.

When you set out to identify your crisis, it is the keystone crisis that you should be seeking. That is what you must identify and isolate before you can begin to manage your crisis. If you can gain control over that one critical element, everything else will tend to fall into place with less resistance and more clarity. When companies fail to identify their keystone crisis, it is often because other fallen pieces obliterate their view of that essential component.

Or, they may be easily distracted by dealing with other issues and ignore the key one.

Picking on poor Wendy's one more time, its keystone crisis was protecting its brand and restoring consumer confidence in that brand.

In my analysis of the Wendy's crisis, it was the company's inability to identify its keystone crisis, or its unwillingness to take a more prominent and decisive role in its true crisis, that led it to cede control to the cops. But the police department's focus was on something entirely different from Wendy's keystone crisis. And ultimately that was Wendy's undoing at the time.

As a comparison, it is worth noting that during the infamous Tylenol crisis of the 1980s, when a terrorist laced bottles of Tylenol capsules with cyanide and killed seven innocent people, the FBI urged parent company Johnson & Johnson *not* to remove the remaining Tylenol bottles and millions of capsules from store shelves across America. The FBI thought the culprit would try again, and this would be the best way to catch him or her. J&J, not wanting to risk another death, refused. Its rationale was simple: we have a responsibility to the public. Let law enforcement authorities do what they do best, and we will do what we do best. Leaving possibly cyanide-laced Tylenol bottles on store shelves would have put the company's customers at risk, and that was something that Johnson & Johnson could not abide. J&J had properly identified its crisis (protection of its customers), isolated its crisis (with a seven-person crisis management team, whose members' laserlike focus was on the crisis to the exclusion of their other regular business duties), which then permitted the company to make vigilant decisions in the successful management of its crisis.[1]

How could this have happened to a successful company like Wendy's? First, being a well-managed company does not mean that a company is well prepared or properly staffed to manage a crisis. More on this in Chapter 27.

Also, it is important to remember that in almost any given crisis, there will be chaos. There will be a lot of extraneous "noise," and some parts of it will be louder (read: clamoring for more attention) than others. If these were children and they were all making a racket, your first instinct might be to want to quiet the noisiest kid first. In Wendy's case, the finger episode was the "loudest kid" and was demanding the most attention—or so it seemed to Wendy's.

But a good crisis manager would have assessed the situation and said, "This definitely needs to be dealt with, but from a company standpoint, it is not the most important thing going on, and solving the crime is not within our job description. There are law enforcement professionals who can do a better job on that issue than we can, so let's focus on what we can do best as a company—for our employees, our customers, our stakeholders, and our franchisees."

If you can't properly assess the situation, you stand a good chance of missing the keystone crisis, and thereby failing as a skilled crisis manager. This is one of the biggest reasons why so many companies stumble and fail to manage their crises effectively: they focus on the wrong thing. Or, to mix a baseball metaphor, they simply take their eye off the crisis ball and either swing and miss or are embarrassingly called out on strikes without ever lifting the crisis management bat off their shoulders.

YOUR CRISIS IS UNIQUE

I always tell my clients that they can learn a lot by watching and analyzing other companies that are in crisis, especially competitors. (As that great philosopher Yogi Berra once said, "You can observe a lot by just watching.") For one thing, if a company in your industry group suffers a crisis, could you be next? Figure it out and govern yourself accordingly.

But, make no mistake, even if what happened to your competitor happens to you, the two crises will not be identical. Every crisis is unique, and every crisis response must be unique. You will never succeed at managing *your* crisis by doing exactly what your competitor did. Each crisis must be managed on its own merits.

I run into this issue from time to time when I am contacted by a prospective client who is interested in having my firm create a crisis management plan for his company. When I outline what is involved in doing that, and the grassroots way we approach the assignment, I occasionally am met by pushback from the prospective client. He may want to know, for instance, why it can't be done overnight, and hastens to tell me that another firm told him that it could have a crisis management plan installed and up and running in a week's time and for less money.

I then explain why "cookie-cutter" approaches to crisis management are doomed to fail. You can't pull one client's crisis management plan off the shelf, change the cover, insert a new client name in all the relevant places, and present it as a crisis management plan that will work for another company. As every crisis is unique, so, too, must every crisis management and crisis communications plan be geared specifically to the company it is designed to serve. Failure to recognize this simple universal truth leads to almost certain disaster when a crisis hits.

In that vein, I emphasize that while studying and learning from other companies that go through a crisis, especially their failures, is useful and informative, in the end, you need to manage your own crisis.

YOUR CRISIS IS SUBJECTIVE

While conducting research for my first book on crisis management, I discovered that a disturbingly high number of companies that had experienced a crisis had not known it until it was too late. How could this happen?

There were essentially two explanations: first, companies would experience precrisis events (known as prodromes, or warning signs, which is the first of the four critical stages in the anatomy of a crisis) but not recognize the immediate or potential significance of them until it was too late; or, second, they missed these events altogether.

(There also was a third explanation: sometimes a manager would spot impending trouble but could not get his superior's attention or, worse, the shoot-the-messenger syndrome was so prevalent within the company that bad news was not allowed to move up the chain and the senior management was never alerted to the impending danger. But dealing with that is more about changing corporate culture within organizations, and we won't cover that here.)

The important thing to remember is that just as every crisis is unique, every crisis is also subjective. What is a crisis for you may be a nonstarter for another company. Just because your crisis doesn't become the lead story on the evening news doesn't mean that it is not a serious issue for you and your company.

For my earlier crisis management book, I created a unique crisis forecasting model that can be used by any company in any industry group to help it understand whether it is in or is about to be immersed in a crisis situation. The advantage of this model is that it allows for, and even is enhanced by, subjectivity.

Assume for a moment that you become aware of a prodrome (a warning sign of possible impending trouble) in your company—some event that may or may not develop into something bigger, something more serious. It may be the first inkling of labor unrest or a handful of unexplained cracks reported in a new product that recently shipped, resulting in its being returned by a still small group of disgruntled customers. The situation needs attention, true, but does it need *immediate* intervention? Is it a crisis? Could it become a crisis? How do you know? How much attention and resources should be thrown at the problem?

To underscore just how subjective a crisis is, let's look at a good working definition of a crisis (which I originally coined in *Crisis Management*, and which is applicable to *any* company of *any* size in *any* industry and in *any* location). A crisis is any situation, such as a prodrome, that, if left unattended, has the potential to:

- Escalate in intensity
- Damage the reputation or positive public opinion of the company and/or its management
- Interfere with the normal operations of business
- Fall under close government or media scrutiny
- Damage the bottom line

Thus, using this five-step litmus test as a pragmatic guide, what may not qualify as a crisis in one manager's estimation could very well be a make-it-or-break-it crisis in another's. It all depends on the company.

In your own particular case, take your company's potential labor unrest or possible product glitch and pose the previous five questions. If you begin to see a pattern of disturbing answers, you have a crisis, and you need to address it.[2]

But those are subjects related to the actual management of the crisis, and our focus is on communications during a crisis.

One more point: even using my definition of a crisis, you may not be convinced that you are in a crisis. The answers you get to those five litmus test questions may be all in your favor. Nevertheless, if your key publics believe that you are in a crisis (for example, there are unexplained cracks in a new product or unintended acceleration), you are in a crisis.

If you are a fiscally sound small bank, and a rumor starts that you are about to be taken over by the Feds for insolvency and that prevailing perception lingers, you are in a crisis. Perception is everything, and it works both ways. Rumors of a crisis can easily trigger a crisis.

ANATOMY OF A CRISIS

One final point on crisis management before we turn our attention back to crisis communications: in conducting research for my crisis management book, which included not only an analysis of pivotal business crises across the country but a confidential survey of the CEOs of what were then the Fortune 500 companies, I discovered that crises usually follow a similar pattern regardless of the industry affected. Understanding this pattern gives you greater control over the management of a crisis because you have a better idea of what lies ahead, and you can plan and manage accordingly.

My research, as reported in that earlier book, concluded that there are four separate and distinct stages to a crisis:[3]

The Prodromal Stage
The Acute Stage
The Chronic Stage
The Resolution Stage

When most people refer to "a crisis," they generally mean the acute stage of a crisis, the time when chaos reigns supreme. However, usually there is a precrisis event that, if it is spotted and managed successfully, will avert the acute stage altogether. This prodromal stage, from the Greek meaning "running before," is actually the first stage of a crisis. One way we often refer to crises is as either "long-fused crises" or "short-fused crises." As the names imply, prodromes—when they exist—are either of long duration or of short duration. Unfortunately, recognition that a prodrome was present often occurs during the next stage, when the dust has settled.

The chronic stage, usually the longest of the four, is where litigation occurs, media exposés are aired, internal investigations are launched, government oversight investigations commence, tell-all books are written, postmortems are conducted, and so on. With some companies and some crises, this stage can go on for years; sometimes it never ends. This is the risk and reward stage.

The resolution stage speaks for itself.

I have two closing notes on this topic. First, not every crisis contains all four of these stages (not every crisis has a prodrome or a resolution stage, for example), but no crisis contains more than these four stages. There was no prodrome to the Tylenol crisis that anyone has ever identified, but the Tylenol crisis itself was a prodrome for every other company that manufactured packaged consumer goods, especially those that are ingestible. From pharmaceuticals to cereal companies, consumer goods packaging today is designed to easily reveal whether someone has opened the product and potentially tampered with it before it is too late. If you have ever cursed at how hard or how messy it is to open a new box of cereal in the morning, you can thank the ripple effects of the Tylenol crisis for that.

And second, the ultimate goal of crisis management is to manage the prodrome so successfully that you go from prodrome to resolution without falling into the morass of the acute and chronic stages. When I give speeches before business groups and I'm asked what was the greatest crisis I ever worked on, I usually tell the members of my audience that they've never heard of it. And that's because while the potential for a full-blown, media-driven crisis was there, it was successfully averted once the prodrome had been identified, and the insatiable media beast was not fed that day.

At least, not by me or my clients.

7

Shaping *Your* Crisis Communications Message

■ ■ ■

As stated earlier (but it is a point worth repeating a thousand times), when there is a difference between perception and reality, perception always wins. Behind the scenes, you and your crisis management team may be doing a bang-up job in wrestling with a megacrisis: successfully keeping disaster at bay, saving towns from impending environmental doom, and protecting shareholder value. But if no one knows about it, your critics and aggressive plaintiffs' attorneys will have a field day belittling your efforts as too little, too late. Worse, they may accuse you of doing nothing and putting people or the company at risk by your lack of action. It's no different from the proverbial tree falling in the forest: if no one hears (about) it, did it really happen? And then when you are finally forced to step out of your bunker to defend your actions, you find yourself on the defensive ... and you wonder why.

Companies in crisis that think that they have no responsibility for keeping their myriad publics informed because they believe they "have things under control," are wrong. I have had clients rankle at having to talk to the media during a crisis for a variety of reasons, but they lose sight of the fact that while they may deem the media an annoying intrusion into their private business dealings, the media are also a fast conduit for reaching the publics that the company *needs* to reach. There are other ways, such as using social media, which we will examine shortly, that are even faster and more direct. But *not* communicating is *never* the right decision.

Effective perception—the impression you want people to have of the way you are managing your crisis—does not happen by itself. The message or messages must be carefully and strategically shaped. For our purposes here, let's operate on the premise that you (your company and your crisis management team) are doing a good job of managing your crisis. (Later we will address the alternative and discuss how to manage your crisis communications message when it's bad news.) Your goal is to ensure that your publics are aware of the job you are doing.

How?

You need to develop key message points that are strategically targeted to your key constituencies, and you should do so proactively. And remember, especially if you will be delivering periodic updates via the news media, your first statement sets the tone for all that follow.

In the limited confines of a book, not every conceivable type of crisis can be considered, but here are some broad topic guidelines for crises that often occur.

In an environmental crisis (oil spill, groundwater contamination, air pollution, train derailment and resulting chemical spill, nuclear reactor accident, and the like), after you describe what you *know* for certain has occurred, your first comments need to address the health and safety of the community and your employees. In describing what occurred, be factual, be truthful, be fast, and be visible. Tell *your* story, and tell it first.

If a portion of the community is at risk, say so, explain how and why, and in the same breath, say what *you* are doing about it. If it is a crisis that involves emergency personnel, as opposed to your own personnel, say so, but add what *you* are doing to aid those teams. Obviously, if no human life is at risk, state that clearly and early. If human life has been lost, say so, express your condolences, and, as there usually is an investigation (internal, external, or both), say so and promise to report back when the investigation has been completed.

These events are rather routine, at least in crisis management circles, but what sometimes is lost is whose message is being put out there. You need to establish control of your own message.

If you have a time frame for closure (say, a highway spill or accident will be cleaned up by rush hour tomorrow morning), say so. Usually, though, the best you can do is promise to provide regular updates, then be sure you do so.

You want to remember to compile your key message points in advance. These message points should also be turned into a written statement for the media, and you need to be sure that what you say tracks what's in the statement. Provide the same information and updates via social media outlets.

Everything you do and say up until this point is proactive. But then the media (or other publics) will ask questions. From this point forward, much of what you do and say is reactive, and this is where you can get into trouble, if you're not careful.

When we work with clients, we conduct crisis simulations (for crisis management training) and crisis media exercises (for crisis communications training). Part of the training deals with staying on message. To the greatest extent possible, you will want to shape *your* message to conform to *your* crisis.

Do not allow yourself to be led down dark alleys by negatively charged questions. Beware, and avoid, questions that put you on the defensive just by their very wording ("Isn't it true that . . . ?" "How can you say that . . . ?" "Do you mean to imply . . . ?" and so on). Treat those types of questions the way you would handle a loaded gun: carefully, and trying to avoid shooting yourself in the foot. And just as you would naturally point a loaded gun away from yourself, do the same with loaded questions.

Take negatively charged questions and turn them around into positively phrased responses, but do not get defensive. Remember that your crisis is being managed well and that this is the perception that you want to create and maintain. Allowing yourself to be put on the defensive eats into and badly erodes that perception.

So, before blindly answering a question that begins "Isn't it true that this accident was both foreseeable and avoidable?" recast the question before answering into something like: "If you're asking if there is anything this plant should have done differently, I would point out, as I did in my opening remarks, that our safety record is the best in the industry. I also stated that we have launched an investigation into the cause of the accident, and that until that investigation is complete, we are not going to speculate on possible causes, and those that do so are being irresponsible. At the same time, I remind you again of the steps we are taking to bring this crisis under control."

From beginning to end, BP never really got control of its crisis communications message. The perception was that the company was as out of control as its gushing oil well in the Gulf of Mexico.

In almost any crisis, the public's safety is paramount, and nowhere is that more true than in a food or health crisis. That is because, unlike a raging fire or rising water, people can't actually see what is causing a food or health crisis, so they're never completely sure that the food they're about to eat is completely safe, or that the person next to them isn't carrying some deadly virus—that is, until they hear your crisis communications messages.

If there is a health scare associated with your food product or your restaurant, you need to get out in front of the story *with* the support of the local or state board of health and any other applicable government agency. While the state or county department of public health will investigate to try to determine the cause of, say, an E. coli outbreak, you need to conduct your own independent investigation simultaneously. Do not wait for someone else to issue a report that will shape your crisis communications message. Assuming that the two investigations mesh, announce the findings jointly. If the government agency is slow to agree to join you, announce your findings *first*, proactively. Remember, it's *your* crisis and *your* crisis communications.

Here's a food contamination crisis example from my own client files.

A few years ago, a successful southern California restaurant chain, Pat & Oscar's, had an E. coli outbreak. The chain, owned at the time by the same parent company that owns the Sizzler Steak House chain, is a family-oriented sit-down restaurant specializing in pizza, salads, and its signature breadsticks.

When the San Diego County public health department contacted the company, and then the media, to report the outbreak and that some people had been hospitalized, restaurant customers stayed away in droves. Overnight, the chain's business plummeted by more than 70 percent.

I was contacted the next day by the chairman of the board of the parent company and retained to handle all aspects of the crisis—whatever needed to be done: crisis management and crisis communications.

There generally are two possible sources for an E. coli outbreak at a restaurant: poor food handling (for example, employees not washing their hands or coming to work infected with a transmittable disease) or contamination from an outside food supplier. We immediately launched our own simultaneous investigation and determined that the source was an outside lettuce vendor. That was "good news" because reporting this information (which soon was corroborated by the health department) and firing and replacing the outside vendor (which we did publicly) sent a strong message that we had identified, isolated, and remedied the crisis. Also, we announced that popular food items that we had previously removed from the menu as a precaution until we knew the source of the E. coli were now available again. Our message points also included the information that we wanted people who ate in our restaurants between certain specified dates to be medically tested, and obviously that we were going to reimburse patrons for any related medical bills.

But the public remained skeptical about returning to the eateries. Business was still off by about the same percentage. The original story ("E. coli outbreak at restaurant chain; people taken ill") was the lead story in all media outlets and commanded people's attention. Our new message ("The restaurant was not the source of the outbreak, and now it's safe to return") was having a hard time breaking through the clutter of all the other everyday news.

Also, our crisis had suddenly shifted, which often happens (remember: a crisis is "a *fluid* and dynamic state of affairs"). Whereas our crisis had previously been the source of the outbreak and all that that entailed, now our focus was on rebuilding the business. It was a classic case of loss of confidence. The crisis communications focus now was on restoring that lost confidence and rebuilding the business. *This* was our "keystone crisis."

We held a media day.

One news outlet at a time, we invited the media into our restaurants and into our kitchens to observe and film our enhanced food preparation procedures, emphasizing and allowing TV cameras to record the extra washing steps that the food handlers were taking with lettuce from the new supplier. The media covered this extensively, and footage aired on the afternoon and evening news all over the southern California media markets. There were live news feeds during the noon news hour, where one reporter was shown sitting at a table and eating a salad for her lunch. Business picked up, . . . but just slightly. A bolder, more impactful crisis communications message was required to show customers demonstrably that it was safe, as well as fun, to eat at Pat & Oscar's again.

That is what is called the takeaway message—the crisis communications message that we want people to take away from what they see and hear. In other words, those who heard or read our message that it was safe to come back may have believed it, but they obviously didn't feel comfortable or safe coming back for a meal. We believed that if we got them to try the restaurant once more, they would be sold. Our market research indicated that business would rebound eventually, but we were interested in a faster turnaround. Simply stated, we wanted people to get back into the habit of eating at Pat & Oscar's before they replaced that option with other restaurants.

We came up with a crisis communications campaign centered around one simple message, "Have a meal on us."

We crafted a full-page newspaper ad that contained just three message points. In big, bold letters at the top of the page, just under the Pat & Oscar's logo and a simple banner headline "A Message from Pat & Oscar's," was a bold subheadline:

FIRST, WE'RE SORRY.

Some of the lawyers were adamantly opposed to our "apologizing" for fear of increased liability, as if the company were admitting wrongdoing. But ultimately we prevailed,[1] and the message began as follows:

> As you may know, San Diego was hit by an outbreak of E. coli two weeks ago and some Pat & Oscar's guests and employees became ill. For that we are very sorry.
>
> We are proud of the fact that we have always received "A" restaurant ratings[2] from the San Diego health department. But, despite the extraordinary care and

precautions we take to ensure that only the highest quality food is served at Pat & Oscar's, a product from one of our suppliers was the cause of the trouble.

While the problem clearly was not caused by our restaurants, but originated from an outside supplier who was quickly identified and replaced, we want you to know how much we regret this incident and how bad we feel for everyone who was affected by it. We have established a toll-free number for people to call to find out how to get reimbursed for any incident-related medical expenses. That number is 1-800-555-5555.[3]

Local health officials were quick to praise Pat & Oscar's for its excellent help and cooperation in identifying the supplier and bringing the problem under control so rapidly. We think the health officials should be praised, too.

So, we're sorry that people became ill. Notice how we weaved into the message that, *Oh, and by the way, it was not our fault, and we've already replaced the vendor.* And pay particular attention to where the outbreak occurred: *in San Diego* as opposed to *at Pat & Oscar's.* This was accurate, since another outbreak had taken place at a local school whose cafeteria had served tainted lettuce from the same supplier, but it never hurts to remind people that the restaurant didn't cause it and that the outbreak didn't start *here.* The toll-free number for medical expense reimbursement had been well publicized by us already.

It's important to note that so far in the ad, we weren't actually saying anything new; we were merely reinforcing messages that we had conveyed previously and in different forms. When we held the aforementioned media day, we selected one regional manager of the chain and, although he had previously had no media training, made him our sole spokesperson. We gave him an intensive, one-day crash course in giving interviews, and we drilled into his head that no matter what the question was, his answer should always begin, "Before I answer that, I first want to say how sorry we are that this incident happened. We take great pride in our excellent and unbroken streak of 'A' ratings from the department of health." So saying "we're sorry" was not the point of the ad, nor was it new information. But a little repetition on this important point never hurts.

Then came this message point:

> **SECOND, THANKS FOR YOUR SUPPORT.**
>
> We are grateful for the many messages and phone calls of support we received from many of our friends and valued guests. You called to say you understood that we were not to blame ... but you also wanted to know why we removed so many menu items.
>
> In order to be extra cautious, we immediately pulled many more items from our menu throughout the chain than we had to—and in many more locations than we had to. But we wanted to err on the side of caution for our guests and employees. Pat & Oscar's immediately halted all food shipments from the supplier in question and new food suppliers were promptly located. Our menus are now back to full strength.

Here we reinforced the idea that the health and safety of our customers was always our top priority. But these first two headlines were just the warm-up acts. The third headline was the real reason behind the ad:

> **THIRD, COME VISIT AND HAVE A MEAL ON US!**
>
> Finally, as a way to thank you for your continued support, and to make up for having disappointed many of you by taking some of your favorite items off the menu, beginning today and for the next three days ...

**We're serving FREE Pizza, Salad and Breadsticks
at every Pat & Oscar's restaurant.**

No gimmicks. No coupons. No purchase necessary.

We couldn't have become the success story we are today
without you, and this is just our small way of saying thanks
for your continued support.

We value your patronage and your trust, and want to do
everything we can to continue to earn both.

Sincerely,

The Pat & Oscar's Team

The ad ran on a Thursday, but we sent advance proof copies to all media outlets the day before. Most of the TV news shows featured and prominently displayed the ad and the "Have a meal on us!" campaign the night before the big day.

When the doors opened at 10:00 a.m. Thursday, there were lines up to two hours long outside of every one of our client's restaurants in southern California, and it continued that way for three solid days. The media covered it as a hard news story for the first 48 hours, often doing live news feeds during their broadcasts. And every customer they interviewed had nothing but the highest praise for the chain. (We gave the media carte blanche to film and conduct interviews in the restaurants as long as they did not interfere with the customers or the restaurant operations and as long as the patrons did not object.)

What people watching at home saw were thousands of happy, smiling patrons jam-packed into the restaurants, with lines far out the door of thousands more waiting to get in. It was a party!

The lines continued non-stop from 10:00 a.m. to 10:00 p.m. Thursday through Saturday, and were heaviest on that final day.

We arranged for entertainment (musicians, clowns and balloon animals for the kids, free breadsticks and breadstick juggling contests, and so on) to keep the people in line entertained while they waited. In three days, we served more than 55,000 people, many of whom had never before set foot in a Pat & Oscar's restaurant. At the end of each day, when there were still people waiting to enter, we gave them coupons for free meals that were good anytime. What? Did you think we were going to just shut the doors on loyal customers at 10:00 p.m. without some sort of token of thanks? The idea was to make people happy, not angry that they had waited in line for two hours and were sent away hungry.

All of the waitstaff—none of whom were laid off during the slowdown; I insisted on that—wore big yellow and black buttons that read either "Have a Meal on Us!" or "Thanks for your Support!" and huge smiles on their faces.

We were asked by a few media outlets if we were trying to "buy" back our old customers and snare some new ones in the process, which smacked of cynicism, but our response never wavered: we wanted to thank people for their support, and this was our way of demonstrating our gratitude.

The one question we refused to answer, and it was asked by almost every media outlet, was how much this was costing us. It was a fair question, and one that we had anticipated, but we knew in advance that providing a dollar figure would become *the* story: "Pat & Oscar's Spends X Millions to Lure Back Lost Customers." Instead, our spokesman's pat response was, "The money is not important. What is important is thanking our customers for being so loyal and standing behind us." Remember, *our* crisis, *our* message; *your* crisis, *your* message. Don't let the media push you around!

Naturally, not only did we successfully bring back our core customer base, but we acquired many new customers, too. Overall, business increased approximately 135 percent.

We also anticipated that there would be many homeless people in line, and we thought this image would send the wrong signal, making it look like a Depression-era soup or bread line. This could have been a touchy issue. We weren't opposed to feeding the homeless—far from it; Pat & Oscar's was well known for being a good corporate citizen of its local communities. However, we were concerned that seeing a line of homeless people waiting to enter the restaurant might be a deterrent to the future paying customers we were trying to reach. To manage this contingency, every morning we delivered thousands of meals to local area homeless shelters, and the word quickly spread among the homeless that they could get the same food at the shelters all day long, without standing in long lines. We received much local media attention for this charitable work, too, which was an unintended bonus.

From the way this particular strategy unfolded, it should be obvious that crisis communications are not limited to verbal and written communications; they also include visual communications. Our first approach, *telling* the public that it was safe to return to the restaurant, while somewhat successful, did not hit the home run we needed. We had to *show* the public that it was safe in a graphic way that made the message crystal clear. So, while the successful management of the crisis made it safe to return to the restaurant, we now needed to make the perception match the reality.

An important cautionary note: the title of this chapter is "Shaping *Your* Crisis Communications Message," with an emphasis on the pronoun. Every crisis is unique, and therefore every crisis management plan and crisis communications strategy must be specifically targeted for the crisis at hand and for the company in crisis. The remarkable turnaround we engineered for Pat & Oscar's was widely reported in business media outlets, and in particular in national print media covering the food service industry. About a year later, I was asked to meet with some executives from a very well-known national restaurant chain—I won't mention its name to avoid embarrassment for it—that had heard of our success with Pat & Oscar's and wanted to talk with me about what we had done specifically for the chain. The executives thought the same plan would work for their company, should it ever need that sort of crisis communications plan. I told them that I didn't think so, since their company was a different chain, it did not have the same type of loyal customer base, and several other reasons that I won't go into here. And I told them what I've just told you: every crisis is unique, and so, too, must the response be tailored for the event and for the company in crisis.

Nevertheless, the executives thanked me for my time, and I never heard from them again. I learned later from someone who had worked for the chain at the time that they thought I had given them the keys to the kingdom, so why should they go to the expense of engaging my firm? They already had the "master plan," which I had "so foolishly given them for free."

As fate would have it, six months later the company had a crisis in a certain region of the country, and the executives tried the same crisis communications strategy we had employed at Pat & Oscar's. However, it backfired on them. Not only did the company still have its original crisis, but the executives had compounded the crisis with what was perceived as a heavy-handed way to bamboozle its customers and influence the government regulators. The strategy was seen as a smoke screen to cover up the real crisis, as well as a form of potential witness intimidation and jury tampering, since pending and future litigation were involved. But that's another story.

One of the reasons President Obama had to struggle so hard to pass his landmark healthcare bill was that someone said the act called for the establishment of "death panels." That was *its* crisis communications message. While that phrase was a completely inaccurate portrayal of one particular provision of the bill, those two words immediately put the White House on the defensive, where it remained for many, many months. If you supported Obama and the bill, it was a massive headache; if you opposed the bill's passage, it was a masterstroke. But either way, it was crisis communications.

Remember, *your* crisis, *your* message. Be wary of those who would deter you from delivering the crisis communications strategy you deem would best serve *your* crisis. The next thing you need to do is figure out who is going to deliver that message, and how.

8

Spokespersons

■   ■   ■

Who is the right spokesperson for a crisis like yours?

Be careful how you answer. Otherwise sound crisis communications strategies have been badly compromised, if not fatally wounded, by having the wrong person out front of a crisis.

As a general rule, your spokesperson should be someone who:

- ■ Is credible (people believe her)
- ■ Is cogent and understandable (can speak in simple, declarative sentences; can explain complex events and terminology in everyday language; avoids "corporate speak")
- ■ Is compassionate (where called for)
- ■ Is likeable (is not condescending; does not talk down to people)
- ■ Is knowledgeable (fully understands the issues at hand and the stakes at risk)

■ Is not easily rattled (especially by hostile or particularly aggressive media representatives)

For starters, all companies should run their executives and managers through comprehensive crisis communications and media training sessions, and the same is true for politicians and anyone else who either is, or may be, in the public eye. This is essential in today's media-intensive environment. Note that this is not the same as being trained to run a shareholders' meeting or to handle routine Q&As following a Rotary Club speech; this is hard-core boot camp.

It is clear that BP never properly trained Tony Hayward for dealing with a hostile media, a hostile community, or the U.S. Congress—a foreign government to Hayward, who was British, remember—made even more hostile by his evasive answers. His responses smacked of being penned by overcontrolling lawyers. Moreover, it is not at all unusual for someone like Hayward (read: a powerful CEO who is often surrounded by sycophants and is not used to having his pronouncements questioned, let alone challenged) to get flustered in the face of a hostile and often belligerent press corps clamoring for answers. This is another reason for intensive crisis communications media training for all potential spokespersons.

And, as stated earlier, while designating the CEO as the spokesperson in any crisis involving the loss of life, severe threat of same, or massive property damage is usually the right course of action, make sure your spokesperson speaks the language of the people. In BP's case, Hayward's tony upper-crust British accent made it hard for him to relate to those who were suffering, or they to him; he seemed aloof because he acted aloof. And, the jarring juxtaposition of his tea-and-crumpet intonations and pinstripe suits against the local Gulf po'boy-and-shrimp dialect only served to underscore this class distinction and the ever-growing divide. The Battle of Waterloo may have been won on the playing fields of Eton, but the crisis communications Battle of Gulf-Oil-Goo was not.

Interestingly, BP already had a top U.S. executive (and Gulf native, coincidentally) in place and in the wings. This person, Robert Dudley, who took over when Hayward ultimately was ousted, should have been BP's point man in the United States from the start. Hayward should have stayed mainly in the United Kingdom, where, if he had had to address the media, at least they pretty much spoke the same language, and what sounded like a foreign accent to U.S. citizens would have sounded right at home in Great Britain.

At no point during the acute stage of the crisis, from the initial oil rig explosion to the ultimate capping of the well to this day, did the public ever side with BP, and that was partly because people had a hard time relating to Hayward and partly because Hayward was perceived as giving evasive responses, as well as being accused outright of doing so. Generally, BP's crisis communications efforts were without form and lacked direction, and that solidified the perception of an "oppositional crisis," meaning that the public was solidly opposed to the company and its management team as a result of the misstatements, obfuscation, and defensive tenor of Hayward's comments. The counter to this is a "nonoppositional crisis," where even though events may be dire, at least the public is rooting for the company to succeed (for example, Johnson & Johnson's first Tylenol crisis or the Chilean mine disaster). The public wanted BP to succeed because the alternative was so tragic and the consequences so ominous, but at no time was anyone rooting for BP as an underdog. If J&J was Dudley Do-Right, BP was Snidely Whiplash.

If your spokesperson doesn't speak the language of the country (like Toyoda) or the language of the people (like Hayward), you're starting at a huge disadvantage. There are always ways to overcome this, of course. For a variety of reasons, I am pressed into service periodically as the "official spokesman" for a client in crisis. But in my view, it generally is more effective to have a good company spokesperson, someone who has a personal stake in the crisis, speak from the heart.

In a media-crazed world, what you say and what you do really matter. It is important that the public be able to like and relate to the spokesperson, who should never come across as "better than you." Leaving the business world for a moment, many people still remember President Obama's gaffe on the 2008 campaign trail, when to show that he was "an ordinary guy," he mentioned shopping for arugula in a Whole Foods grocery store. This made him appear aloof and out of touch with the people. For better or for worse, this is a nation of Big Macs and fries, not arugula salads. True, he won the election, but he took his lumps at the time for a comment that gave the perception that he wasn't one of the people. Similarly, Massachusetts Senator John Kerry, the Democratic nominee for president in the previous election, was chided for campaign-provided pictures that showed him participating in a favorite pastime: windsurfing. The idea was to communicate Kerry is athletic, but windsurfing is not a sport that most people can relate to. Kerry, by the way, lost. And switching parties, if only to demonstrate that these verbal faux pas are nonpartisan, Mitt Romney's immense personal wealth has for years made it hard for him to relate to the common person and even harder for him to get people to view him as "one of us." Stumping in his home state of Michigan in the winter of 2012, and wanting to illustrate how he supported Detroit and the beleaguered U.S. auto industry, he famously said that his "wife drives a couple of Cadillacs." Romney, who has replaced the silver spoon in his mouth with a golden foot, also said that he "like(s) being able to fire people," described his personal net worth as "between 150 and 200 some-odd million," and told a CNN interviewer that he was "not concerned about the 'very poor.'"[1]

It's not the Cadillacs, it's that she drives "a couple of" them; it's not his wealth, it's that while people all across America are having trouble making ends meet and are losing their jobs and their homes, he so cavalierly makes an offhand comment like "between 150 and 200 some-odd million," as if that extra $50 million is so insignificant as to be not worth counting more closely; and it's not that he likes to fire people—well, maybe it is. Who knows?[2]

And let's not forget his famous blunder behind closed doors that was captured on a cell phone video when he essentially wrote off 47 percent of the country in a demeaning and cavalier way. He later tried on more than one occasion to restate and correct his remarks, but the damage was done. Romney lost the 2012 presidential election and one of the reaons, according to many pundits on both sides of the aisle, was that he wasn't likeable enough. Communications gaffes like these certainly didn't help him win over the voters.

Is a political campaign a crisis? Only every single day. Everything that happens on the campaign trail is a turning point for better or worse—the classic definition of a crisis.

Returning to business, keep in mind that there is no rule that says that you must have a single spokesperson. It is perfectly acceptable, and sometimes even highly advisable, to have multiple spokespersons, depending on the nature of the crisis.

If your crisis is of a technical nature, say a potential automotive defect resulting in fatalities, the CEO may be present as the face of the corporation who expresses compassion, but you also may benefit from having an automotive engineer on hand to help explain mechanical issues to the media and to the public. If your crisis deals with a possible food contamination issue, you may also want a quality assurance expert or even an epidemiologist fielding some of the questions to explain how the problem was first spotted and what steps the company is taking to resolve the crisis and ensure the public's safety. If yours is a geographically dispersed company with plants or offices all across the country, and the crisis is local as opposed to companywide, you may want the local plant manager or local company official in charge to be the spokesperson. Each crisis is different, and each crisis communications strategy, including the spokesperson, is different, too. A crisis is a fluid and dynamic state of affairs, and your responses and your communications efforts should mirror that. Be flexible and try not to lock yourself into just a single strategy or a single spokesperson simply because "that's how we did it last time." Each time and each crisis is different. And whoever your spokespeople are, be sure that their messages can be easily understood by all audiences, especially in complex or highly technical crises. Otherwise, you just compound your problem.

During the 2011 Japanese earthquake and the resulting tsunami that crippled one of the country's nuclear power plants, Dr. Michio Kaku, a physics professor at the City College of New York, was a frequent guest on national news shows. He had a particularly effective way of restating complex technical issues, including the use of simple visual aids, that made what was going on thousand of miles from home understandable.

When we help companies build proactive crisis management and crisis communications plans, media training is part of the recommended process. One of the strategies we cover with potential technical spokespersons is how to translate complicated techno-jargon into laypersons' terms. And because we never know exactly who the spokesperson will be until the crisis hits, we try to cast a wide net and train as many logical possibilities—and backups—as we can.

How do you decide who *your* spokesperson will be? Well, those just discussed are only a few of the possibilities, and in each case the decision almost makes itself. But you can, and should, plan for this as part of your crisis simulation exercises. In a crisis, where speed is of the essence, you don't want to be casting about for, and training, spokespersons when the clock is ticking. You may not be able to anticipate every conceivable crisis that might occur—nor should you try to do so; that's an exercise in futility—but you can certainly do so in broad strokes by categories (recalls, safety, environmental, and so on) and anticipate who your very best spokespersons would be, as well as the target audience, for each broad scenario and each message.

We may never know what was going through the mind of Mickey Arison, CEO of Carnival Cruise Lines, the parent company of the infamous *Costa Concordia*, the ship that ran aground off the Italian coast not far from Rome in the spring of 2012. The ship was longer than and more than twice the tonnage of the famed *Titanic*. It was the worst peacetime Italian passenger vessel disaster at sea since the collision and sinking of the SS *Andrea Doria* in 1956.[3] Even though 32 people died,[4] a number that includes some bodies that were trapped underwater for days as the world anxiously watched and waited to see if rescue divers might miraculously emerge with survivors instead of corpses, Arison's initial crisis communications messages consisted of a few tweets on his Twitter account and a brief statement. He then said that everything was being handled by the company's Italian subsidiary and *Concordia* operator, Costa Cruises. But it wasn't.

There was so much finger-pointing going on and so many conflicting stories that it seemed that the only way to sort it all out was for the parent company to take charge, rather than continually shirk its responsibilities. However, Arison opted to stay secure and largely silent in his corporate office in Miami, Florida, although the rudderless local operation in Italy needed a real leader to take charge.

Note that earlier I advocated that in cases of multinational companies in crisis here in the United States, when the CEO does not speak English or the language of the people, he should stay at home and not be the spokesperson, so on the one hand I can't fault Mr. Arison's decision not to fly off to Italy. After all, while I may be wrong, I do not believe he speaks Italian, so the same rules regarding the CEO as spokesperson should apply without affecting a double standard.

However, he could and should have been more visible here in the United States, speaking to U.S. media outlets and offering condolences in English to the families of the U.S. cruise ship passengers who perished. The perception was that he was not in charge, and the question soon became, is anyone?

The ship's captain, who was placed under house arrest, started blaming his employers for ordering him to sail close to shore to afford passengers better coastline views, a charge that was promptly denied by Costa Cruises.

Even the news media took the company to task for its botched crisis management and crisis communications. "Carnival Fails Crisis 101 in Costa Response," blared one headline. In that story, a reporter asked me if I would give Carnival an F for its crisis response report card. "To give them an 'F' acknowledges they even took the test [on crisis management]; they haven't even shown up to take the test," I replied.[5]

Wall Street was equally harsh. Carnival's stock plummeted 15 percent, its steepest drop in more than a decade.

When it's your crisis, you need to take charge of it, and your spokesperson needs to be proactive in her crisis communications messages. Even when law enforcement personnel are handling the forensics or rescue/recovery operations at the scene of the crime or disaster, you need to make sure that your company's interests are being served without interfering with others who are performing vital emergency or forensic services.

The cruise ship business has had its share of crises in recent years, so you'd think that the CEO of arguably the world's biggest cruise ship company would be trained in crisis communications. The Carnival crisis is an example of how the perception of things so far outweighs whatever the reality is, and in the blink of an eye.

Forward-thinking companies, regardless of the business they're in, should look at examples like Carnival and ask themselves: "Are we ready for our own crisis? Do we have crisis communications people and plans in place? How would we fare if this were *our* crisis?"

How are crisis communications and media training performed? How do you train someone to be a credible spokesperson? Is it even possible? Can *anyone* be trained?

We train company spokespeople to manage crisis communications messages the same way we train companies to manage crises: through simulations or crisis inoculations. The premise behind the term *crisis inoculation* is the same as in the medical field, where an inoculation against, say, measles gives the patient a very small dose of the disease—not so much that the patient gets sick, but just enough so that his body's immune system builds up natural antibodies to ward off the disease later in life should he be exposed to the virus.

Psychologists initially developed this technique while studying the effects of stress on the human body and used stress inoculations to measure results. In our case, we subject clients to stress via realistic crisis simulations and run potential spokespersons through simulated media attacks and interview scenarios. We may, for example, create a simulated crisis and provide the spokesperson candidates with a list of the key message points we wish to convey. After they "Meet the Press"—which may take the form of a press conference, a one-on-one TV interview, or even an "ambush" interview, and where the interviewer is asking loaded questions provided by us—we evaluate together how our candidates performed.

Were they believable? Did they make their points? Did they make their points *cogently*? Did they get rattled? How did they handle rude questioners who didn't let them finish their responses? Were they answering what was asked? Were they successfully able to recognize negatively charged questions and recast them into positively phrased questions? What were their strengths? What were their weaknesses? Did they sweat (literally) on camera and under the lights in a studio setting? Did they look at the interviewer? If they were being interviewed in a hallway with a gaggle of reporters and TV cameras, did they know *where* to look? When multiple questions were thrown at them at once, did they know what to do, which questions to answer, and how? If we conduct focus groups (which we sometimes do), what did our focus group think of the spokesperson candidate? Did he genuinely convey empathy for the victims, or did it come across as lip service? And to all of the foregoing, if we use the first simulation as a baseline, do the candidates improve or decline in subsequent exercises?

Before leaving the preceding litany, here are answers to a few of the trickier questions:

- **How did they handle rude questioners who didn't let them finish their responses?** You do *not* want to "get into it" with a rude reporter. Some reporters are naturally abrasive; others will interrupt you to throw you off your game, sometimes intentionally. If the crisis is huge, the reporter is often under enormous pressure from her editors to "get the story" and "get it *now*!" If the reporter gets under your skin, the tone of your response speaks for the company, so you may need to bite your tongue and moderate your response and your tone of voice. However, at some point, it is permissible to say, "I am trying to answer your questions, but I cannot do so if you continue to speak over me. Please let me respond and then ask your next question. If not, we will have to end this interview for now."

- **Were they answering what was asked?** This was a loaded question to the reader. Sometimes, for any number of reasons, you do not want to answer the precise question that was asked. Try to recast the question and provide the answer you want to offer. Also, untested spokespeople often forget that it is perfectly acceptable *not* to answer a question (just as long as you don't say "no comment"). Or, you can always defer by simply saying, "I don't have that information right now, but I will see if I can find out and get back to you." Or, you can look for openings to recast the question into one that you *do* want to answer.

- **If they were being interviewed in a hallway with a gaggle of reporters and TV cameras, did the spokesperson know where to look?** Focus on the reporter whose question you are answering; do not look at the camera. It avoids confusion on your part. It's good manners, and it is easy to remember: simply look at the person you're talking with.

- **When multiple questions were thrown at them at once, did they know what to do?** Answer the question you want to answer. Look at the reporter who asked you that question, and answer it. Answer the easiest of the questions first, but at the same time start formulating your responses to the other questions.

These are just some of the techniques we help client spokespersons develop. After an initial session, we play back the video (if we are recording the session) and critique it with the candidate, pointing out where he could have improved. Then we do it again until he becomes more inured to the process, and then we ratchet up the intensity of the questions. Once the session is concluded, periodic refresher courses are often helpful.

Some candidates "wash out." There is no shame in that, but now we know whom we will not use as a company spokesperson if a crisis breaks.

I am often asked to be the spokesman for a client in crisis, but I try to decline. I feel it is always better to have a representative from the company, rather than a "hired gun," out front.

In the Pat & Oscar's crisis discussed earlier, I mentioned that we took a regional manager for the company and made him the company spokesman. He was very nervous and was reluctant to take on this important role, but I assured him that he'd be fine, and we put him through a crash course in media relations. He was still nervous and somewhat tentative in his responses at the outset, but I insisted that he could do it and that he would do it very well—and he did. But, it was important to boost his confidence in the beginning.

There were other people I could have used, but George had all the right attributes: he had worked for the company for a long time, he was a district manager, he was a native of the community where the outbreak took place, he was one of the first people to get the call from the health department, and he came across as genuinely compassionate. He really did take the crisis personally. When he said to reporters, "I couldn't believe this was happening to Pat & Oscar's. We take such care in our food preparation and have always had an 'A' rating," he was sincere and believable. And his comments on that point were his own.

His early nervousness soon gave way to confidence after having one or two interviews under his belt, and he was very effective for us because it was obvious that he was an employee who was speaking from the heart.

When you pluck someone from relative obscurity and put the spotlight on him, as we did with George, sometimes coworkers will resent it: *why him and not me?* This happens more often than you might think, but we anticipate it and watch for warning signs. Why? Because sometimes that jealousy turns into mischief, or worse. In this case, despite our admonition that no one except the designated spokesperson was to talk to the media, we discovered that someone was leaking information. I should point out that the information that was leaked was not damaging or contradictory; it was just information that was known only internally and that we wanted to stay that way. We quickly discovered the leaker's identity and we "benched" him for the duration of the crisis.

At the time, senior management asked me why I insisted that this person not be fired. I said that if he's unhappy and causing trouble now, just imagine what damage he might do if he were fired. That old truism, keep your friends close and your enemies closer, has much merit.

During your crisis, you may want to consider discreet public opinion polling to find out how the public perceives your handling of the crisis, and whether it likes and believes your spokesperson and her messages. If you find that your spokesperson is not connecting with your constituencies, replace her. If your message is not connecting with your constituencies, tweak it so that it does.

Take control. Determine early exactly who is the right spokesperson for a crisis like *yours*. Remember, it's *your* crisis, *your* message, and *your* spokesperson.

Social Media and Digital Communications—or, Truth/Lies at the Speed of Light

■   ■   ■

The good news: YouTube is here!

The bad news: YouTube is here!

And both statements have huge implications for crisis communications.

If the previous chapter covered what have become known—rightly or wrongly—as "old media," this chapter deals with the newest and most revolutionary crisis communications tool in modern times, and potentially the worst: social media and digital communications. And while it is the proverbial double-edged sword, the way that sword swings is, in large measure, completely in your hands. Pun intended.

Let's first consider the awesome power of social media in the hands of "the people." Tools—weapons in some hands and in certain situations, some would opine—like Facebook, Twitter, YouTube, blogs, instant messaging, and so many others,[1] including even tools that seem old hat today, like basic e-mail and plain old texting, have caused a massive sea change in the crisis communications landscape in recent years. And there's no sign that this revolution will slow down anytime soon. If your company is in crisis and you haven't prepared your social media network well in advance for this eventuality, this could be your death knell.

For anyone who is not completely up to speed on the current crop of social media outlets, here is a primer I literally swiped from the Internet that will give you a fast working knowledge of how social media are used today in the real world. Think of it as Social Media for Dummies:

Social Media Explained:[2]

Twitter: I'm eating a donut.
Facebook: I like donuts.
Foursquare: This is where I eat donuts.
Instagram: Here's vintage picture of my donut.
YouTube: Here I am eating a donut.
LinkedIn: My skills include donut eating.
Pinterest: Here's a donut recipe.
Last FM: Now listening to "Donuts."
G+: I'm a Google employee who eats donuts.

If the so-called Arab Spring proved anything, it is that nothing is as powerful as an idea whose time has come to be posted or tweeted. It is no exaggeration to say that Facebook helped bring down the Egyptian government of Hosni Mubarak; Twitter helped corral, capture, and dethrone Libyan dictator Muammar Khadafi;

and, tying it all together, Google Maps pinpointed the upcoming sites of fast-breaking citizen uprisings and protests throughout the volatile Arab world in the game-changing spring of 2011—all of which heightened the intensity and solidarity of the unrest by mobilizing protesters in real time.

"[G]lobalization and the information technology revolution," soaring to new heights thanks to the social media explosion, is "the single most important trend in the world today," according to columnist Thomas Friedman.[3]

Dethroned dictators, however, would beg to differ, saying that social media are lethal weapons in the hands of lawless thugs; champions of democracy would disagree with the despots and say that in those and similar instances, social media were effective tools that accomplished, in the crucible of acute crises, in a matter of days or weeks what shuttle diplomacy by scores of bloviating political functionaries had been unable to achieve for decades. It's a matter of perspective as to who's right.

More recently, on the subject of brutal dictators, the viral YouTube video outlining the atrocities of Ugandan strongman Joseph Kony, leader of the guerilla group the Lord's Resistance Army, has, as of this writing, garnered more than 96 million hits, or views, and growing, and has sparked a worldwide movement to make his face as well known as those of the world's biggest celebrities, and thus—in theory—make it easier to bring him to international justice.[4]

A case of social media playing the role of hero.

Here in the United States, the overhyped "Occupy" protesters were marshaled like hapless drones in city after city by concealed leaders controlling BlackBerry Messages, Twitter, and other instant texts. In fact, it almost seems that new social media apps are being created on the fly to fill real or perceived demands. Like Vibe.

Vibe comes closest to Twitter in the social media spectrum, but unlike with Twitter and most other outlets, a Vibe user does not need to create an account to read or send messages. This allows for completely anonymous postings. All Vibe requires is the user's location, which a GPS-equipped mobile phone will provide automatically. Thus, where Twitter essentially broadcasts globally, Vibe broadcasts to people who are near the sender, and the person doing the posting can set the geographic radius for who can respond, thereby making it easy to communicate more directly with protesters in the Occupy movement and actually organize and stage local events and protests.[5] Had police been monitoring Vibe and other social media outlets, they could have known in advance where the next protests were going to take place and deployed personnel as needed to keep the protests and the protesters from getting out of hand.

In fact, if the police wanted to be surreptitious in their surveillance, all they needed was a Twitter account and a basic knowledge of hashtags (#), which give a user the ability to monitor and follow any given discussion without actually "following" any one individual or making his presence known. During the early stages of the original Occupy Wall Street movement, for example, the hashtag #ows (for "Occupy Wall Street") was widely followed and helped rally people at specific times and locations.

Law enforcement's apparent lack of social media skills early on was evident from the way protest after protest seemed to gain the upper hand. Law enforcement had better learn fast.

In Los Angeles, a rapper called "The Game," (real name Jayceon Terrell Taylor), tweeted the phone number of the Compton branch of the Los Angeles County Sheriff's Department and told his half-million mindless followers to call the number. Almost immediately, and for the next three hours, the Sheriff's Department's emergency lines were jammed, preventing people with real emergencies from getting through and getting the help they needed. Authorities, as of this writing, are deciding whether to file charges against Taylor, and if so, with what to charge him.

Following riots and looting in London, organized largely by BBMs (BlackBerry Messages), British Prime Minister David

Cameron actually proposed shutting down social media access for anyone suspected of criminal activity. That sort of police-state threat was never carried out.

In San Francisco, following the police shooting of a knife-wielding man, social media quickly organized a protest on a subway platform. This caught surprised cops flat-footed, so they blocked cell phone service at the station. Undeterred, the protesters used social media to organize protests that completely shut down operations at other BART (Bay Area Rapid Transit) stations.

"Twitter and other social media have made it much easier to mobilize large crowds quickly, and police are struggling to keep up," according to reporters Robert Faturechi and Andrew Blankstein. "Some police departments are beginning to assign officers to monitor Facebook, Twitter and other sites in search of crime and also to understand how social media work."[6]

Indications are that the learning curve for law enforcement, while steep, can pay off.

When the Los Angeles Police Department saw a pattern of tweets indicating that the band Red Hot Chili Peppers was going to hold an impromptu free summer rock concert on the popular Venice Beach, it sent additional police into the area early to keep the crowd from getting too rowdy.

"'It could have easily gotten out of control, but we got information from Twitter that allowed us to front-load officers down there, mitigate traffic and drinking, check permits and address the large crowd,' [LAPD Commander Andy] Smith said. 'If we weren't there when this started, it could have been a disaster.'"[7]

The power that social media have to influence opinions and even actions cannot be overstated. Even small, off-the-radar blogs can move mountains, and Jon Fleischman is a good example.

Fleischman, a Sacramento, California–based political gadfly, runs an activist conservative website, FlashReport.org. After a late-night legislative session not too long ago, in which leaders of both major parties and of both chambers thought that they had finally made enough cuts to hammer out a budget compromise, someone leaked word of the deal to Fleischman. Almost immediately, his "obscure, but influential website . . . slammed the deal as 'fat' and 'bloated' and likened it to 'putting lipstick on a pig.'

"'I knew as soon as I saw that post go up that the deal would collapse,'" Adam Mendelsohn, then an aide to [then Governor Arnold] Schwarzenegger said. . . . 'Maybe an hour after that, we got a call: There wouldn't be a vote that night. Here we were in the biggest state in the union and important policy was being dictated by a blog post at midnight.'"[8]

Fleischman makes no bones about his Republican leanings. His reportings are biased—he admits that; he generally puts his own spin on facts.

But what happens when social media are used for *purely* nefarious purposes? Just ask South Carolina Governor Nikki Haley, whose latest politically-motivated-by-enemies crisis post went viral in a matter of minutes. Literally.

At 12:52 p.m. one day in 2012, a political adversary created and posted a blog saying that Governor Haley was about to be indicted for tax fraud. At 1:14 p.m.—22 blazingly fast minutes later—the item was retweeted by a reporter for the *Washington Post*, who violated one of the cardinal rules of journalism: check the facts. As the minutes ticked on, other media outlets followed suit, and at 3:29 p.m., the *Drudge Report* featured this jaw-dropping headline: "Report: DOJ May Indict SC Gov. Haley for Tax Fraud." And the next day, South Carolina's largest newspaper—a sad example of old media playing a desperate game of catch-up to new media—breathlessly featured the story on its front page.

But there wasn't a shred of truth to the story.

Incredibly, even as this story was spreading at full tilt, exactly 20 minutes after the first blog appeared, a *USA Today* reporter with a brain used old technology—the telephone!—to call Governor Haley's office to find out if the story were true.

And *still* the false story spread unchecked.

"What is abominably clear is that this sort of thing can happen to anyone at any time," wrote columnist Kathleen Parker in the *Washington Post*. "And much worse things can be said that can't easily be disproved. Haley extinguished this fire by releasing a letter from the Internal Revenue Service stating that there was no investigation. But what if, instead, the rumor were that a candidate was once suspected of child abuse?"[9]

It would be a lot tougher to get *that* toothpaste back into the tube.

This is also known as "cybersmear," a relatively new tactic that can ratchet up the crisis stakes immeasurably and with devastating speed. And when damaging stories are concocted out of whole cloth, the victim is forced to resort to all sorts of contortions to try to prove her innocence, and sometimes even more damage ensues as a result.

Parker laments the "failure of legitimate news organizations to turn the rumor over and examine its underbelly before reprinting it,"[10] despite the fact that *USA Today* seemed to be heading down that very righteous path 20 short minutes after the story first appeared. Then why did the story continue to grow anyway? As Parker put it, "Indictments spread like wildfire; corrections couldn't roast a marshmallow."[11]

Some refer to this as "new journalism," but I categorically reject that appellation. Journalism, by and large, is an honorable profession, made up of men and women whose writings or broadcasts are (or are supposed to be) subject to various layers of review and fact checking by editors and others before a story goes public. If you or your company is the target of an "old media" story, you may not like what's been written, but by and large, reporting rules were followed, or at least they were *supposed* to have been followed. There are, of course, exceptions to every rule, and too often political biases overshadow the remnants of what once was referred to with pride as "objective reporting." Drastic budget cutbacks resulting from shrinking advertising revenue, spurred by advertisers flocking to digital advertising outlets, have resulted in staff reductions among print media that severely limit editorial manpower and fact checkers in newspapers across the country. Also, it's cheaper to hire wet-behind-the-ears so-called reporters to replace veteran newspeople, so many of whom opted for buyout packages and early retirement that newsrooms were depleted of warm and experienced bodies. So while the fact-checking model remains in theory, the reality in practice is that many stories that haven't been completely vetted or properly written or edited are rushed into print.

A case in point: a recent front-page postelection story in the *Los Angeles Times*, ostensibly about the San Francisco Bay Area's two newly elected female Asian American mayors, carried in its lead paragraph this head-scratching phrase in a passing, non sequitur reference to the state's then newly minted lieutenant governor: "Gavin Newsom, who has taken his gelled hair and actress wife to Sacramento. . . ."[12]

What in the world does Mr. Newsom's hair, gelled or otherwise, have to do with a story on new Asian American civic leaders? In fact, the article had nothing whatever to do with Newsom. And since when is it acceptable journalism to use a sobriquet ("actress wife") without also mentioning her actual name somewhere in the article? To say nothing of the fact that in Los Angeles, which the *Times* calls home, half the town has gelled hair and the other half has actress wives (or actor husbands).

The immature writing of the two reporters, Maria La Ganga and Lee Romney, who write as though they were dropped from their high school papers, was bad enough, but where were the seasoned editors who are supposed to review copy before it's printed? The snarky, pejorative phrasing in the story raises two important questions: what was the paper's ulterior motive behind the cheap shot, and is it no longer accurate to call the *L.A. Times* "an objective paper"?

On the other hand, those who have an agenda and who tweet have no such filters at all, and with no accountability, they are nothing more than modern-day bushwhackers—no better than those old Western movie cowards who'd shoot a man in the back without thinking twice.

To be fair, there are digital media outlets that do check facts before a story runs. But the entire landscape of social media is more akin to the Wild West, where lawlessness (read: blogging agenda-laden rumors instead of facts) reigns supreme.

However, the Internet makes it easy for rumors and cybercrises to arise. And whether they occur on purpose or by happenstance, they must be dealt with immediately, before they spread unchecked. What you want to do is drive a stake through the rumor's heart quickly, but even that doesn't always work. Once something is on the Internet, it has a way of rematerializing when you least expect it. Still, you need to be aggressive and try. "This will blow over" as a mantra or security blanket always fails.

This is where you can and should use your company's social media skills to set the record straight. If people want to attack you or spread rumors about you, they're going to do it. If the rumors are false and you know who is spreading them, you may have some legal recourse. However, as long as the rumors continue to spread in cyberspace, you will be damaged, and your crisis communications challenges become more like trench warfare. "The only way to put out a social-media fire is with social-media water," according to Ramon DeLeon, a social media maven.

So it's important that you keep your guard up at all times and monitor social media 24/7 to learn as early as possible if you or your company is under attack by a blogger. But sometimes it is possible to be too aggressive when throwing up your shields. That's a lesson that Kansas Governor Sam Brownback learned the hard way when he brought out the big guns to swat an 18-year-old high school student's tweet.

"Ending a battle that could only have taken place in the brave new world of social media, Kansas Gov. Sam Brownback on Monday apologized for an incident involving a teen who had maligned him on Twitter," wrote a *Los Angeles Times* scribe in a story that the paper trumpeted: "Teen Tweeter 1, Kansas Governor 0." What did young Emma Sullivan do? She tweeted that the governor "sucked."[13]

The story began with a small white lie. Emma had attended a Youth in Government program at the state capitol where the governor had made an appearance, and tweeted that she had just told Brownback to his face that "he sucked." In truth, she hadn't done so, but perhaps she projected her true feelings, as opposed to her actions, in the tweet, which was seen by the governor's overzealous aides. They contacted the youth program, which contacted Emma's high school principal. Emma, then a senior at Shawnee Mission East High School at Prairie Village, Kansas, was summoned to the principal's office, where she was directed to write a letter of apology to the governor. Suggested writing points were provided, and a Monday morning line-in-the-sand deadline was decreed.

Emma refused, and made it clear that she had no intention of apologizing.

As word spread and this became a freedom of speech cause célèbre, offers of help for Emma came pouring in. Prior to the incident, Emma had had about five dozen Twitter followers; which quickly mushroomed to more than 11,000. Brownback on his best day had only about 3,300 followers of his Twitter musings.

Soon the school district, wisely deciding that it had had enough of the can't-win imbroglio, backed down and acknowledged that "a student's right to freedom of speech and expression is constitutionally protected" and that Emma "is not required to write a letter of apology to the governor."[14]

Brownback, trying to save face, posted on Facebook, "My staff overreacted to this tweet, and for that I apologize. Freedom of speech is among our most treasured freedoms."[15]

The school district's statement, acknowledging the times we live in, concluded, "The issue has resulted in many teachable moments concerning the use of social media."[16]

Left unclear in the backtracking statement is exactly who needs to be taught what.

But enough about brutal dictators, ego-amped rappers, stick-in-the-mud educators, sloppy "journalism," full-of-themselves politicians, drive-by tweet victims, and teenage fibbers who hold their ground against weak-kneed, holier-than-thou school officials.

Let's talk about *you*.

If you are a publicly traded company, you may remember wistfully those days of yore when the only time you had to meet your public was during the public comments section of your annual meeting. And no matter how rough the questioning at the meeting became, when it was over, you were fairly well insulated for another 12 months. No longer. Today, your public uses every conceivable social media outlet to bring the fight to you, day in, day out, and in the most public and private (say, your front lawn) forums imaginable. And if your company is undergoing a crisis, this ratchets up the ante considerably. If you're fortunate, the attacks on you, your company, or your product will at least be of a type that affords you a reasonable counterargument to put forward to your constituents—your side of the story, as it were. But today, with so many tweeters with so many agendas, sometimes people just make stuff up, and before the brakes can be applied, serious damage is done.

Just ask Governor Haley.

It's like that old conundrum question for which there is no right answer: yes or no, do you still beat your wife?

Even on a good day, every company has enemies—bitter competitors, unhappy customers, disgruntled current or former workers, soured shareholders, unpaid vendors, and so on. But when you are a company in crisis, and the *perception* of your handling of the crisis is negative, the number of those in opposing camps can take on mythic proportions, real or imagined.

And every single one of them is armed with her own mega-sized barrel of ink: her personal social media outlet.

Faster than you can say Mark Zuckerberg, Facebook attack pages, where you and your company are denounced as (insert pejorative expletive of your choice here), can be created and launched, and thousands if not tens of thousands of people can visit the page, leave their own disparaging comments about you and your company, and, like emperors of ancient Rome, decide your fate by turning their thumbs up or down with "likes" or "unlikes." And when one person "unlikes" you or expresses a scathing opinion about your company with a "comment," his Facebook friends are notified of his negative views or opinions, and then *their* friends are notified. In such an everyday occurrence, such posts grow exponentially and seemingly instantaneously. Before you know what hit you, you're as vilified as Bernie Madoff at a meeting of his former investment clients.

Suppose you leave your house for work one morning and find yourself confronted by an angry mob of protesters. If you say just one discouraging word, let the slightest inkling of your temper flare, accidentally bump into someone who is blocking your path to your car, or hell, just look cross-eyed at someone, the entire incident will be caught on cell phone video and posted on YouTube before you get out of your driveway and go viral before you arrive at work.

People who have nothing better to do tweet all day long; and people who are on a mission against the perceived heavy-handed way you are mismanaging your company's crisis and driving your company and its stock prices into the ground will tweet like two thumbs possessed. And those tweets are retweeted until they span the globe. All too often—especially when vendettas are involved—truth and facts are left bleeding and dying on the sidewalk, victims of drive-by tweeting.

More than a century ago, Mark Twain famously quipped, "A lie can travel half-way around the world while the truth is putting on its shoes." Imagine what he'd say *today*!

Bloggers—think Twitter without the 140-word message limitation—are generally on a mission of some kind, and the original blog and the multitude of comments find a permanent home on the Internet. Having a blogger as your enemy while you are trying to manage a crisis is an irritant that sometimes festers. Bloggers want action; they demand attention; they try to get in your face. You may believe that you cannot accommodate their needs while you are in the midst of a crisis, but if you ignore them, the headaches they cause only grow more acute.

Add to all of this the weight of the celebrities and politicians who jump on some of these social cause bandwagons. It is not that their presence makes the stories being peddled any more or less true, but that their celebrity status gives the stories more visibility. If it is a YouTube video, that translates into more views, or hits. And more visibility can affect the *perception* of reality.

Not too long ago, one of the plaints often heard was that someone was misquoted or something she said was taken out of context. You were, by and large, at the mercy of a reporter and that reporter's accuracy and professionalism. This hasn't changed: when you're speaking with a reporter, print or electronic, everything you say is edited by the reporter and the reporter's editors (or is supposed to be). Even live interviews can be "edited" to conform to a biased editor or producer's viewpoint, and this can happen even to people who are experienced in granting interviews.

Like me.

It's no secret that Fox News has a strong conservative bent, and it's also no secret that conservatives generally favor more oil drilling in the United States. Just listen to any of Sarah Palin's speeches about drilling for oil in northern Alaska and her "Drill, Baby, Drill!" mantra. As the BP Gulf oil spill was still raging, a Fox News producer asked me if I could spare 20 minutes to do a live interview regarding the spill. Since I did not have time to get to the studio, we agreed to conduct the interview via Skype. The oil was still spewing, and I was told that the interview would concern my views on how the crisis was being managed. I had had some involvement in the *Exxon Valdez* oil spill crisis in Prince William Sound, Alaska, some years earlier, and I am considered a crisis management expert, so asking to interview me on this subject made sense. I agreed to the interview.

The first—and only—question put to me in this 20-minute scheduled interview was: "What advice would you give BP to help the company convince the people of the Gulf region that drilling for oil is safe?"[17]

I began—operative word, *began*—my response as follows: "That question presupposes that I agree with your basic premise that drilling for oil is inherently safe." Before I could say another word, my microphone and my picture went dead, and through my earpiece I heard the interviewer say, "Thank you, but I'm sorry we're out of time."

The Fox News producer *thought* she knew what I was going to say, and apparently my *supposed* comments flew in the face of her or the network's conservative corporate doctrine, so she told the interviewer to end the session with me immediately. Actually, Fox News had no idea what I was going to say and never gave me a chance to offer my views. The show's producer's conservative paranoia led her to literally pull the plug on the interview before it ever began.

The point of this anecdote is simply that I give media interviews fairly often and have for many years. If something like this can happen to me, it can happen to you.

Today, every company has the ability to level the playing field, if not tilt it in its own favor, by using the ever-growing arsenal of social media programs, platforms, and apps to communicate with its constituents and get its messages out *directly*. You don't have to own a newspaper or buy ink by the barrel to do so. With relatively little money and a decent Internet connection, you're pretty much in business.

The greatest tool that social media provide to businesses that need to get their message out is the ability to leapfrog traditional media and get the company's messages through to its constituents in a direct, highly targeted, unedited, and unfiltered way. The importance of this ability to communicate directly with constituents during a crisis cannot be overstated.

If crisis communications has the ability to shape the perception of how well a company is managing its crisis, the effective and strategic use of social media is one of the most powerful ways *you* can shape that perception.

This gives you more control over your own destiny. This is power to the people to the nth degree. Don't run from it; embrace it.

HOW?

Your marketing people will give you all the reasons why you want to have a prominent presence in the social media world, starting with perhaps the most basic element: a Facebook page.

In a perfect world, where there are no crises to worry about, your Facebook page is a repository of information and updates about the company and events at, or sponsored by, the company. But this is not a perfect world, and when a crisis befalls you, using the goodwill you have created and the names, e-mail addresses, user names, and so on of your customers that you've captured in your social media outlets, or of people who have just "liked" you on Facebook and will receive news from you whenever you add to or update your page, will enable you to reach your constituents immediately and explain the crisis from *your* perspective. You will be able to say anything you want and put your crisis into a perspective that you fashion.

If a blogger, for example, is criticizing your actions or nonactions, it may be because he really doesn't like you or your company, or it may be because he is unaware of the true facts of the situation. You may not be able to turn his mind around, but this is your golden opportunity to set the record straight with the world without having your comments severely edited for content or truncated for lack of space. There may be some give and take ("he said, she said"), but at least your message is being disseminated directly to your key constituents, while the rest of the world peeks in.

You may even find it beneficial to engage in an online dialogue with your antagonist. Doing so may help to defuse a potentially explosive situation if you come across as rational against your aggressor's shrill rantings. This is a tool that mainstream media do not offer, so make the most of it. Listen carefully to the criticisms and see what you can learn. A crisis is a fluid and dynamic state of affairs; your ability to respond must be equal to the task. However, beware of engaging with extremists and "legitimizing" them in the process.

You can record your unedited, unfiltered message on YouTube and post that all-important crisis communications video message on your Facebook and Twitter accounts, to name just two possibilities. Anyone who has ever given a taped interview will tell you that no matter how the interview seemed to go, you're lucky if 15 to 30 seconds of it ever gets used on the air. Sometimes that's because of biased editing, but often it's just a lack of unlimited time. YouTube solves that problem. And if you're a company in crisis that has been accused of manufacturing a life-threatening product, and you have a good explanation of why that story is false, wouldn't you welcome the opportunity to tell your full side of the story directly to your publics in general and your customers in particular? That's especially true if you have a crisis media–trained, telegenic CEO who can look directly into a teleprompter and speak with sincerity.

You also have the ability to update or add to the information conveyed in that video each day, or even each hour, if necessary, as new facts emerge. For example, if you are involved in a life-threatening crisis, you should use every means available to update your constituents as frequently as possible.

Most businesses of a certain size have a staff or management position of director or vice president of communications. Within that framework, there should be a manager of social media, preferably as a full-time position. This is not a dilettante position—it's not the part-time summer position you give to your wife's teenage nephew as a favor to her sister. If it is set up properly and strategically, this individual or department will be one of your most valuable assets in the heat of an acute crisis.

A social media manager should spend the majority of her time each day online, monitoring key media outlets—including the websites of newspapers and radio and television stations—to track stories that are of interest to your business or that concern your business. Think of that task as reactive. But in order to build a following, you need to be proactive and post stories that are favorable to the company. If your company is tweeting or posting only once or twice a week or less, you may as well shut down the site. You don't want to overwhelm your followers with too many alerts, but you do want to stay in front of your constituents and make your postings relevant.

Today, the third most active social media site is Pinterest, which calls itself an online pinboard. You usually will find photos and fashion items on the site, but if your company falls into any of the broad categories used for interest levels of Pinterest subscribers, you can build new and loyal followers of your messages. Yes, this is good for your business, but it also will be helpful in getting out your messages in a crisis.

Google Alerts, a powerful tool in its own right and one that has been around for some time, allows users to enter search words or phases (for example, the name of a company or individual); whenever one of those search terms appears in a media outlet around the world, the person who created the search gets an e-mail alert from Google with a link to the actual story. So far, however Google Alerts is primarily used to monitor mainstream media.

Google Reader, however, is one of several social media apps that monitors websites across the globe for keywords and subjects that you request. Google Reader then provides RSS (Rich Site Summary) real-time information on what is being said or written about in a news feed, eliminating the need for you to open an e-mail, click on a link to visit a website, and perhaps having to register on a new site before you can see the content fully. Bloglines and My Yahoo! are two other popular web-based news feed readers.

Another alternative tool called Jami, which is based in Asia, monitors social media outlets and also provides alerts via live RSS feeds, as well as translations (if needed) with the push of a button.

HootSuite, another similar and helpful app, provides users with their own customized dashboard to help them monitor and keep track of multiple social media networks. HootSuite allows users to see all activity of interest in one place, as well as providing them with the ability to post their own messages and even schedule postings in advance.

Collective Intellect, recently purchased by Oracle Corp., is another social media tracking service that is designed to help companies monitor and respond to actual consumer conversations on various sites, such as Facebook, Twitter, and so on. Sites like these can help an astute social media director to spot troubling trends—*prodromes!*—and try to resolve a potential crisis before it erupts into an acute crisis.

And there are many more services, some of them strategically sporting the word *reputation* in their names. Their claim is that they will search the Internet, including all possible social media sites, for postings about your company and help you gauge any damage to your online reputation. And, naturally, they can help you repair it if necessary, . . . for a fee. A full-time social media person can probably accomplish the same thing, but if you are a small- to medium-sized firm, outside resources like these can prove helpful.

This discussion could go on and on, but here's what's important to keep in mind. First, this is the tip of the social media iceberg. Every day, more apps are being created. As little as a decade ago, all you had to do was pick up the local newspaper or maybe the *Wall Street Journal* or the *New York Times* to find out what people were saying about you. Not any more. You've got to monitor the blogosphere continuously, and the operative word is *continuously*. The apps listed here are just the beginning, and your social media director can and should be aware of others as they go live.

Second, this cannot and should not be done ad hoc. There is so much stuff being said "out there" that a social media–savvy person or department needs to be specifically given the task of keeping tabs on it all, at least as it pertains to *your* interests. This would be a perfect job for a smart, young, social media–adept college grad with an English degree and an ability to write.

Third, this is a perfect opportunity to create dialogues and build bridges. If the blogosphere is carrying misinformation about your company or its crisis, this is where you can find out about it fast, set the record straight, and build important bridges and open dialogues with those who have a different mindset before firmly entrenched opinions are created. But, as with anything related to social media, speed is of the essence.

It is important to understand and acknowledge that that recent college grad I just mentioned is probably not qualified to speak for the company on his own. However, he can bring the negative stories and trends to the communications chief, who, in swift consultation with the powers that be, can fashion suitable responses—which should be done with dispatch. The approved messages then can be posted by your social media director.

The ability to leapfrog over mainstream media in a single bound is pure gold. After so many years when you were at the mercy of those who buy ink by the barrel, social media have leveled the playing field in your favor. You can now take your message directly to the people without fear of being misquoted.

But be forewarned: the playing field has also been tilted *against you* and in favor of those who would oppose you. The advantages granted to you by the social media gods have also been bestowed upon your adversaries. This simply means that you and your social media director need to be ever more vigilant. Remember: extinguish social-media fires with social-media water.

For example, political websites and bloggers on both sides of the aisle are rampant. If you are a company that has a real or perceived liberal agenda or that contributes to left-wing causes, you may find yourself the target of conservative bloggers and websites such as Fox News, the Drudge Report, the Breitbart website, the Daily Caller, the Weekly Standard, and many more.

On the other side, if you and your company support right-wing issues, sites such as the Huffington Post, Slate, Politico, the ACLU, the Democratic Underground, and so on may target you.

It is possible to nip something in the bud in these circumstances. Realistically, if you're dealing with a blogger with an agenda, your direct efforts to convert the miscreant will be for naught. However, knowing what is being said out there allows you to post the truth—or at least your version of the truth—on your website, Facebook page, Twitter account, and so on, and to do so early, before the naysayers have gained a foothold in the blogosphere. Do not go radio silent when you are under attack. Make your voice and your story heard. Take full advantage of the myriad social media avenues that are open to you.

By acknowledging on your own social media outlets that misinformation is being posted about you, and now here's your side of the story, you are taking some of the wind out of that opposing blogger's sails. Moreover, if you have, over the years, cultivated a reputation for being a "straight shooter" and have taken the time and put forth the effort to create deep reservoirs of goodwill, you will be making great strides in your overall crisis communications strategies.

We will delve a little deeper into the concept of reservoirs of goodwill later, but for now it is important to know that such valuable assets can be accrued through an active and meaningful social media presence. If your company has a Facebook page, for example, no matter what else is going on in the company on a routine basis, that page and those friends who have "liked" you in the past are now part of your active crisis communications arsenal if and when trouble breaks. If they "liked" you on Facebook, that means that they are already favorably disposed to you as a company. Given that assumption, they are likely to be allies in the opening volleys of a crisis, and you should communicate with them early and often.

On the subject of "often," as you post things on various social media platforms during noncrisis times, remember that you shouldn't make a pest of yourself and overload your followers with an endless stream of banality. Keep your posts varied and targeted to the largest common denominator of followers. That said, memories are short, especially on social media, where there is just so much information streaming at you and demanding your attention 24/7, so you need to keep your presence in the forefront of your constituents' minds. Three to five informative posts a week is sufficient to keep your followers engaged. These posts should be carefully planned out in advance—say at the beginning of the week, and perhaps tied in to something else that's going on at the company, such as a sale for a retail business or the grand opening of a retail outlet. And the tone you adopt should reflect and be aligned with the nature of your business. Your posts could be serious, funny, dietary, casual, intense, academic, financial, or something else. If you are a bank, for example, or any other "serious" business, you don't want to communicate in a cute or flippant manner that would befit, say, a coffee shop. Know who you are, know who your audience is, and don't talk down to it. This is where having a creative writer in your social media position is vital.

Of paramount importance is this: if you are wrong in a crisis (for example, one of your products has a defect), say so via social media (and other media outlets) and explain what you are going to do about it, especially what you are doing to protect the public. Keep uppermost in your mind that you are now speaking directly to the people who may have been affected by this issue, and if they think you are stonewalling them, they will be your most ardent critics. Give your followers accurate, swift, and reliable information direct from "the horse's mouth." This will help reduce the length of time that the story stays alive, whereas lies and cover-ups will only prolong it when the truth eventually comes out, as it always does.

None of the foregoing is to suggest that the mainstream media be ignored or overlooked in a crisis. Just understand the meaning of an "oppositional crisis."

I usually counsel clients that one way to classify crises is by whether they are oppositional or nonoppositional. This is an important distinction, and one that you had better have clear in your mind as you engage your crisis communications strategies. A nonoppositional crisis—the better of the two—is one in which the world is on your side and wants you to succeed. Perhaps the most famous nonoppositional crisis, mentioned a little earlier, was the Johnson & Johnson Tylenol crisis of the 1980s, when a terrorist slipped cyanide into Tylenol capsules and seven people in the greater Chicago area died. This was a heinous and cowardly act, and as the FBI tried desperately to catch the culprit and pundits were writing off J&J's chances of saving the brand, almost everyone was hoping that the terrorist would be caught and rooting for the company to succeed. There have been others, too, including the Chilean mine collapse, also touched on earlier. It was nothing short of a miracle when 33 miners were discovered alive, but trapped, some three weeks after the disaster. During the rescue, the world waited and prayed for a successful rescue.

In a nonoppositional crisis, the world is hoping that you succeed. The world is on your side.

Conversely, an oppositional crisis is one in which you have your side of the story and others have their side. An objective reporter will record and publish your answers to her questions, but she also will interview and report on the views and opinions of your opposition. You see this all the time in crises that result in litigation, at shareholder meetings, or in the case of accidents.

And what I always tell clients is that they will not like these stories because they will feel that the reporters are giving too much time and attention to the company's adversaries. Actually, they probably aren't, but it is human nature to read those "balanced" stories and see only the negative things that are being said about you, completely discounting all the positive things that were said. Therefore, it is natural for you not to like those stories.

As this chapter has demonstrated, with the global reach of social media, it is easy to subject the world to your version of the facts in a completely direct and unfiltered style. Why, then, clients occasionally ask me, should they agree to sit down with, say, the *New York Times*? The reporter is only going to give your critics a chance to attack you, so why should you cooperate with a print or TV or radio or online reporter?

That's a reasonable question, perhaps, until your understand the consequences of not cooperating with the interviewer's request.

Ignoring the mainstream media is tantamount to giving your opponent an open field, a chance to score a touchdown without any opponents—*you!*—on the field to block his forward progress. Why would any rationale person do *that*?

No, the pragmatic solution is to use all relevant facets of social media to communicate directly with your constituents, while still playing ball with the mainstream media. But you can be judicious in deciding which interviews to grant, since you now know that the mainstream media are not your sole means of crisis communication salvation.

In a crisis, your communications people can, and should, have a strategic plan to get your message out to all of your targeted audiences. You should use YouTube and other such outlets to post taped, rehearsed, and polished comments from you, speaking *directly* into the eyes of your constituents. Learn how to use and get comfortable with a teleprompter.

If an antagonist posts something adverse about you, your company, or the manner in which you're managing the crisis, your social media people should promptly post accurate and respectful rebuttals. At the same time, they should look for trends that may tell you how you and your management of the crisis are being perceived by the public. This knowledge will help you determine whether you need to modify or strengthen your key message points. Remember the importance of perception: even if you *know* you're right, if the perception is that you're wrong, you *are* wrong. Or, at least, you're wrong in the eyes and minds of those who matter. Your goal now is to figure out how to change that perception, and social media can play a pivotal role in doing that.

There are new risks and rewards in using social media during a crisis, but then again, there are risks and rewards inherent in every crisis. Remember: *wei-ji*, the Chinese word for crisis, contains characters representing both danger and opportunity.

One final note on the power and swiftness of social media and why whether they are a tool or a weapon depends on your perspective:

When the five young Cordell siblings living near Boston pestered their folks for a puppy, to little avail, the kids offered a challenge. What if we get a million "likes" on Facebook, they proposed. Can we get a puppy then? Overconfident no doubt that such a thing was impossible, dad Ryan Cordell readily agreed. The photogenic kids posed behind a large handmade sign that read:

Hi World.
We want a puppy!
Our dad said we could get one if we get 1 million Likes!
He doesn't think we can do it!
So "LIKE" this!

They posted it on Facebook and went to sleep. The post went viral, and the kids got one million "likes" in only 13 hours. As of this writing, they're at 2.6 million "likes."

No word yet on whether Dad will keep his word. The kids think Facebook is a great tool; Ryan may think it's a "beastly" weapon.[18]

Shakespeare Was Right: *"The first thing we do, let's kill all the lawyers."**

■   ■   ■

n a crisis, lawyers generally fall into one of two camps: those that are helpful and those that are obstructionists. Those in the latter category usually don't favor talking to the media; "no comment" is the mantra they have tattooed on their foreheads, and woe

---

* William Shakespeare, *King Henry VI*, Part II, Act IV, Scene 2. Shakespeare actually meant this line as a tribute, not a curse, to the legal profession. His point was that lawyers were a formidable defense against those who would overthrow a democratic form of government. Thus, to topple a government, first weaken one of its strongest defenses—lawyers—by slaying the whole lot of them. The current connotation of this classic line says more about the low esteem in which lawyers are held than it says about Shakespeare. Whatever the Bard's original intent, the line has come down through hundreds of years to infer that lawyers stand in the way of progress. And, regrettably, sometimes in the way of crisis management and crisis communications.

to any client who doesn't cleave closely to their holy pronouncements about not communicating in a crisis.

Many lawyers treat the law as stark, draconian, and largely black
and white, and those who have been trained that way respond accordingly in a crisis. Crises, on the other hand, exist in the vast complexity
of the gray, with much more texture and nuance. Effective crisis communications uses that gray to the communicator's advantage to shape
the perception of how a crisis is being handled.

Lawyers have a tough enough job to do, but it's like the old
adage, "If all you have is a hammer, every problem looks like a
nail." Consequently, lawyers sometimes just don't—or won't—
see the bigger crisis picture; instead, they view most crises exclusively through the myopic lens of possible litigation. If lawyers are
unmoving or unreasonable when you are trying to communicate
the company's position to your constituents, this can hamper your
best crisis communications intentions. But there are ways to skirt
these annoying roadblocks.

In a crisis, narrow-thinking—not narrow-minded—lawyers
sometimes get tripped up by their own legal training. I have actually seen lawyers who were more interested in winning a legal battle in court than in saving the company in the marketplace. These
Pyrrhic victories are a travesty at best and a disaster for the company in crisis at worst.

In short, as a general rule, lawyers are not trained crisis
communicators.

Some of the most successfully managed crises I've been
involved in have included excellent working partnerships between
lawyers and my firm. When everyone is working for the same
goal—managing the crisis toward a successful conclusion—the
client usually comes out on top. But then there are times that just
make you shake your head.

One of the more unusual crises I was asked to consult on concerned
a very prominent Fortune-listed company that was being sued by

a single individual in the rural Deep South. The company, which must remain nameless, is a large manufacturer, and by-products of its manufacturing process spewed into an adjacent river by design. The company had all the proper environmental permits. This discharge caused no harm or health consequences, but a man living downriver of the plant was nevertheless fearful that he *might* contract cancer as a result of what was being pumped into the river. He was perfectly healthy, but he sued anyway. The basis of his suit? Fear.

A nuisance suit, I can hear you saying.

Since the case was being tried in the Deep South, the company hired a local "good ol' boy" law firm in Mississippi to handle the defense. The local media, alerted by an aggressive plaintiff's attorney who was peddling his client's tale of fear wherever and whenever he could, picked up on the story and contacted the defense attorney for comment. He refused any comment at all. The reporter, undaunted, contacted my client's public relations department, which was known for being open with, and helpful to, the media. However, the company had already been put on notice—and I do mean put on notice—by the good ol' boy lead attorney in the case. He told the company that he knows "these folks down here, and they don't wanna read any comments in the papers from some high-salaried corporate suits from the big city."

And then he went so far as to threaten the company's most senior management: if they said one word to the media, he browbeat them, he would refuse to take any responsibility for the outcome of the case, which he predicted the company would then lose. The client well knew that many other plaintiff's attorneys and potential litigants were watching the case with great interest, and that if the first plaintiff won, it would be open season for a raft of class-action lawsuits against the client from every Tom, Dick, and Billy Bob who lived downstream from any of the company's plants anywhere in the country.

Sufficiently chastened, the client acquiesced to the lawyer's demands, and while it pained them, its personnel refused to make *any* comment to the media.

The company lost the case anyway.

The company appealed the case and retained the same attorney and his firm to handle the appeal. The media were still looking for any comment from what was now being referred to as the "cancer-causing company," but that same attorney warned them again: I will not take any responsibility for the outcome of this appeal if you speak one word to the media.

The company lost the appeal.

It was at this point that I received an emergency phone call from the senior vice president of corporate communications. The company sent a private corporate jet to pick me up in Los Angeles and fly me cross-country for a meeting with three people: the chairman of the board and CEO, the chief corporate counsel, and the head of corporate communications. It was surreal.

The four of us met in the company's massive boardroom on the top floor of its corporate office, sitting at a highly polished mahogany table that could have accommodated dozens. The chairman paced nervously and gazed out the window at a panoramic vista of the city as the corporate attorney addressed me.

"We want to tell you our situation and then ask your advice, which will boil down to one question," she began, and then proceeded to lay out in great and methodical detail the story I have just recapped very, very briefly. She explained that the company was planning to appeal again, and acknowledged that other litigation from other plaintiffs and other attorneys had already been filed. She also told me that the good ol' boy attorney was expecting to handle not just this appeal, but the defense of the other cases, too.

And with each new filing came more and more media requests for interviews.

She spoke nonstop for nearly two hours as the chairman continued to pace and take in the view; no one else said a word. She went into great detail about what the plant in question manufactured, how it manufactured the product, and what was being pumped into the river. She showed me independent lab reports and EPA reports attesting to the noncarcinogenic nature of the emissions and by-products. She showed me environmental permits. Finally, when she had finished, the chairman sat down opposite me and said simply and in a very soft and concerned voice: "What would you recommend we do?"

"Fire the attorney," I said, "and hire a new one that understands the importance of communicating in a crisis. Then, put on a full court media blitz to explain why you are a good company and a good corporate citizen that provides jobs, security, and valuable products and *that you do not cause cancer*. Tell the media what you just told me. Take them on tours of the plant."

I then explained that because the company had not defended itself against previous attacks in the media, the public was turning against it, including some of its own employees. Because it had lost two cases, *the perception was that it was guilty of causing cancer, and perception trumps reality*.

My final advice: "Do whatever you need to do, but change the perception to match the reality."

There was an audible sigh of relief, most notably coming from the head of corporate communications, who I could feel was just waiting for someone to unshackle her. It was, and still is, a solid company, and it had never run from controversy in the past. The gag the local attorney had placed over its mouth was just killing it.

The bottom line was, the company followed my advice (only a thumbnail of which just I related), hired a more enlightened attorney, communicated openly and proactively with the media about its operations, openly shared its own and independent safety and environmental tests assuring that no carcinogens were present, and beat back the appeal and all the other cases that had been filed. In fairness, this company knew what needed to be done all along. The executives *knew* that the lawyer's advice was wrongheaded— the company didn't become a global leader in its field by being dense—but they blindly followed the lawyer's "no comment" dictate because "he's our lawyer."

They just needed to have what they already knew confirmed by a crisis communications expert from outside the company.

There is, of course, more to the story than I just relayed and that confidentiality prevents me from disclosing, but what always struck me as odd (and a little sad) was that even though the executives at this extremely large and immensely successful company knew exactly what they *should* be doing, they still allowed themselves to be bullied into submission by this one attorney and his bombastic threats. Such is the aura that a powerful (or at least blustering) attorney can convey, and some companies never challenge that assumed authority.

That is a mistake.

Curiously, I fully understood the lawyer's position, and I understood his reasoning. But unless you are under a court-imposed gag order, there usually is nothing to be gained by remaining completely mute while the other side is beating your brains out in the media every day, as was the case with the opposing plaintiff's counsel. After all, why would you willingly allow someone to attack you? It's human nature: if someone starts to beat you up, don't you want to defend yourself?

It's a simple perception equation: attacks in the absence of a well-reasoned rebuttal equal guilt. If someone is putting out incorrect information about you that is causing the public's perception of your company to sour, mount a crisis communications strategy that sets the record straight. But even if the lawyers tell you to clam up, there are still ways of getting your points across.

Perhaps no one put it better than former New Jersey Governor Christie Todd Whitman, who, probably under orders from attorneys not to comment on some ongoing lawsuit, nevertheless quipped to reporters, "We don't, as a rule, comment on litigation, no matter how baseless or pathetic it is."

Around the same time, I had another client, a national construction company that was building a new high-rise office tower in downtown Los Angeles. During the erection of the structural steel, one of the fifth-floor bays collapsed under the weight of the just-loaded 80 tons of steel beams, and three workers rode the steel to their deaths, down through five levels of corrugated sheet metal flooring to ground level, and then through three subterranean concrete garage levels. It was a tragedy so extreme that it took 24 hours for the bodies to be cut loose from the twisted steel.

There was a very real possibility that the district attorney's office might file criminal charges against my client (negligent homicide, and worse, was discussed), but we felt that when the full facts of the case were known, liability would lie elsewhere, and the D.A.'s office would not prosecute our client. In part, this had to do with the structural steel subcontractor, whose contract dictated that everyone except his direct employees leave the job site when steel was being raised and installed. In short, at that time, it was not my client's operation, nor was it my client's workers who had perished. This fine point was lost on the media, who (typically) target the biggest name and deepest pocket around: in this case, my client. Plaintiff's attorneys do exactly the same thing.

My firm was promptly engaged to manage the crisis as well as the crisis communications. Others on the crisis team included two attorneys; one was the head of litigation from a very well-known, high-profile Los Angeles–based international law firm that represented the client's worldwide interests, and the other was from a small, local firm that was new to me.

If I told you that one of the attorneys gave me trouble, which would you guess it was? The high-priced guy or the low-rent guy?

In my experience, smaller law firms often love to talk to the media. It raises their own profile, which may lead to more business for them. Other, more established law firms, which sometimes look down their noses at the ink-stained wretches of the Fourth Estate, are the ones who favor the "no comment" route.

But in this case, it was the opposite.

Thus, whenever the media wanted an interview or whenever we tried to issue a written statement, the litigator from the big firm was fully onboard with our crisis communications strategies. But the small firm vetoed everything, and without unanimous consent on public statements, our hands and the client's were tied.

At one point, the families of the three victims filed the inevitable wrongful death suits—we were expecting them—and my firm had prepared a written statement defending the client, explaining why the wrongful death statue did not apply, and so on. Everybody okayed it . . . except the small law firm.

Why? It made no sense. Since the workers did not work for my client, but worked directly for the company that had caused the accident, we felt this was an important point to make to the public, as well as to the D.A.'s office through the news media.

I met with that attorney and, in so many words, explained that if the client didn't "defend" its actions, and in particular explain briefly why it was not liable for the accusation of wrongful death, it would look as if the client was admitting to it by its silence. My argument fell on deaf ears.

It was then that I realized that this attorney was *not* representing my client's best interests; he wasn't even representing the same client as I was. He was an insurance company attorney. The client's insurance company, based in New York, had hired this local firm to handle the coverage aspect of the case, and its job was not to spend the insurance company's money by going to court. Its mandate was to settle claims, write a check, and be done with it, and let the reputational chips fall where they might. Statistically, the insurance company knew that in many instances, it is cheaper to settle than to go to court, and *everything that particular lawyer did or said was driven by how much it was going to cost*. At no time did that lawyer ever consider what was best for my client—only what was best for the insurance company, his employer. Meanwhile, my client's reputation was being thrown under the bus, and the D.A. was licking his chops in that election year.

This type of conflict of interest is an ever-present problem; fortunately, there are avenues of relief in most states.

In California, for example, a 1984 landmark case[1] ruled, in very simple terms, that where a conflict of interest exists between the insured and the insurance company, and where the insurance company reserves its right to deny coverage at a later date, the insured may substitute out the insurance company's defense attorney—hired and paid for by the insurance company—and engage an independent counsel of its own choosing. The insurance company is still on the hook to pay for the defense. In California, this is known as a Cumis counsel, named for the insurance concern that was the target of the initial suit.

The conflict of interest clause varies by states, and it is important to note that "A mere possibility of an unspecified conflict does not require independent counsel. The conflict must be significant, not merely theoretical, actual, not merely potential."[2]

But note that this does not apply across the board, and, in fact, "a number of courts recognize that the insured does not have the right to select independent counsel at the insurer's expense in all cases."[3]

(Recognizing the irony of what I'm about to suggest, consult an independent attorney to review your specific situation and circumstances in your specific jurisdiction. Just be aware of whether or not your best interests are being served and govern yourself accordingly.)

In this case, the conflict was obvious and actual. We did an analysis and discovered that customers that had previously asked our client to bid on new buildings year in and year out were suddenly leaving its name off of bid sheets. In other words, not only was my client losing business, but it was losing the opportunity to bid on new business. And we were able to determine that, in large measure, this was the result of all the negative media stories. Some sizable past customers of my client felt that while they had been fortunate to dodge a bullet in the past, why take unnecessary chances with a construction company that had a string of fatalities on job sites and was facing a possible criminal investigation by the district attorney's office? Would you do business with a company like that? The perception of wrongdoing and possible criminal negligence was a strong stench to overcome. And the insurance company's defense counsel was making it nearly impossible to eradicate it.

After the insurance company's defense attorney was fired, the other firm that was already involved in the case was asked to take on the added duties. All outstanding matters were resolved in 90 days. We were able to successfully—if belatedly—mount a successful crisis communications campaign with key constituents, and no criminal charges were filed against my client.

So, you might think from reading the foregoing that every time a lawyer tells you not to talk to the media during a crisis, he is wrong, and you should ignore him.

No. It's not that simple.

It's important to understand *why* lawyers often don't want their clients talking to the media before and during litigation. You've probably watched enough cop shows to be familiar with the phrase, "Anything you say can and will be used against you." That is true in civil litigation, too.

Opposing counsel will pounce on every single thing you say to a reporter and try to use it against you. You will have to defend your every utterance as it relates to the crisis at hand, either in withering depositions or blistering cross-examinations in court, as your own team of lawyers tries to put out multiple fires that you have caused. Since a lot of crises result in litigation, attorneys often want to muzzle their clients during the crisis itself, merely in anticipation of litigation.

In short, many attorneys feel that the more you say, the more complicated their job defending you becomes. I won't deny that this is an important and valid point.

But here's the thing: remaining completely mute in the face of damning accusations carries the real risk of making you look guilty simply by virtue of your silence. It's often tantamount to a tacit admission of culpability. If you don't offer *some* response, the *perception of guilt will outweigh the reality of innocence.*

So it may be the case that attorneys don't want you to say anything that could jeopardize the case, but rather than explaining that and seeking help from professional communicators to craft safe and acceptable messages that will help, not hinder, the defense, they just mount a blanket "no comment" strategy.

And that is woefully shortsighted.

In some of the most successfully managed crises I've been involved in, a healthy working relationship between the lawyers and me and my firm enabled us collectively to determine what could be said, how, and by whom. The lawyers felt that their legal interests had been heard and heeded, and those of us handling the crisis communications felt that our client's overall interests were being served.

Fortunately, many companies today are fairly enlightened on this point and understand that winning the legal case, while obviously important, must be balanced against the real risk of losing the business. If, in winning a legal case, you alienate and lose your customers, what good is that hollow victory? In the case cited earlier, the company did not pick up the unfortunate nickname "cancer-causing company" because it lost the case; it acquired the erroneous appellation because it did not engage in crisis communications and defend itself in the media against the wild and baseless accusations perpetrated by the plaintiff's attorney. Remember, the initial lawsuit didn't so much allege the presence of carcinogens as claim that the plaintiff *feared* he might get cancer.

Also, if there is concern about your spokesperson's being thrown a curveball question in a media interview, this is a good time to play the social media card, as your attorneys can review your YouTube video script before it goes live to vet it for possible problems. You can even say something like, "Because of the sensitive nature of this matter and the ongoing investigation, our attorneys feel very strongly that I should not sit down for long interviews that may be subject to biased editing. However, this issue is so important to us, and we care so deeply about our customers' well-being, that I wanted to at least take a few moments here to tell you what I can about the situation."

Crisis management and crisis communications are team activities. All voices should be heard, and then the CEO or the crisis manager needs to make a decision and act. Lawyers often have a vital role to play in a crisis, but the problem I've seen on many occasions is that management blindly defers to the lawyer's wishes for no other reason than "he's our lawyer, and we'd better follow what he says." That is not always the wise course to take, especially when the lawyer's point of view is strictly on the legal issues at hand, to the exclusion of bigger companywide issues, including how the company in crisis is being perceived by its key constituents.

One final word on using a lawyer as the spokesperson for a company in crisis: be careful.

Rightly or wrongly, using an attorney as your spokesperson often makes it look as if the company is hiding behind its lawyer's skirts, and maybe the company has some culpability after all.

If the questioning deals with a legal issue (for example, "What do you think about today's courtroom testimony, counselor?"), the lawyer is absolutely the right person to be standing before the microphones on the courthouse steps. Of course, circumstances permitting, I'd like some time alone with the attorney first, to prep him for the sort of questions we might anticipate and to cover the best ways to respond, as well as ways to anticipate and then deflect problematic questions and provide the responses that will serve the best interests of the client with the client's larger group of constituents. But sometimes, despite your best efforts, a loose cannon is still a loose cannon.

A case in point: some years ago, I was managing a crisis for a successful midsized business in the medical field that at the time was under investigation for alleged money laundering* by the FBI, the IRS, the California Fair Political Practices Commission, and the local district attorney. We knew that there would be media at the courthouse for the hearing, and we briefed the local attorney on what questions to expect and how to respond.

Instead of following the party line that we had provided and the client had okayed, standing on the courthouse steps with every local television camera, and radio and print reporter waiting for his comments, he dismissed the entire lot of very serious accusations—charges that carried the potential for significant prison time—with a dismissive and arrogant wave of his hand and declared the charges "nothing more than garden-variety fraud."

The way the media reported it made it seem as if the client was condoning "garden-variety fraud" as acceptable behavior, trivial, and wondering why on earth the FBI, the IRS, the FPPC, and the DA would waste their time with such frivolities. Worse, the lawyer was essentially implicating our client in having actually *committed* fraud, garden variety or otherwise.

Lesson: a cocky, grandstanding attorney can be dangerous as a media spokesperson in a crisis.

And even though, as stated earlier, sometimes an attorney is the person you want and need to have speak for you, in most crises, I'd prefer having my client speak for herself—after she's been properly media trained and briefed on what to say and how to say it. If this is done properly, her message carries more sincerity to the client's key constituents. A client who can speak from the heart in a crisis involving loss of life, for example, is worth her weight in gold.

---

* Lest you think I was representing a Colombian drug lord, the client was charged with reimbursing his employees who had used their own money, at his suggestion, to attend political fund-raisers for candidates that the company was supporting. By reimbursing the employees, the company masked the true identity of the donor of the money. The legal term for this act is money laundering.

During the infamous Jack in the Box crisis, where four young children died from eating hamburgers that contained a deadly strain of the E. coli bacteria, the company was under heavy attack at its first news conference, including a particularly tough line of questioning on why it had waited so long to speak publicly and why it had not apologized to the families of victims. The perception was that the company was cold and uncaring toward the families of the young victims, which certainly was not accurate. The Jack in the Box executive at the microphone was not doing very well with those pointed questions, and then, suddenly and without warning, the very frustrated chairman of the board, who was not supposed to speak, jumped up from his seat, grabbed the microphone, and delivered an extemporaneous heartfelt entreaty, in which he started off by saying something like, "I am a grandfather, and my heart breaks for the families that lost children." He personalized the deaths in a way that made it clear that this was a tragedy that hit him hard as a caring person, and this was a company that cared and regretted the loss of life in the most profound way. This was a loss that was felt personally by people who worked at Jack in the Box, people at the highest level. No lawyer could have delivered that message as effectively.

And the company bounced back.[4]

Remember, when it is *your* crisis, you need to do what is best for you and your company.

Lawyers can and should play a pivotal role as members of the crisis management team, but it is a team, and the lawyer's judicial concerns must be weighed against the overall crisis strategy and the overall best interests of the company.

11

Protecting Your Brand

■　■　■

A brand is a promise. It is not tangible. It is more than your reputation, which by definition exists in the past tense. A brand is a reminder of the past, but it is also a promise for the future. It exists only in the minds of your publics. And yet, it is one of your most valuable assets. In fact, the brand is everything. Thus, in a crisis, you need to respect and protect the promise of the brand at all costs.

Coke, Apple, McDonald's—they all have brands. The hundreds of millions of dollars these companies spend on advertising are to advertise their brand.

If you enjoy drinking Coke (or Diet Coke), you expect that every single time you pop open the top of a can and take that first sip, it will taste just the way it did the last time you drank it. The advertising that Coke does is to remind you of that taste and the brand's promise that it will still be there waiting for you whenever you're thirsty. Coke even used to advertise the very intangibility of it all when it touted: "The pause that refreshes." What exactly *is* a "pause that refreshes"? That intangible, ephemeral promise is Coke's brand. And it made them beloved, to say nothing of wealthy.

The same may be said about Apple products. Apple has built a remarkable global reputation as a company that designs and manufactures slick, sleek, must-have creative hardware and software that redefines the cutting edge and the "coolness factor"—products like the iPod, the iPhone, and the iPad. In each instance, Apple was there—in the marketplace—first, and when it brings out its next product, the promise of the Apple brand is that it, too, will be cool, creative, and a must-have product for the masses . . . and will soon be copied and imitated by Apple's competitors. Apple's brand is such that the company has developed a niche in introducing products that at the time nobody actually needed or even knew they wanted (such as the iPad), but nonetheless creating an incredible demand for them. Other than at an Apple store, when was the last time you saw customers lining up around the block to get into a store and be one of the first to purchase the latest version of something or other? Even when consumers already had a similar product—say, the iPhone 4—people lined up to buy a slightly different iPhone 4S. Why? Because of the promise of Apple's brand. How strong is Apple's brand? How many other products can you name whose strong appeal spans three or more generations?

When you see a McDonald's ad on TV, can you smell and taste those golden french fries? Does it make your mouth water? Some people crave them, and the promise of the McDonald's brand is that you can walk into any McDonald's restaurant and enjoy the same tasty french fries that you've come to enjoy at your local McDonald's (whether or not they're good for your waistline or your arteries). Its brand is not so much the Big Mac or the fries as it is the promise that when you return, your taste buds will be just as satisfied as they were the last time you visited.

The same can be said about any company in any industry. If you manufacture superior widgets at a fair price and on time, the promise of your brand is that you are a reliable company. If I do business with you, I know what I'm going to get in the future, and I will be satisfied. Of course, the reverse corollary also hold true. For example, BP's current brand is "environmental screwup." Hopefully, that will eventually change for the better.

When you reaffirm a brand, you increase its value; when you tarnish a brand, you diminish its value.

Here's another example: when I lecture on crisis communications at graduate schools, I occasionally flash a picture of automobile tires on the screen and ask, "What is this company selling?" Of course, the answer is obvious: tires. Next, I flash that famous Michelin photo of a very young child in a diaper sitting in the middle of a tire and ask, "What is Michelin selling?" Answer: safety. That is Michelin's brand. So far, it's working, but should anything adverse happen, such as the devastating Firestone tire recall in 2000 because of safety issues, then Michelin would be likely to be ridiculed if it trotted out that ad with the kid again. Protecting its brand, to say nothing of protecting its customers, is of paramount importance to the company.

"Our brand-love research shows that loved brands reflect and symbolize deeply held personal values, such as Apple does for creativity,"[1] according to University of Michigan marketing professor Rajeev Batra, author of an article entitled, "Brand Love."

Such is the all-important promise of *your* brand.

And so it is critical that you understand that in a crisis (no matter what else is going on, and there will be a lot of other things going on; trust me!), your brand is under attack, too, and you need to defend and protect your brand at all costs. If you weather the crisis storm but your brand winds up in tatters, you may find yourself out of business, or on the ropes until you can rebuild your brand.

While it's not quite a case of not seeing the forest for the trees, it's close. I have seen companies in crisis that are so myopically focused on a single issue that they have ignored the damage that is being done to their brand.

It is important to note that there are ways to bulletproof your brand so that it is more impervious to the residual effects—friendly fire, if you will—of an assault on your company in the form of a crisis. We will delve into this in more detail when we talk about reservoirs of goodwill, but for now, just know that your brand requires constant attention, and that if the company is in a crisis, it becomes even more important to protect your brand from attack and erosion.

Remember, too, that when your company is immersed in litigation, the brand also is on trial. Whatever the facts of the case being litigated inside the courtroom may be, the unstated fact is that the action also puts the brand on trial in the court of public opinion, and a verdict will be rendered in that trial, too. The higher the profile of the case, the more media that cover it, the higher the stakes—meaning, the more the brand is at risk.

And while the impaneled jury must render its verdict based on very strict and usually narrowly worded judicial guidelines, the *other* jury—your constituents—will be rendering its verdict on your brand in the marketplace. In-house corporate counsel often fail to instruct the outside litigators they retain on what else is at stake in the trial, as in the case of the "cancer-causing company." And even when they do, conflicts between corporate counsel and the outside hired guns sometimes occur.

So, while the attorneys argue their case and draw blood *inside* the courtroom, the crisis communications team must present, or reinforce, its case concerning the continued efficacy of the brand *outside* the courthouse and inside the minds of the company's constituents.

How do you resolve this dilemma?

Often the answer is a carefully structured and even more carefully worded settlement. While it is not possible to issue a blanket rule that fits all contingencies, this much can be said with certainty: each case is unique, and the appropriate strategy to employ must be based on the particulars of each case. If the risk to your brand is too great, consider how much you may lose even if you win the litigation, and then render your decision accordingly. While facts are currency in court, never lose sight of the importance of the currency of perception in the marketplace.

In general, there are two likely explanations for a sustained attack on your brand: either the crisis has, in fact, damaged the brand (for example, Coke switches formulas, and the new taste is horrible—remember *that* crisis?), or the brand is still fine, but the *perception* is that the brand has been tarnished. Whichever is the case, reality or perception, you have your work cut out for you.

As you strategize about how to manage your crisis, part of your crisis communications responsibilities is to protect the promise of your brand.

What's being said about you and/or your brand? Is it accurate? If not, what are you going to do to change the public's perception?

Are you carefully monitoring what's being said on the various social media outlets? And, are you responding swiftly to correct any and all inaccuracies, squelch rumors, and so on? All those tweets can add up to some big chinks in your brand's armor.

It is too easy to dismiss occasional tweets as being under the radar; instead, you should look for discernible trends. If you can visualize your brand as the proverbial dike, it is easy to imagine how a chink here and a chink there can one day cause leaks. It's better to service your brand each day with ongoing fresh coats of "Teflon cement" that will provide long-lasting protection against brand erosion. After all, you only have ten fingers to plug any dike.

Be mindful, however, that if you engage in social media brand protection only when you are in a crisis, your publics will have no frame of reference by which to judge you. Proactive crisis management and crisis communications mean proactive social media use. The last thing you want in a crisis is a clean slate. Rather, your slate should already be well filled in so that your publics have a good and positive sense of who you are and who your company is. If you wait until the crisis hits to begin to engage your publics and shore up weak spots in your brand, you have given your opposition the very same clean slate to do its damage. And, if you are a large and lumbering giant of a company, your opposition can move much faster than you can.

Again: when you are in a crisis, your brand is under attack. Count on it.

12

Telling the Truth

■   ■   ■

N
o one said it better than Mark Twain: "Always tell the truth; that way you don't have to remember anything."

It's good advice that too few follow. Why?

Crisis communications miscreants fall into two general categories: idiots and liars. One is painful, the other lethal. Remember, in a crisis—as in life, I suppose—it's not what you *know*, but what you *do* that matters, and character counts. As Ella Wheeler Wilcox penned many years ago:

> One ship sails east and another sails west
> With the self-same winds that blow.
> Tis the set of the sail and not the gale
> Which determines the way they go.
> As the winds of the sea are the ways of fate
> As we voyage along through life,
> Tis the act of the soul that determines the goal,
> And not the calm or the strife.[1]

It doesn't take someone with my three decades of experience to tell a company that's in trouble not to lie. If we stipulate that "everyone knows *that*," the relevant question becomes: *then why do so many companies in crisis lie anyway?*

The stakes in a crisis today are higher than ever—so much so that shareholders and corporate boards could easily consider failure to know and to effectively practice solid crisis communications skills as malfeasance and a breach of fiduciary responsibility on the part of a company's management and hold managers accountable if the company or its bottom line suffers. Thus, the knee-jerk, go-to position seems to be lying: tap dancing, half-truths, obfuscation, smoke screens, misdirection, memory loss, willful ignorance, plausible deniability—*lying*.

I often earn my pay, in part, by showing a client *how* to tell the truth without losing his job, his reputation, or his company.

Some executives believe that a lie is often the most expedient path to relief; it's not, and it never will be. Telling the truth—as painful and as terrifying as that path may sometimes be—is actually *good* for business in the long run, . . . as long as the truth is told the *right way*. And if you enter a crisis already having a reputation for not being candid, this will make almost any crisis communications effort an exercise in futility as you try to convince the public and the government that you are speaking truthfully. This is especially critical during high-stakes crises where lives are at stake, such as the devastating crisis that befell TEPCO's Fukushima, Japan, nuclear reactor plant.

It was TEPCO (Toyota Electric Power Co.), you will recall, that owned the plant that was ravaged by the earthquake and tsunami off the Japanese coast in 2011. When crises happen to critical companies, such as utilities, it is essential that the crisis communications operation is already geared up to dispense truthful information that is vital to the public. Even if the information is negative, and especially in a life-threatening crisis, brutal facts are more important than "spin," a lesson the Three Mile Island folks learned the hard way.

Almost from the outset, TEPCO was "being criticized by people around the world, including the Japanese prime minister, for lacking candor—and not for the first time."[2]

TEPCO and other Japanese utility companies have for many years been accused of withholding information and not telling the truth about safety violations and past accidents, but TEPCO seemed to be the worst of the lot. An engineering professor at the University of Southern California who has studied the Japanese nuclear industry for the last 10 years describes TEPCO as being "mired in secrecy."[3]

But even average Japanese have learned to be wary of anything that TEPCO says, and the company's reputation is decidedly mixed, at best. "And even people who feel more forgiving this time because of the extensive nature of the disaster still expressed frustration at the lack of reliable updates.

"'They're trying very hard, but we're not sure about the information,' said a resident of Japan. 'We need more detailed information from Tepco and the government so we know how to respond.'"[4]

But when a TEPCO spokesman protested and declared that the company wasn't hiding anything—*that it was telling the truth!*—people viewed that proclamation with doubt and suspicion. Remember the little boy who cried wolf?

Here's a hint: if you have to proclaim forcefully that you're telling the truth, that means that you're not being given the benefit of the doubt. And if you're not considered a source of reliable information on a good day, you've got an incredibly tough mountain to climb when you're in a crisis.

Things are chaotic enough during a crisis that you need every advantage you can muster. If a reputation for honesty is not in your communications quiver, ask yourself *why*, and do it now, before the crisis hits. Then set out a strategy to remedy the problem.

It's frightening for some people—some company executives—to tell the truth during a crisis. There is so much at stake, and they fear dire consequences if "the truth" emerges. Sometimes they're right, but often they have blown the perceived consequences way out of proportion. Either way, telling the truth has a cathartic effect on people. I've had clients whose hands I have held during this process tell me later how relieved they felt at having been able to get past a particularly precarious interview or government investigation simply by looking the questioner in the eye and spouting the truth, and knowing deep down to their toes that they were, in fact, telling the truth.

Lawyers (here we go again!) sometimes advocate the "no comment" mantra just to avoid the possibility of a client's lying. A lie *will* come back to haunt you, or hang you. So, if you are going to communicate—even if you have surrogates speaking on behalf of the company—telling the truth is the way to go. It's simply the right thing to do, and if you have a reputation for honesty, you avoid the Liar's Enigma, which poses this riddle: "If you ask a known liar if he is telling the truth, do you believe him if he says yes . . . or no?"

And "don't lie" also means don't fib, fudge, fabricate, stretch the truth, cross your fingers, and so on.

Or, as a Yiddish proverb wisely observes, "A half-truth is a whole lie."

But does that mean you have to spill your guts? *No!*

What it does mean is that everything that comes out of your mouth (or your crisis communications spokesperson's) should be accurate and verifiable; it does not, however, mean that in a media interview, for example, you are obligated to volunteer information that is potentially harmful to you or to your company, *unless the public's safety is at stake.* It is perfectly acceptable to emphasize certain portions of the truth to the exclusion of others, provided that by doing so you are not presenting a false and dangerous picture as a result of your omissions.

Assuming that you are not on the witness stand, you do not have to "tell all." And even when you are (or in news interviews), you do not have to volunteer information, unless doing so advances your cause. (A later chapter will discuss granting interviews and answering problematic questions posed by the news media.) Litigators prepping their clients for depositions or trial testimony always say, "Less is more," meaning don't volunteer information. In such instances, the correct answer to "Do you know the color of the sky?" is a simple yes, not "Blue," unless you are specifically asked for the sky's tint.

A good crisis communicator can anticipate the tough questions that will be asked in an interview and will spend a sufficient amount of time prepping the company executives who will be answering the reporter's questions. And, time permitting, that prep-time role-playing scenario will be videotaped for immediate playback and candid critique by professional communicators. This is no time to flatter the boss's ego; if he really bombed during the exercise, tell him so and fix it, fix him, train him. Of course, the operative phrase here is "time permitting," and when you're in a crisis, time is not usually on your side. This is why crisis media training should be an ongoing, proactive process at companies.

The crisis communicator's job is to help prep the executive for the most effective ways to field thorny questions that adhere to the truth without sinking the ship.

And the single most important corollary to "tell the truth" is "a lie *will* be found out." Count on it. Telling the truth up front avoids explaining the cover-up down the road. If you find yourself in that predicament, your new brand is Liar. Plain and simple. Time and again, history has demonstrated that it was not the act, but the cover-up or the mountain of lies that brought down a leader or a company.

Look no further than the recently disgraced and currently unemployed Yahoo! ex-CEO, Scott Thompson, who was publicly accused of falsifying his résumé, and hence his credentials.

Even though he mounted a full-throated denial of the accusations, the smoking pistol that he could not adequately explain was that his actual résumé and official company biography, which were included in SEC regulatory filings, stated that he had earned degrees in accounting and computer science from Stonehill College, whereas he had actually earned only the accounting degree. The "embattled chief executive . . . told the company's senior management . . . that he never submitted a résumé or falsified his academic credentials."[5] But, in fact, he had not earned a degree in computer science—a degree program that was not even offered at the small Massachusetts college while he was a student there.

What "at first seemed a small and improbable allegation from an annoying dissident shareholder turned into a major crisis, thanks largely to Mr. Thompson's own evasions and missteps. In the end, the board had little choice but to sever ties with its chief executive of only five months."[6]

In the face of evidence indicating that this falsification had gone on for years and had begun at previous places of employment, in "just 11 days . . . Mr. Thompson's credibility with the board was in shreds . . . and [he] was out."[7]

Once you get on that slippery slope, there's little or nothing for you to hang on to.

How serious is résumé fraud? While some of Mr. Thompson's defenders claimed that the résumé debacle had to have been an "inadvertent error,"[8] in an interview I gave during the Yahoo! turmoil, I said, "There's nothing inadvertent about putting something down on paper that you know you didn't earn. I think it speaks to the man's character."[9]

I suspect Yahoo!'s board knew it, too, even though it went through the motions and appointed a three-person committee to investigate. I told another reporter at the time, "When was the last time you heard of a special committee being formed where some heads didn't roll? In my opinion, the handwriting's on the wall: He's on his way out. And if he is, I would say do it sooner rather than later. For the board to be diverted from their main mission is a distraction they don't need."[10]

Thompson's creative writing apparently began when he was employed at Visa and eBay and continued at Yahoo!. At some point, you have to ask the man who claimed he did not embellish his own credentials, "Aren't you reading your own résumé?"

More than 20 years ago, as the keynote commencement speaker at a major university, I cautioned the graduating class about the perils of résumé fraud—and that was well before the age of the Internet and the ease of checking up on someone with a click of a mouse button. You would think someone working in the technology industry would be especially mindful of *that*.

> Thompson's fib has many people questioning how resume fraud continues to go unnoticed by some of the world's biggest organizations, especially since it has been making headlines for well over two decades.
>
> In 2006, former RadioShack CEO David Edmondson resigned after he was caught erroneously stating on his resume that he received a Bachelor of Science degree. Veritas chief financial officer Kenneth Lonchar resigned in 2002 after he was exposed for lying on his résumé about an MBA from Stanford, and long-time Massachusetts Institute of Technology dean of admissions Marilee Jones was forced out in 2001 for falsely padding her credentials.[11]

In addition to embarrassment, there often are financial consequences for the company involved. "When Veritas, which was acquired by Symantec for $13.5 billion in 2004, discovered the fraud behind Lonchar's resume, its shares took a 14% dive."[12]

Even professional liars (read: members of Congress) sometimes get caught with their pants down. Literally.

The story of former U.S. Representative Anthony Weiner has become a stale punch line by now. But there may still be a lesson or two to be gleaned from his falsifying cliff-dive from grace.

For those with short memories, Weiner was a prominent congressman, a rising star in the Democratic Party, and widely touted as the next mayor of New York City. For reasons tucked far into the recesses of his fevered brain, Weiner, a married man with a pregnant wife at the time, began a "sexting" affair with a teen-age college student, among others, that included texting her closeup photos of his crotch. Other pictures depicted his face and bare chest.

(Weiner's wife, Huma Abedin, was at the time a top aide to Secretary of State Hillary Clinton. Abedin, who was pregnant at the time the scandal broke, gave birth to a baby boy in December 2011. And the man who presided at the Weiner-Abedin nuptials was none other than former president Bill Clinton, who is well known for having had his own problems keeping his pants zipped. As I said in Chapter 1, you can't make this stuff up!)

When the story broke—"Flash! The Story Will *Always* Break!"—Weiner's go-to response, not surprisingly, was flat-out denial at the top of his articulate and affronted lungs. Note: it's usually those silver-tongued charmers (Bill Clinton, John Edwards, Anthony Weiner, Lance Armstrong, and the like) who invariably think that they can talk their way out of anything. They can't. They believe that if they just look you in the eye and lie, you will believe any yarn they spin. They're wrong, as history has demonstrated time and again. But still, the fools try.

Weiner then claimed that his Internet account had been hacked. But if you go back and play his responses to certain questions, he deftly sidestepped answering direct questions, and instead tried to parse his lawyerlike responses with enough wiggle room that he could always claim he didn't actually lie. As I said a moment ago, you don't have to tell all, as long as your omissions don't give a wrong impression. When he was trying to float that "hacking" tale, rather than answer directly whether it was a picture of his own crotch regardless of who sent it, Rep. Weiner coyly said that he couldn't say whether it was or it wasn't, when he knew damn well that it was. And he also knew that if he owned up to it, his goose was cooked.

After that strategy of deceit failed, he tried to throw the next stone he grabbed in his pouch: he started to attack the questioners.

When Weiner was being interviewed by ABC News senior political correspondent Jonathan Karl, Karl asked him, "Is it inappropriate for a member of Congress to be following young women on their Twitter accounts?" Instead of answering the question, Weiner went into full attack-dog mode, asserting that the question was "outrageous" and that the "implication was outrageous." And then, throwing down the gauntlet to Karl, he challenged the reporter: "Do you really think that's a fair question?"[13] As it turned out, of course, it was perfectly fair and on point, which no doubt was why Weiner got so exercised, and his outbursts only made him seem all the more pathetic and deceitful when the truth finally came out.

As the layers of the onion began to peel away, it ultimately was learned that Weiner had had sexting relationships with at least six women, including college students, single moms, and porn stars, and was all too happy to take indecent and suggestive pictures of himself and send them to women he didn't really know.

Sir Walter Scott's crystal ball must have had Rep. Weiner in mind when he penned, "Oh what a tangled web we weave/When first we practice to deceive!"

One of the most important lessons to keep in mind is that anything that goes on the Internet lives forever. That includes e-mails, text messages, and raunchy pictures. *For-Ev-Er*. That this was done by a prominent member of Congress who thought it would never come out raised Weiner to the pedestal of Full-Fledged Imbecile. And yet, in short order, another prominent simpleton will take center stage and have his humiliating public comeuppance. They never seem to learn.

But should Weiner have lied?

That's the question, really. He was caught in a crisis of his own making, and one from which there seemed to be no possible escape. He knew that telling the truth would probably end his career, so he thought his only fallback position was that age-old, triple-threat strategy: denial, denial, denial.

There's actually a line of dialogue in the 1997 movie *Wag the Dog* that says just that. Robert DeNiro's character tells a political operative that, when trapped, the first rule is: deny, deny, deny. That was a movie; Weiner was a sad real-life soap opera.

Remember, when the Weiner story first broke, it was just one photo and one woman. At the time, though, Weiner knew full well the complete depth of the story and should have been smart enough to know that people would be coming out of the woodwork on this story, and that others would be digging for more dirt. It's the old "where there's smoke, there's fire" maxim, and conservative bloggers like Matt Drudge and the late Andrew Breitbart were loaded for bear and kept turning up the flames under Weiner and his tales. In more ways than one, Weiner's chestnuts were in the fire, and his persistent lying only intensified the heat. And the more he lied, the more of the real story was revealed until, inevitably, he admitted everything and resigned in utter disgrace.

If we were to diagram this on a chalkboard, what did Weiner actually do wrong? Well, besides *that*, I mean.

Embarrassed at having been caught with his pants down, Weiner, a lawyer by training, took a page from the BP playbook and decided that he shouldn't say anything that could be used against him later. Thus, he created incredibly tortuous and convoluted denials without actually denying anything or admitting anything (to paraphrase: I'm not saying that it is or is not my crotch or whether I have or have not ever seen this crotch before or whether it has or has not been digitally enhanced, nor am I saying whether the message did or did not come from my Twitter account, which may or may not have been hacked and sent to someone whom I may or may not know . . .).

As a *Los Angeles Times* editorial described it so colorfully, "Weiner . . . responded by temporarily losing his mind, lying to the media . . . and spreading a bizarre conspiracy theory that an intercepted photo of his crotch might have been digitally altered."[14]

To further define our terms, *lying* during a crisis is also crisis communications—it's just stupid crisis communications.

It was painful to watch Weiner twisting and squirming, thinking that he was successfully covering his tracks, all the while knowing that the clock was ticking.

Three weeks after his first lie (and there were many), he resigned his seat in Congress amid massive pressure from both sides of the aisle in both houses of Congress, the White House, and general public opinion.

So, what should Weiner have done?

It is entirely possible that Weiner could have kept his seat in Congress had he admitted to the story from the beginning. All he had to say, in so many words, was, "Yeah, I did it. It was an incredibly stupid, juvenile prank, and I am so embarrassed by this rash act. I apologize to my wife, my family, my constituents, my colleagues in Congress. I assure you that it will never happen again. I ask for privacy while I undergo spiritual counseling and I try to make amends to my family."

If you admit to it, you are taking the wind out of the sails of those who'd come against you. It will be embarrassing—hell, *yes*, it will be embarrassing—but you and the public will probably get over it, even if you did it more than once. After all, adulterers—Newt Gingrich, anyone?—have cheated on their spouses and still retained their seats in Congress and their clout. Weiner, for all of his weird sexual predilections, never broke a law or a commandment. Gingrich broke one of the Ten Commandments at least twice and mounted a serious campaign for president of the United States!

Get out in front of the story, and do it fast. There is life after shame.

What brought down Richard Nixon was not the Watergate break-in; it was the lies and cover-ups.

Weiner and his indiscretions were always going to be a story; what made it a big story was the way the congressman mishandled it. Strategic crisis communications would have helped. Had Weiner decided that he wanted to try to avoid the crucible, he could and should have resigned his seat immediately, not after dragging out this sordid story, playing a bad hand in hopes of filling an impossible inside straight. That strategy, which also served to elevate and prolong the story, only added to his woes by laying on him the additional burden of being a "bald-faced liar," not just kinky.

He could have resigned his seat in Congress "for personal reasons," entered a sex addicts rehabilitation clinic of some kind, and saved his wife and family from heaps of disgrace and pity. His public life might then have been over, but he could have had a long and lucrative career in the private sector. After all, considering some of the things that *do* go on in the private sector, some of which directly lead to crises, "sexting" would be considered relatively mild by comparison.

In fact, you need look no further than the recently rehabilitated and largely publicly forgiven Eliot Spitzer, former governor of New York. One of the more intriguing aspects of a crisis communications comparison will be an examination of how this once-prominent elected official—who was caught in an FBI sting and admitted to having committed multiple acts of adultery with a high-priced call girl and having used public money to pay for sex—is today viewed somewhat kindly, whereas Weiner—who committed *no* actual acts of infidelity (outside of lusting in his heart) and used *no* public funds and broke *no* commandments or laws—is still considered a despicable creep.

And more recently, the General David Petraeus scandal demonstrated the crisis communications art of the swift resignation, a tactic that Weiner ignored. Through a bizarre and convulted chain of events that we need not recap here, it was revealed that Petraeus had been having an affair with his official biographer, Paula Broadwell. He admitted it immediately and resigned as head of the CIA *ahead* of the story breaking. And Petraeus is still highly regarded in Washington, despite his acknowledged affair.

Yes, Weiner's bigger crisis—a crisis solely of his own making—began when he started to lie and cover up as his go-to crisis communications positions. Weiner had options; lying was not one of them.

None of which answers the more compelling question: why do companies (or company executives) lie during a crisis?

We'll leave any discussion about pathological liars to the clinically trained and professionally licensed Ph.D. psychologists. Our question is more nuanced: why would a successful company willfully engage in a falsehood during a crisis? If history informs us that most liars eventually are caught, what is to be gained from what is usually a short-term and hugely embarrassing lie?

There are some people who choke under pressure and resort to lying as a safety valve. "Choking under pressure is poor performance that occurs in response to the perceived stress of a situation,"[15] according to psychologist and University of Chicago professor Sian Beilock. And nowhere does stress manifest itself more than when you are suddenly thrust into the cyclone of a crisis. High-pressure environments cause physiological responses, such as an increased heart rate, shortness of breath, and a spike in adrenaline, and the fight-or-flight phenomenon sets in. Not everyone can handle the stress brought on by a crisis.

In Chapter 28, we will examine the best way to make decisions during periods of crisis-induced stress, which will help your crisis communications in those ultra-tense moments. We know that many people who can offer sound advice to someone else who is in crisis may have difficulty handling a crisis of their own. This is not at all unusual. When I am asked how I handle the stress of managing crises for clients, my usual reply is simply that they are not my crises. I have the advantage and the ability of remaining objective, and therefore, I can help guide a company in crisis through the minefields of making sound, vigilant decisions. My unbiased decisions and my recommendations are based on years of experience in what will work best for the company, not my personal emotions because of my roots in the company.

In the case of Yahoo!'s Mr. Thompson, giving him zero benefit of the doubt, his lie would probably have been fostered in the belief that résumé fraud would land him a better-paying job. But in the case of a company in crisis, it's much more complicated.

During times of crisis, the effects of stress on a company's management team are almost incalculable. You are experiencing an event (1) the likes of which you may have never experienced before, (2) in which you probably have received little or no training, and (3) where the risks and penalties for failure are palpable. In short, you are under a ton of chest-compressing stress.

Take a deep breath. Cardiac arrest can happen when you are under loads of stress during a crisis.

Based on my professional obvsersations over the years, the simplest explanation for why companies in crisis knowingly lie is fear of loss. Whether it is loss of money, market share, market value, careers, businesses, or prestige, companies often panic and turn to desperate measures to, at a minimum, maintain the status quo and retain what they already have. I understand the rationale. I understand the motive. I understand the emotions.

But I can tell you that of the two options available to you, only telling the truth gives you any hope of retaining what you have, and lying will provide only a fleeting wisp of hope that will quickly fade as the truth seeps out, often magnifying the lie out of all proportion, and spinning that well-known tangled web of deceit.

In other words, as bad as the crisis seems to you at the moment, telling the truth about whatever went wrong gives you the peace of mind and clearheadedness to face the situation head-on. Take your lumps early and get it over with. Something may have happened on your watch, but owning up to it will earn you big points with your constituents and earn you a reputation as being an honest and forthright company. This reputation will serve you exceedingly well the next time trouble strikes.

It will also buy you time when people are clamoring for answers. When you have a deserved reputation as a straight shooter, if, during a crisis, you tell a reporter that you don't have the answer to her question yet, but your team is working on it, and you hope to have something more definitive to report within, say, the next 48 hours, you have a better chance of gaining a breather.

Conversely, if you are a company that is not known for being candid when candor is called for, saying that you hope to have better answers in 48 hours is likely to lead to snide media comments: "The company *declined to answer* our reporter's questions, but said they are 'working on it and hope to have an answer soon.'" The nuanced perception in that type of reporting is that you're either fabricating or stonewalling.

But note well: there is no guarantee that telling the truth in a crisis will save your company, its reputation, or your job, and I am not predicting that it will; what I *am* saying is that a lie will almost certainly be exposed eventually—even years later—and then you will have to explain why you misled the public. If you lied or withheld critical information in the first place to protect the company's reputation or its assets, you just blew it.

Sometimes the reasons for lying are purely mercenary. Two of the most blatant examples from the automotive crisis archives involve Firestone Tire and Rubber Company and the Ford Motor Company.

Firestone's debacle involved the then-popular 500 series of steel-belted radials, which, according to the National Highway Traffic Safety Administration, were prone to blowouts, tread separation, and a number of other dangerous conditions and even deformities. By the company's own testimony at the time, the tires had been responsible for some three dozen deaths and hundreds of accidents. Wouldn't that be enough reason to recall the tires? One would think so.

But Firestone engaged in a delaying strategy that had the company challenging every single government complaint, sometimes forcing the government to reexamine its own findings. This delaying ploy allowed the company to continue to manufacture and sell the tires, and thereby remain profitable, while the investigation dragged on and on and on.

So what's wrong with challenging the government's findings, you may ask? Nothing, but if the company admitted that keeping the tires on the road had lethal consequences, the least it should have done was voluntarily recall its tires pending the outcome of the investigation, as a proactive safety measure. Firestone would have been better perceived as a caring company with a crisis communications message along the lines of, "While we dispute the government's accusations and are launching our own full-scale investigation with independent tire safety experts, the public's safety and peace of mind are too important to ignore, and we'd rather err on the side of caution and our customers' peace of mind."

Ford's infamous gas tank explosions in its once-popular and inexpensive Pinto set a new low in corporate greed. For eight years, Ford dragged its feet on a government-ordered redesign of its deathtrap cars while between 500 and 900 unsuspecting lives were lost in fiery deaths when the Pinto victims' rear-mounted gas tanks erupted into balls of flame after rear-end collisions. Why? Pure cost-benefit economics. According to reports at the time, Ford bean counters apparently had determined that it simply was not cost-effective to redesign the car and retool the assembly line until a sufficient return on investment had been reached.[16] Henry Ford even threatened to shutter a plant and put hundreds of workers out to pasture if the company was forced to accede to the government's demands. The company's business model apparently dictated that it was cheaper to pay (or have its insurance companies pay) hundreds of wrongful death claims than to redesign the car to protect the public.

And then there is Dow Corning's reprehensible cover-up concerning the dangerous and even lethal consequences of leaks from its silicone breast implants. At the time, I authored an op-ed piece for the *New York Times* that laid out the company's lies and deceits:

The Dow Corning Corporation revealed itself last week to be a company adrift without a moral compass.

It finally released memos showing that for two decades it had known silicone can leak from its gel breast implants into some women's bodies. Accompanied by a shakeup of top management and the long-overdue pledge to cooperate fully with Federal safety investigations, these mea culpas and the new candor are promising. But putting truth on the bench to be called on only if deception strikes out is a crisis management error of potentially lethal proportions.

By becoming forthright only after obfuscation, denial and rationalization failed, the company demonstrated that honesty had been relegated to a backup position . . .

From the beginning, Dow Corning relied too much on heavy-handed lawyering. Lawyers in product liability crises often take the view that everything revolves around the law and its loopholes. What becomes obscured is the ultimate crisis management objective: to have a company left to manage after—or if—the crisis passes.[17]

But while these examples have some dust on them, it is important to bear in mind that none of these cases happened during the Internet age. Just imagine what would happen to any company that tried to use those delaying tactics today, when a single tweet has the potential to bring a company to its knees. In other words, while we'd all like to think that companies' moral compasses have become properly aligned over the years, the truth in too many cases is just that companies realize that there is a greater likelihood of being exposed today than there was a decade or more ago.

And still they try to get away with one every now and then, even companies we have come to admire. Perhaps some of these companies feel invincible because they are on such a high pedestal. Wrong.

Highly regarded Apple Computer had its own "antenna-gate" crisis not too long ago, in which its then newly designed iPhones had antennas that were so poorly located that users' hands naturally covered them while they were holding the phones and they had difficulty making or receiving calls. As its customers raged, the company's initial cavalier dismissal of the problem created a larger, hugely embarrassing public backlash when the firm was slow to engage in much-needed crisis communications. Eventually, the company addressed the problem and created a suitable workaround until the next generation of iPhones was created.

Handmaidens to liars are those leaders who have been fed misinformation by subordinates, either deliberately or inadvertently, and who act publicly and embarrassingly on incorrect information. The reason for this often centers on the organizational culture that exists. It is essential that leaders and managers be willing to *hear* the truth, and that they abolish the shoot-the-messenger culture if one exists. One of the most effective ways to practice sound crisis communications strategies is first to establish the kind of corporate culture that encourages the truth to come forward and creates a wide and sunny path by which bad news can emerge from the shadows. Managers need to listen to those on the front lines without a filter and encourage staff members to tell the leaders what they *need* to hear, not what someone thinks they *want* to hear. (See the next chapter for a tragic example of how the wrong corporate culture played a role in putting innocent children at risk.)

The reasons why such cultures exist are myriad, but at the heart of the problem is denial and the gut-wrenching fear engendered by the huge stakes involved. Why? As Upton Sinclair once sagely put it, "It is difficult to get a man to understand something when his salary depends upon his not understanding it."

Help in motivating corporate culture change—encouraging companies to tell the truth during crises—might be found in research conducted by Dan Ariely, a Duke University professor of behavioral economics. In conducting research into cheating patterns, in which study subjects had the ability to cheat on a test without getting caught and without any consequences, he and his colleagues stumbled upon a surprising revelation in an experiment using 450 UCLA college students. The group was evenly divided, and each half was given the same math "test" in which the researchers had seen repeated patterns of cheating previously, with this difference: prior to the test, those in one group were asked to recall and write down, from memory, the Ten Commandments, whereas those in the other group were asked to list the last ten books they had read. The results were startling: in the second group, the "books" group, the researchers observed the usual pattern and percentage of cheating. However, in the "commandments" group, there was absolutely no cheating at all.

"This experiment has obvious implications for the real world," said Ariely. "While ethics lectures and training seem to have little to no effect on people, reminders of morality—right at the point when people are making a decision—appear to have an outsize effect on behavior."[18]

And at some level it circles back to the university Mea Culpas study[19] cited earlier in this book.

If one reason companies lie is fear of loss, the joint study by researchers at the University of Michigan and Stanford graduate business schools makes a compelling case for telling the truth in a crisis and owning up to your own blunders. Rather than relying on anecdotal evidence or focus groups, that study demonstrated that the stock prices, tracked over a 20-year period, of selected companies that accepted the most blame for their own negative past stock performances outperformed, in the long run, the stock prices of other studied companies that blamed external factors. The difference in performance was between 14 and 19 percent.

Telling the truth, taking responsibility, and letting your myriad publics know that you are on their side is not only a good crisis communications strategy, but a good business strategy, too.

As Twain also said, "When in doubt, tell the truth."

13

Say It Ain't So, Joe![1]— The Penn State Crisis

■   ■   ■

One of the worst crises ever to occur at a U.S. college happened at Penn State University. I refer, of course, to the horrific sexual abuse crimes against some ten minor children, committed for years by a former assistant football coach, Jerry Sandusky, who in June 2012 was convicted of 45 of 48 criminal counts of child sexual abuse, some of which occurred on campus. On October 9, 2012, Sandusky was sentenced to 30 to 60 years in prison, guaranteeing that the 68-year-old man will die behind bars, should the appeals fail.

The public revelations of pedophilia in 2011 shook the university and the entire Penn State community to its very core, shocked and repulsed the nation, and resulted in the public firings of legendary football coach Joe Paterno and university president Graham Spanier and the removal of two other school officials.[2]

(Full disclosure: In addition to receiving my undergraduate degree from Penn State, I also was invited back some years ago to deliver the keynote commencement address to the graduating class; the subject of my talk—ironically—was honesty and doing the right thing. I also was invited to be the guest of then–university president Spanier and join him in his Beaver Stadium luxury suite at the Penn State–Illinois game of October 29, 2011, in what turned out to be Joe Paterno's final game as head football coach of the storied team. Paterno, 84 at that time and with more victories (409, following that game) than any other major college football coach, had been head coach since 1966; Spanier had been president since 1995. My schedule, however, conflicted, and I did not attend. Despite my past ties to the school, my comments on the school's crisis communications are, I believe, objective. But you'll have to draw your own conclusions, armed with the information contained in this paragraph.)

Following the revelations contained in a Pennsylvania grand jury presentment against Sandusky in 2011, it was reported that the first time anyone had been aware of Sandusky's perversion was in 1998. At that time, a report of Sandusky showering with a minor child surfaced. The incident was investigated by campus police, a child welfare caseworker, and a local district attorney. No action was taken against Sandusky, and no charges were brought.

Three years later, in 2001, ten years prior to the grand jury action, a graduate student assistant football coach, Mike McQueary, who as an undergraduate in the mid- to late 1990s had also been the team's quarterback, reportedly saw a naked Sandusky molesting a young boy in a shower at the football facility. The next day, McQueary reported the incident to Paterno, who promptly reported it to his superiors: President Spanier; Tim Curley, the athletic director; and Gary Schultz, the school vice president in charge of administration and the campus police. The initial criticism leveled against Paterno was that he didn't do enough to stop the then-alleged abuse and, in fact, subsequently acted to protect Sandusky and actively participated in a cover-up with his superiors to shield the school from "bad publicity." Paterno was never accused of any sexual abuse.

Let me be clear: there were failings all around in the way in which this crisis was bungled, beginning at the very top with President Spanier and including Coach Paterno, Messrs. Curley and Schultz, and the *entire* Penn State board of trustees. You don't need someone with my expertise to tell you what *should* have been done. Had the 2001 allegations of sexual abuse been properly investigated and reported to the appropriate law enforcement authorities, there would have been a crime and a criminal behind bars, *but no crisis.*

But—and this is important—this book is not about crisis *management*, it is about crisis *communications.* On that subject, once the crisis was made public, Penn State officials made numerous and costly missteps, but four enormous crisis communications blunders in this most regrettable tragedy stand out most egregiously.

When the grand jury presentment became public in November 2011, the school's shocked and dazed board of trustees huddled late into the night to discuss its options, including what, if anything, to do with Paterno. There were only three games left in the football season, and Paterno offered to resign effective at the end of the season. No doubt, he was trying to shift focus away from himself. "At this moment the Board of Trustees should not waste a single moment discussing my status," he said. "They have far more important matters to discuss. I want to make this as easy for them as I possibly can. This is a tragedy. It is one of the great sorrows of my life. With the benefit of hindsight, I wish I had done more."[3]

Something that was not known publicly at the time of Paterno's self-serving statement, but that was revealed subsequently, was that earlier that year he had renegotiated his contract, which had been due to expire in 2012. Under the new deal, Paterno had agreed to voluntarily step down as coach one year earlier, at the end of the 2011 football season, in exchange for more than $3 million.[4]

It is not known whether the board of trustees considered or even heard Paterno's plea, but in one of the most bizarre (many have said cowardly) acts ever carried out by a public body, the trustees dispatched a messenger, Fran Ganter, the associate athletic director for football, to Paterno's home at about 10:00 p.m. Ganter carried an envelope that contained a phone number on a slip of paper. After waking Paterno up, Ganter handed him the envelope, told him to call the number, and then departed.

Paterno dialed the number and spoke on the phone with Penn State trustee John Surma, chairman and CEO of U.S. Steel. Surma was brief: "The board of trustees has determined effective immediately you are no longer the football coach."[5]

Then Paterno hung up, and the board convened a hastily called press conference to announce his and Spanier's firings.

Paterno's rabid fans will debate for some time whether he should have been fired then and there or been allowed to step down voluntarily either at that time or at the end of the season (as he was secretly planning to do anyway). This topic has been, and will be, well covered by others; there is no shortage of armchair quarterbacks on this sideline issue.

In the wake of what the later investigation reported, I believe it was right and necessary for Paterno's football career to end at that time. But remember, at that point, the investigation had not even been announced; the board was responding only to the grand jury presentment, which had charged Paterno with . . . *nothing*.

I believe the board felt enormous pressure coming from the media frenzy, and it was apparent that there was no one at the university who was experienced and qualified to manage the crisis, and especially not the self-inflicted crisis communications maelstrom. It's common to make poor, hypervigilant decisions when barbarians are storming the gate; easy to throw some sacrificial red meat over the fortified battlements to try to keep the hordes at bay.

However—and this is where I take the board to task—the tone-deaf board of trustees' abject failure to practice sound crisis communications led directly to widespread student riots, fires, and property damage on campus and in adjacent State College as roving mobs of angry students violently protested Paterno's firing and the coldhearted and late-night manner in which it was carried out.

Unless you are ordering an immediate evacuation of a town to prevent imminent danger (such as a rapidly encroaching fire, the impending bursting of a dam, or a gas leak or toxic spill from a railroad train derailment) and possible loss of life, or you are a state governor issuing a last-minute reprieve of someone on death row, or you are dealing with something else that has time-sensitive urgency, *never hold press conferences or issue statements in the middle of the night!* It sends the completely wrong crisis communications signal. It gives the impression of unnecessary panic, anxiety, and urgency in what is being said and done.

It's the act of someone—in this instance, an entire board of some-ones—who mistakenly believes that doing something under cloak of darkness will somehow shield him from public scrutiny and back-lash. This is both wrong and wrongheaded. It is a crisis communications error of epic proportions, and it shifts attention away from the subject (*what* is being done) and onto the verb (*how* it is being done).

When you have bad news to report during a crisis—and we will discuss in a later chapter exactly *how* to convey bad news during a crisis—what is needed are bold leaders who are not afraid to plant their feet in front of the public in the harsh glare of daylight and camera lights and say what needs to be said. These were the worst nighttime firings since the infamous Saturday Night Massacre dur-ing the Watergate crisis, and they were a direct cause of the very predictable—and preventable—rioting and property damage that resulted. Consequently, now the school was not just being labeled a shielder of one man's perversions, it also was tagged as a gang of hooligans.

All of which only further inflamed the media firestorm.

What was needed that night was a crisis communicator who should have had the courage and the gravitas to say to the board, "*Wait!* There is no urgency that mandates a late-night announce-ment. No one is at risk right now, least of all any children. We can accomplish exactly the same thing at noon tomorrow, and in a much more controlled environment."

Given the explosive nature of this firing and the wholly predictable campus backlash, holding that press conference in the light of day would have helped convey the message that the board was calm and in control as it delivered hard and hard-to-hear news.

Put yourself in the place of the Penn State crisis communicator, and ask yourself: What critical moment would have been lost had the board of trustees waited until the next day to publicly render its decision? What was so imperative that the announcement had to be made near midnight, following an impersonal phone call to Paterno? Was anyone, especially children, at risk of immediate danger? Were lives hanging in the balance?

These are important questions to ask yourself when you are faced with your own crisis. Your messages are important, obviously, but so, too, are the timing and the method of delivery, which are key parts of your overall strategy. Try not to have your message overshadowed by other events that are well within your control.

I recall a few years ago when my firm's automated after-hours phone system tracked me down to return a call that had come in at 9:00 p.m. Pacific Time on the Friday before Labor Day. When I looked at the area code, I saw the call was coming from Toronto, where it was then midnight. When I returned the call, the chairman of the board of this worldwide company told me he was in the conference room with his entire board of directors. They were in a major crisis. But after hearing their plight, I assured them that there was nothing that would be served by acting or issuing statements immediately. (They were also unaware it was the eve of a U.S. holiday.) In fact, I assured them that any action taken by us that night would only serve to escalate the crisis in the minds of their customers and the media. Fortunately, they heeded my advice and we sprang into action the next morning, and the crisis was soon resolved.

Paterno should have been summoned to campus early the next morning and given the news of the board's decision in person. *Some consideration was due a man who, during his 46 years as head coach, had done so much for the institution far beyond football.* In a positive way, he was almost single-handedly responsible for raising the out-in-the-middle-of-nowhere school's national visibility and heightened stature as a leading educational establishment. But even if you discount that, some consideration should have been given to the predictable backlash. If your goal is to terminate someone, and you are the crisis communicator on the scene, part of your decision-making process should be to strategize about the most effective way to (1) accomplish your goal and (2) do so in a way that does not cause a crisis, or a larger crisis. This applies to all companies faced with announcing unpopular decisions. *Don't be rash; be strategic.*

Hence, once the board had made the decision to fire Paterno and Spanier—crisis *management*—the next question should have been how and when to deliver the blows. This is crisis *communications*. Obviously, someone—maybe the entire board?—wanted to wash his hands of the mess as quickly as possible, and made the ill-conceived determination to act immediately without considering the consequences.

The board should have realized that not only were its actions going to be scrutinized on a national level, but the manner of delivering the message would also be debated. This was an abject failure of proper crisis communications skills. And it was only to get worse.

Next, a *joint* statement should have been issued—one that reported on a mutual decision that Paterno would leave his position—which, if it had been delivered in the light of day and while students were in classes, would probably have either prevented or severely mitigated the rioting. Plus, with the advance warning, the local and campus police would have had time to prepare for any unrest, just in case. This is proper crisis management as well as crisis communications. The knee-jerk decision to fire Paterno with a late-night phone call was a misguided move by a timorous board filled with fear and trepidation. It backfired on them, and it will backfire on you.

However, *if* Paterno had refused to cooperate, then he should have been fired summarily by the board.

Note that none of what I am saying here should be construed as either a whitewash of, or an apologia for, Paterno—quite the contrary. Once the board had made a *crisis management* decision ("Joe must go"), the *crisis communications* decisions that followed should have been focused on how to deliver that decision in a manner that would be in the best interests of the school, while not causing a crisis backlash. *This* was the board's first crisis communications failure.

In hindsight, one might look back and say that given Paterno's alleged knowledge of events and his alleged participation in shielding Sandusky, he deserved no better. However, at the time of his dismissal, these elements had not been established, and even today they are somewhat muddled. Part of the reason for this may be attributed to the voraciousness of the media, which pushed some stories ahead of established facts. Given the manner in which the firing took place, the media deemed this open season on Paterno.

The rioting that followed served only to further besmirch Penn State's reputation (if that were even possible) and gave the perception of a student and alumni body that wanted to protect a man who may have failed to protect young, innocent children.

Immediately thereafter, the school realized that it had serious crisis communications damage control to perform. College acceptance letters had gone out to thousands of high school seniors, and one immediate priority was to reach out to each of those high school seniors in case they or their parents were having second thoughts about whether to enroll at Penn State in the wake of the scandal. In late November of that year, the newly named university president, Rodney Erickson, autosigned a "personal" letter to each accepted student, which read, in part: "Recently you received an offer of admission to Penn State and I want you to feel a sense of pride in your accomplishments as well as a sense of excitement for the opportunities that await you as part of the Penn State Community." Then, in the only direct reference to the tragedy, he wrote, "Over the course of recent weeks, the character and resilience of Penn State have been tested in ways we never could have imagined. To their great credit, the students have reminded us that the Penn State community is compassionate and strong."[6]

The letter, which contained no other reference to the crisis, may have served its purpose. Reportedly, the number of college applicants increased slightly in the year immediately following the sexual abuse revelations, and some 36,000 undergraduates occupied Happy Valley in the fall of 2012. Additionally, the school took in more than $208 million in donations in the 2011–2012 fiscal year. The gift giving, mostly from students and alumni, was the second-highest take in the school's history, which the school cited as proof that it still had strong support despite the disturbing revelations.[7]

One of the school's other crisis management and crisis communications moves in the wake of the scandal was to appoint former FBI director Louis Freeh to lead an independent investigation into the entire affair, including the university's alleged role in a cover-up following McQueary's initial report. Freeh has his supporters and his detractors, but as former head of the FBI and a former federal judge, his perceived professional reputation for justice and impartiality immediately communicated to the world that the school was serious about investigating the events and any possible cover-up by school officials.

Freeh's 267-page report on the university's failings was released publicly on July 12, 2012, following an eight-month investigation.[8] It was immediately embraced by some, and just as quickly denounced by others.

Among the harshest criticisms was that the evidence presented in the report did not support the hyperbolic seven-page news release that Freeh read publicly at a national press conference. In other words, critics alleged that Freeh jumped to some sensational and unsupported conclusions and discounted or ignored testimony resulting from a very lengthy interview with Spanier.

One of the most damaging findings, according to Freeh, was that in early 2001, following McQueary's description of what he had seen in the shower, Spanier, Curley, Schultz, and Paterno were at first in favor of turning Sandusky and the whole matter over to Pennsylvania's Department of Public Welfare, the agency responsible for the protection of children. However, an e-mail from Curley soon thereafter said that he had changed his mind after talking with "the coach," and he now recommended that, for humanitarian reasons, they should talk with Sandusky and help him get professional help rather than report him. Freeh says that Spanier caved and did not direct anyone to report Sandusky to the authorities.

But who, exactly, did "the coach" refer to?

It must be noted that the Freeh commission did not have subpoena powers, that several pivotal individuals—notably Curley, Schultz, and McQueary—declined to be interviewed by the independent investigation committee, and that Paterno never had the chance to do so. Only Spanier agreed to be interviewed, and he underwent a five-hour interrogation.

This serious deficiency has been cited by critics of the report, pointing out that it cannot be complete without the sworn testimony of these key players, and that absent sworn testimony of any kind and judicial rules of evidence, the bulk of the report includes much hearsay, with leaps to conclusions that leave room for doubt—had anyone bothered to look carefully at it or speak up.

Moreover, another broadside has been leveled against certain conclusions drawn by the report, including that Paterno was never directly tied to the "smoking pistol": the aforementioned e-mail from Curley to Spanier in which he says he spoke with "the coach." As presented, those holding this position argue, the "coach" was likely to have been Sandusky, not Paterno (who was usually called "Joe" by contemporaries, and certainly by those at the Spanier, Curley, and Schultz levels), and only Curley—who has "lawyered up"—can shed needed light on this crucial point. And there were other instances and e-mails in which Curley said he spoke with "Coach Sandusky" about bringing boys into the showers. It is fair to argue that the use of "coach" in this instance is somewhat ambiguous and leaves room for questions—but certainly was not ambiguous as Freeh emphatically characterized it, which is part of the strongest criticism of him: that his press conference and news release connected dots that the report did not.

Jay Paterno, Joe's son, granted several media interviews, in which he also pointed out that lack of testimony under oath was a serious shortcoming in the report, and vigorously defended his father as a man of integrity who would never have shielded a pedophile. Many others, including some on the board of trustees, say the same thing, and a mini-documentary available on YouTube, called "The Framing of Joe Paterno," paints a more graphic picture of problems with the Freeh Report. John Ziegler, a talk show host and the man behind the video, has also penned a lengthy screed that goes into more detail of how he claims the media participated in the framing. There are valid points made in support of a rush-to-judgment accusation.[9]

And, predictably, Graham Spanier, the man at the top of the pyramid, has attacked the report, and his portrayal therein, vigorously. In a letter that Spanier wrote to the board following the release of the report, he forcefully labeled "[t]he Freeh report . . . egregious in its incomplete and inaccurate reportings of my 2011 discussions . . . and the recounting of unfolding events of 2011."[10]

Spanier claims that he told Freeh and his investigators in no uncertain terms that he was never informed of Sandusky's "child abuse, sexual misconduct or 'criminality of any kind,'"[11] but Freeh ignored his vehement denials.

The former Penn State president has nothing but contempt for the report, saying: "The Freeh report is wrong, it's unfair, it is deeply flawed, it has many errors and omissions."[12]

Given how Spanier comes across in the report, it would be in his own interest to try to rehabilitate his badly damaged reputation. But certain facts, even as he portrays them, defy credulity. For example, he denies any knowledge of any specific accusations of sexual impropriety concerning Sandusky, but admits to hearing from Curley and Schultz in 2001 of a report of a naked Sandusky "horsing around" in the showers with a naked minor boy.

"'I recall asking [Curley and Schultz] two questions,'" Spanier says he reported to Freeh. "'Are you sure that is how it was described to you, as horsing around?' Both replied 'yes.'

"'Are you sure that that is all that was reported?' Both replied 'yes.'"[13]

So, Spanier had been informed more than a decade earlier that a grown man, a former university employee of a certain senior stature, and a minor child were naked and were "horsing around" in the showers—and he did nothing to investigate? Isn't the fact that a grown man is naked and "horsing around" with a young child in the football shower facilities on campus enough of a red flag? How much more do you need to know to understand that something is wrong, and that something needs to be done?

And are those the *only* two questions you'd want answers to?

Spanier just went on about his business that day, his two "probing" questions asked and answered.

Later in the same letter, Spanier tries to shift responsibility to his own general counsel, Cynthia Baldwin, saying that she told him "very little" of how she was handling the situation, and quoting her as saying that the Commonwealth of Pennsylvania was then on its "third or fourth Grand Jury," but not to worry, she said. There was no involvement of the university, "and . . . the Attorney General did not seem to have any evidence to suggest that something happened involving Penn State. She had, she said, spoken several times to Attorney General staff. I [Spanier] was never told by her of any materials being subpoenaed from the University, or even that I had been subpoenaed to testify."[14]

It is almost inconceivable that a competent attorney, and especially the general counsel of a major enterprise like Penn State, could not learn through normal channels the focus of a grand jury probe. Spanier points out that even Freeh faulted Baldwin's lack of due diligence in failing "to seek the advice of a law firm with quality criminal experience to advise her of how to deal with the Attorney General and the Grand Jury investigation. I [Spanier] have learned this is a standard procedure when corporations or other large entities are served with Grand Jury subpoenas."[15]

One more example of university ineptitude across many levels.

And maybe more than meets the eye. In a bizarre wrinkle in this part of the saga, Baldwin drove Curley and Schultz from the Penn State campus to their grand jury testimony in Harrisburg, Pennsylvania, and back—about a four-hour round-trip drive over a total distance of some 180 miles. When asked individually during the grand jury proceedings if they were represented by counsel, both men said yes, and named Cynthia Baldwin. Baldwin denies that she represented either man, and when asked for the record during the proceedings, she said that she represented "Penn State." But she never corrected either man, or the record, at the time or anytime thereafter.[16] However, it is indisputable that she was in the grand jury courtroom during Curley and Schultz's testimony—raising the question of how she would not know the precise focus of the grand jury probe and fail to warn Spanier, her client, of the precarious position on which the entire school was perched.

Spanier concluded by saying, "the report is full of factual errors and jumps to conclusions that are untrue and unwarranted."[17]

Nevertheless, in context, the conclusions of the report, as presented by Freeh at his press conference, seem to leave little room for doubt. And it also should be noted that other than Spanier, no one has come forward to discount or take issue with anything in the report, which did manage to successfully interview 430 people.

One of the most damning indictments of the university from Freeh was when he said, "Our most saddening and sobering finding is the total disregard for the safety and welfare of Sandusky's child victims by the most senior leaders at Penn State. The most powerful men at Penn State failed to take any steps for 14 years to protect the children who Sandusky victimized."[18]

Of these, I would lay blame most especially at Spanier's feet. When you are the CEO—the president of a major university—it is your job to listen to the advice of your counselors and subordinates, but then do what needs to be done. In almost any crisis, conflicting voices will demand to be heard, and opposing points of view will be argued. That leads to healthy debate and the hope that all views are being expressed. But it is the person at the top of the food chain whose job and ultimate obligation it is to ask the questions that need to be asked and make the tough decisions that need to be made. There is a time for debate and a time for decision. Spanier should have demanded more information about the "horsing around" incident, and he certainly should have rejected Curley's second suggestion as not being in the best interests of the university or the victims and followed through with the original plan: report Sandusky to the authorities.

For whether or not "coach" referred to Paterno or Sandusky in that earlier discussed e-mail, no one disputes that Spanier was the recipient of the message, so he had knowledge of, and participated in, the discussion about not reporting Sandusky.

It was Spanier's role to make the call and his obligation to do so, but he failed to act. Why? Why did he balk?

That was the second huge crisis communications collapse.

According to Freeh, "In order to avoid the consequences of bad publicity," Spanier and company "repeatedly concealed critical facts relating to Sandusky's child abuse from the authorities, the board of trustees, the Penn State community, and the public at large."[19]

Others have pointed out, anecdotally, that Paterno wielded so much influence on campus that Spanier was afraid to go up against him. If that was so—I have no independent knowledge of this—but if it was so, Spanier was unfit to be a university president. Where was his backbone? If a university president cannot control a football coach, one of them needs to go: the subordinate.

Remember, a bad story will always get out, with or without your help; it is just a matter of time, even if it takes a decade or more. Trying to keep something under wraps in order to avoid "bad publicity" *never* works. If you are in charge of communications during a crisis within your organization, you should count on this as a universal truth. A story may be "bad" or "embarrassing," but attempts to cover it up are always worse when ultimately they are exposed. While Penn State managed to avoid bad publicity related to the heinous nature of Sandusky's actions for 14 years, just consider how much worse it was after the revelations of the cover-up at the highest levels of the school were revealed.

This can easily happen to you should you try to follow such a perilous path.

Think, on the other hand, how the school would have been lauded if it had stepped up in 2001 and reported Sandusky and the abuse following McQueary's eyewitness account. Had school officials acted more forcefully against the popular Sandusky in 1998 or 2001, think how many innocent children might have been spared. Think how Paterno's reputation would have been burnished even brighter for having "done more."

This lesson is worth remembering during *your* crisis moment.

But how should Spanier have known a crisis was brewing?

Back in Chapter 6, "Understanding *Your* Crisis," and under the subheading, "*Your* Crisis Is Subjective," I outlined the five issues that identify a crisis; had Spanier asked *relevant* questions about these issues, he could have nipped this crisis in the bud.

By asking the *right* questions—not the two lame and pointless questions that he did ask—he would have seen that this prodrome could escalate in intensity, could come under close government or media scrutiny, could damage the positive reputation of the university and its leaders, and so on—that is, could lead to a crisis. And armed with that foreknowledge, Spanier could have accomplished the ultimate crisis management hat trick: going from prodrome to resolution without suffering the acute or chronic phases of a crisis.

Of course, careful followers of this story already know that a local district attorney *did* investigate the 1998 incident and concluded that there was nothing there to act on. Perhaps, but the previous incident, on top of the McQueary report, suggests that "where there's smoke, there's fire" and should have been even more impetus for Spanier—and Curley and Schultz—to probe deeper.

It is important to note that other key opportunities to halt the molestations also were missed. In the last chapter, I referred to corporate culture and suggested that you ask, honestly, whether your organization is one that encourages bad news to be reported, or whether it "shoots the messenger." As it turned out, sadly, such an open environment did not exist at Penn State. The Freeh report recounted the lamentable tale of two janitors assigned to the Penn State football locker room who observed Sandusky sexually molesting a young boy in 2000—one full year before McQueary's observation. Because they were lowly janitors and knew well who the powerful Sandusky was, they feared that they would lose their jobs if they reported what they saw, according to the report.

One janitor said that if they reported it, "they'll get rid of all of us." The other agreed, saying that reporting it "would have been like going against the President of the United States [meaning Paterno] in my eyes." This janitor, so far removed from the top of the power pyramid, nevertheless astutely observed that "football runs this university" and predicted that the school would close ranks to protect the football program.[20]

In a broader context, what the janitors witnessed could be classified as a prodrome. In some client organizations, we install Prodrome Review Committees, which allow employees at all levels to raise a red flag if they see something amiss, and to do so anonymously, if they choose. You need the right corporate culture for this concept to succeed, which clearly was not present at Penn State. One of the aims of a Prodrome Review Committee is to ensure that word gets to the top to enable a crisis management decision, and hopefully before an acute crisis erupts. However, this corporate culture also must extend to and from the top. In Penn State's case, the head of the entire university, and others in leadership and key management roles, *were* aware of the prodromes—and willfully chose to ignore them.

And there was at least one other person who was fully aware of the sexual abuse allegations against Sandusky and did absolutely nothing to stop it: Tom Corbett, governor of Pennsylvania.

Prior to his election in November 2010, Corbett had served as the state's elected attorney general from 2004 to 2011,[21] and it was under his regime that the Sandusky investigation was launched and multiple grand juries were convened to hear testimony from victims of the predator's abuse. In all, Corbett knew of the abuse allegations against Sandusky as the state's highest law enforcement officer, the attorney general, and as its highest elected official, the governor, for at least three years. *And he did nothing to stop it!*

In addition, the governor of Pennsylvania automatically serves as a member of the Penn State board of trustees. So, from January 2011, when he was installed as governor, to November 2011, when Sandusky was arrested, *Corbett still did nothing*, even as a member of the Penn State board of trustees. Said nothing. Protected no child. Whispered nothing into anyone's ear—not even at the Second Mile, the charity Sandusky started for underprivileged youth, where the pervert apparently recruited his victims in a sick sort of farm system.

When Freeh pointed the finger at "the most powerful men at Penn State," he missed one of the big ones, one of the most powerful men in the Commonwealth of Pennsylvania: Tom Corbett.

Corbett is not some lowly janitor who is fearful of losing his job. If it is the responsibility of people in positions of authority to protect innocent children—*and it is*—then Corbett had a legal and moral responsibility to act. His woefully shameful and pathetically anemic response was that his hands were tied until an arrest was made. To which I, and others, have said: *So make the arrest! Get Sandusky off the streets! Protect the kids!* Waiting three years to make an arrest—giving Sandusky three more years of freedom to continue his depraved acts—is as inexcusable for Corbett as it is for Spanier. You can't fault one without faulting the other.

In fact, Corbett actually knew a great deal more than Spanier, since he was privy to confidential grand jury testimony. Not to make any excuses for Spanier, but essentially all he had was the McQueary account. Corbett, as the attorney general leading the investigation, had it all, including the testimony of, and access to, the victims. *And still he did nothing.*

Even though the Sandusky trial has ended and a harsh sentence has been imposed (pending appeals), Penn State is far from out of the woods. As the deep pockets in this tragedy, it faces mountains of litigation and various possible criminal charges, and the school's primary liability insurance carrier, Pennsylvania Manufacturer's Insurance Co., swiftly moved to deny coverage.[22] With each new twist of the screw, the crisis will be revisited. So, in a ham-fisted way, the school tried to limit further stories by offering to settle with Sandusky's victims even before anyone ever mentioned compensation.

The day after the Sandusky verdict was announced, University President Erickson issued a crisis communications message that read, in part, "While we cannot change what happened, we can and do accept responsibility to take action on the societal issue of child sexual abuse—both in our community and beyond."[23]

That is an interesting sentence construction—not accepting responsibility for the abuse, but accepting "responsibility to take action on the societal issue of child sexual abuse."

However, the paragraph that jumped out at me even more was where Erickson said that the university wanted to compensate the victims, who at the time of his writing had not yet filed suit (some did later, as was predictable), and do so out of the public eye.

> Now that the jury has spoken, the University wants to . . . do its part to help victims continue their path forward. To that end, the University plans to invite victims of Mr. Sandusky's abuse to participate in a program to facilitate the resolution of claims against the University arising out of Mr. Sandusky's conduct. The purpose of the program is simple—the University wants to provide a forum where the University can *privately*, expeditiously and fairly address the victims' concerns and compensate them for claims relating to the University.[24] (Emphasis added.)

This attempt to silence the victims, while blatantly transparent, is not altogether a bad idea, from a crisis communications perspective. The school has already opened its checkbook and taken the cap off its fountain pen, and is just waiting to see how many zeroes are required. In litigation like this—meaning litigation in which, no matter what happens, the university's reputation will again be tarnished with each new development—the sooner the school can put a coda on the public's rehashing of the sordid details, the sooner things can return to a semblance of normalcy, the better (although anything resembling normal at Penn State will be years off).

But I take issue with the decision to announce publicly that you want to pony up some bucks, even before you've been sued. A post-trial message from the university's president was appropriate, but inasmuch as the victims were all represented at the trial by private attorneys, if the school truly wanted to provide a forum to discuss the question of victim compensation "privately," this very public letter was not the way to do it. The school could have had discussions about compensation with those attorneys, in private. Often, communicating *privately* rather than *publicly* is the more strategic crisis communications option.

Thus, yet again, the school's delivery of an important crisis communications message was upstaged by the method of its delivery, which was amateurishly transparent.

Erickson's disingenuous letter, which appears to have been scripted by some PR person who was completely devoid of competent crisis communications skills, was designed to send the message: *"Hey, look what we're doing! Aren't we great?"* The targeted audience was not the victims but others, such as opinion makers, state and federal legislators, criminal prosecutors, the NCAA, the Big Ten conference, the media, future students and their parents, football recruits, and so on. The time for the school to act responsibly had long since passed.

But if the school hoped to influence the NCAA, it failed.

The worst penalty the NCAA had ever handed down previously was the so-called death penalty leveled against Southern Methodist University in 1987. In that case, it was uncovered that SMU football players were being paid thousands of dollars from a slush fund that had been created by boosters and was administered by school officials, including former Texas governor Bill Clements. The NCAA sidelined the football program for the entire 1987 season, and it was more than 20 years before the program returned to any semblance of prominence. In 2009, SMU received its first bowl game bid in 25 years, since 1984.[25] When the bid was announced, Steve Orsini, SMU's athletic director, proclaimed, "We've proven there's life after death."[26]

For months, Penn State—school officials, football players, students, and alumni—waited anxiously to learn whether the same fate awaited them. On July 23, 2012, the sentence was imposed.

It was, in many ways, much worse and, in many more ways, completely unprecedented.

The NCAA levied the following sanctions against Penn State:

- A four-year postseason ban (no bowl games) for the football program
- A reduction in football scholarships from 25 to 15 over four years
- A $60 million fine
- A five-year probation period for *all* school sports
- And, vacating from the record books all Paterno victories from 1998 to 2011

Mark Emmert, the NCAA president, characterized the case as the most painful "chapter in the history of intercollegiate athletics" and said that the punishment meted out was arguably "greater than any other seen in N.C.A.A. history."[27] The loss of 111 "Ws" means that Paterno is no longer the major college career leader in football victories.[28]

In announcing the sanctions, Emmert also made it clear that the record $60 million fine was not to come at the expense of non-revenue-producing sports or academics. The money is to be used as an endowment to serve the victims of child abuse nationwide.

He also said that current Penn State players could transfer to other schools at once and not lose eligibility (rather than be "red-shirted," or held back from play for a year), should they so choose, a tacit sanction that also hurt Penn State. Not wasting any time, about one week later, on July 31, junior star tailback Silas Redd was the first to leave; he agreed to play for the University of Southern California in the fall of 2012. Eight more players, including some prominent starters, soon followed Redd's lead and found homes on other gridirons across the nation, causing some pundits to question if Penn State would be able to field a competitive team in the fall.[29]

Later the same day, the Big Ten conference, of which Penn State is a member, announced its own sanctions: banning the football team from appearing in any Big Ten championship games for four years and stripping it of financial participation in any shared conference bowl revenues—an estimated $13 million per year.

One day earlier, Erickson—without consulting his board, students, or alumni—made the unilateral and highly controversial decision to move the iconic seven-foot-tall bronze statue of Paterno from the entrance to Beaver Stadium to a secret location. One astute observer commented that if the powers that be at the school had given as much thought to flesh-and-blood children as they did to a 900-pound, inanimate statue, they wouldn't be in this mess.

It is telling to note some unusual, if not bizarre, characteristics of Penn State's response, or lack thereof, to the Freeh report and the NCAA sanctions, for they speak volumes about the school's total lack of understanding of crisis communications. Mere hours after Louis Freeh released his commission's findings, Erickson and Karen Peetz, newly minted chairwoman of the board of trustees, held a press conference in which they said that the school accepted Freeh's report unconditionally, all the allegations it contained, and the more than 100 recommendations it proposed. The board questioned nothing; it challenged nothing; it investigated nothing. The Penn State faithful can only be grateful that Freeh did not also accuse the school of complicity in the Lincoln assassination.

Freeh conducted his press conference in Philadelphia, as the board was meeting in Scranton, Pennsylvania, that same day. How carefully did the board, which reportedly had no advance copy of the report, actually review and digest the devastating 267-page document before accepting it unconditionally? Did anyone even raise a question about certain perceived inconsistencies in the report, or about conclusions drawn from tenuous facts? Not likely, and yet they rushed to drink the hemlock. This sends the wrong sort of crisis communications message. Blunder No. 3.

Erickson should have received the report and dismissed Freeh and his team after having thanked them for their service, and then the board should have taken the necessary time to read and fully digest the report. If there were follow-up questions, a board committee should have broached them with Freeh and his team for clarification. And when the report then was made public, which would be proper, it should have been at a joint press conference with Erickson and Freeh together. But Erickson accepting the report and all of its findings unconditionally sent the already reeling university stumbling down another treacherous path.

Typically, when the NCAA looks into alleged abuse of any kind at a school, its painfully slow multistep investigative process can take years, and it is usually followed by a formal listing of the allegations, a lengthy amount of time to allow for a response from the school, a rendering of the punishment, and inevitable appeals from the school. For example, when the NCAA first began looking into allegations that USC's star running back Reggie Bush and his family illegally accepted $100,000 from a sports marketing agent, it took so long to conduct the investigation that by the time the report was complete, the Heisman Trophy winner was already a star running back for the New Orleans Saints.[30] The NCAA's July 23 decision followed the release of the Freeh report by less than two weeks. The NCAA chose to sidestep its own rules and issue its sanctions without even waiting for the criminal and civil actions surrounding the Sandusky case to play out, another unusual step. Emmert said that since Penn State had accepted the findings of the Freeh report in full, without challenge of any kind, the athletic authority used that report as the basis for imposing the stiffest sanctions in NCAA history. For the NCAA to impose sanctions, let alone those of this severity, without conducting its own independent investigation and completely bypassing its own Committee on Infractions is completely unprecedented. It also deprived Penn State of due process.

In the real, as opposed to the academic, world, it is not uncommon to have a defendant appear in both criminal and civil cases for the same alleged crime (think O. J. Simpson). Typically, the criminal case is tried first. Even if he is convicted in a criminal trial, the defendant is still entitled to his day in civil court. It is *never* the case that if the defendant is found guilty in one court, the other court will save time and money by just imposing "justice" based on what happened in the first case; no defendant in his right mind would agree to that. But that is exactly what happened here, meaning that you could posit that Penn State was so stunned by events that it was not in its right mind at the time. We've already discussed certain procedural deficiencies with the school's former general counsel; perhaps this is more of the same.

As for the sanctions, the school accepted them, too, without a whimper. Penn State also entered into a formal consent decree with the NCAA, stating that the school not only agreed with the sanctions but abdicated any right to appeal them. Blunder No. 4.

Remember, in a widespread crisis like Penn State's, every utterance from all concerned falls under the broad heading of crisis communications, and the NCAA is no exception. In that sense, vacating 111 football victories has been criticized for being purely punitive and even vindictive. The only people such a move hurts are innocent student athletes for the past dozen or so years. Their legitimate achievements on the football field have been eradicated from the record books, but why? Why should the NCAA punish innocent student athletes? Toward what end? The NCAA severely punished Penn State with four of its sanctions. If it wanted to inflict punitive punishment on Paterno's legacy, it could have struck his name from the College Football Hall of Fame or put an asterisk next to those 111 victories in the record book with some sort of footnoted annotation. *Explain* history; don't rewrite it.

It was a crisis communications decision that the supercilious NCAA may one day rue. It inadvertently crossed a Rubicon by taking what it viewed as an expedient shortcut, and in effect compromised the integrity of its own future investigative authority. Others have claimed this NCAA bitch-slapping of Penn State was a way for Emmert to bolster his own persona.

Conversely, more than 20 years ago, Pete Rose was banned from baseball for life by then MLB commissioner A. Bartlett Giamatti for betting on games while he was a player and later a manager, including games in which he was actively involved. And yet, Pete Rose still holds the official all-time record for most career hits—4,256. Major League Baseball deemed that a record is a record and a miscreant is a miscreant, and Rose's record was not vacated, nor has he been enshrined in Cooperstown.

Paterno, not innocent players, should have been the target of the NCAA's corrective actions, if they felt Paterno was somehow culpable. The NCAA's crisis communications message regarding vacating wins and punishing the innocent was wrong and displayed a lack of crisis communications sophistication and blatant pettiness, or worse.

So, too, was the sanction to put *every* Penn State sports team on probation for five years. That severe disciplinary action penalized some 30 teams, coaches, and hundreds of kids who were and are completely innocent of any of the wrongdoings involving Sandusky or football. This sanction, too, is purely punitive and vindictive and displays a mean-spiritedness on the part of the NCAA—and Mark Emmert—that previously was kept well hidden.

Apparently, that's not the only thing the NCAA keeps hidden.

In a scathing front page indictment of the NCAA's investigative methods, the *Los Angeles Times* wrote that several disturbing incidents have dragged the normally secretive NCAA into the harsh glare of the spotlight, raising serious questions about the organization's own brand of unilateral ethics and how it polices athletes and coaches, as well as its inconsistency in meting out punishment.

"'The NCAA does not operate like a prosecutor's office or a police department where there are clearly understood constitutional limits,' said Geoffrey C. Rapp, a University of Toledo law professor and editor of the Sports Law blog. 'They don't have a structure in place to ensure consistency.'"[31]

Or fairness.

In one case, where the NCAA lowered the boom on a former USC assistant football coach, who then turned around and sued the sports organization for defamation, a Los Angeles County Superior Court Judge, after hearing the evidence, labeled the NCAA investigation "malicious," "over the top," and demonstrated "ill will or hatred" toward the defendant.[32]

In another recent case, this time involving unspecified charges against a top-recruit UCLA basketball player, Kyle Anderson, Jr., it was revealed that the NCAA investigator assigned to the case had prejudged the player's "guilt" well before all of the facts were in, when the boyfriend of the investigator allegedly told an airplane seatmate that his girlfriend would make sure Anderson never became eligible. This occurred well before the player's parents were interviewed or any financial records examined. When the boy's father later asked what his son was supposed to have done, the NCAA investigator said "they were not at liberty to say." The investigator soon was fired and the case went away.

In addition to Penn State, critics have noted inconsistencies in the enforcement sanctions the NCAA has handed down against Ohio State, Auburn, and USC.

The attorney representing the UCLA player cited above observed ruefully that America's judicial system was founded on the basic tenet of people being presumed innocent until proven guilty. "The NCAA gets it backwards."[33]

Normally, the NCAA undertakes its own lengthy two-part investigation involving first, scrutiny by its Committee on Infractions, and then adjudication. Neither prong was followed here. So, why did Penn State embrace the NCAA sanctions so quickly?

Erickson said that the choice was either to accept the sanctions as presented, no questions asked, or to face a four-year death penalty, meaning no Penn State football for four years. This choice, which was essentially blackmail by a brass-knuckled bully, was confirmed by Emmert. So, when faced with that choice, Erickson

entered into intense and secret negotiations with the NCAA—
again, without informing his board.[34]

The school administration formulated a crisis management and
crisis communications tactic that consisted of doing everything
possible to distance itself from these horrific events as quickly as
possible in an effort to find that elusive thing called closure, but
without any strategic decision making in the process. However, to
make such a momentous decision without consulting the trustees
left many on the board fuming and forged yet another layer of crisis
distraction that the school certainly did not need. Moreover, it created a déjà vu moment: the board of trustees had been kept out of
the loop when Spanier was president, and was also being systemat-
ically kept out of the loop under Erickson's freshman regime.

Said one board member, "'I am frankly outraged as a member
of the board of trustees that the university entered into a consent
decree without discussing it with the Board in advance of signing,'
Anthony Lubrano told *USA Today* Sports. 'If I'm going to be held
accountable, I feel like I should've been part of that process.'"[35]

Lubrano, an unabashed Paterno supporter, went on to say that
other board members are similarly upset. He said that the board
"rolled over and played dead"[36] because the school wanted so badly
to put Paterno in its rearview mirror.

And a group calling itself Penn Staters for Responsible
Stewardship, looking to oust the school's current leadership,
blamed the board for the severity of the NCAA sanctions. For the
NCAA "'[t]o rely upon such a report [the Freeh report] to issue
punishment is beyond reckless, and should not be supported by the
leadership of Penn State,' said the group. 'By agreeing to these sanctions, every single member of the Penn State Board of Trustees has
blatantly failed in their fiduciary responsibilities to the university.
With each passing hour we are gaining additional alumni support
in our demand to have them resign immediately.'"[37]

Around the same time, a credible report circulated that the
board had convened a meeting to discuss whether Erickson even

had the authority to agree to such sanctions without board approval. According to one source, "Some trustees have expressed concern that Erickson violated a board rule that says the board must authorize the signing of 'contracts, legal documents, and other obligations.'"[38]

And another group from the board reportedly started a move to sue to vacate the NCAA ruling.

While these types of grassroots movements seldom succeed, our purpose here is to analyze the effectiveness of "rolling over and playing dead." What kind of crisis communications message does *that* send?

A mixed message, at best. The board and the school's senior administrators previously did not lead when they could and should have done so, nor did they exhibit any crisis communications leadership qualities in the latest round of lashings. They seemed to be openly asking to be flogged, as if a greater number of scars would somehow help the healing process. And with each action the school took in its feeble management of its crisis, it sent to the world crisis communications messages that only served to underscore that no one was running the asylum—least of all the board, which has the responsibility and is obligated to do so.

Looking ahead, NCAA's Emmert said, "[A]ll universities must now contemplate whether their own athletic programs had become 'too big to fail,' or, even more troubling, 'too big to challenge.'"[39]

"At our core, we are educators," he said. "Penn State leadership lost sight of that."[40]

Then, in a moment of obvious head-in-the-clouds wishful thinking, he went on to lamely predict, "Football will never again be placed ahead of educating."[41]

Of course, if the unenlightened Emmert had bothered to check his own NCAA website, he would have seen that Penn State's GSR (graduation success rate) for football players is an impressive 87 percent, second only to Northwestern in the Big Ten and tied with Stanford for tenth place nationally.[42]

Uninformed and erroneous comments like Emmert's are a common crisis communications problem when people speak for sound bites rather than from facts.

What Emmert undoubtedly meant was that football on many university campuses has become too dominant—or, as he put it, "too big to fail" and "too big to challenge"—and that's because of the big business/big money aspect of the game today, some corners are cut at colleges that should remain sacrosanct. Football may have been placed ahead of many things, but at least at Penn State, it does not seem that education was one of them, and the president of the NCAA, of all people, should know that.

The problem with empty bromides such as Emmert's is that the NCAA is as responsible for that culture as the individual schools, perhaps more so. College sports are driven by money. A successful football program like Penn State's can generate tens of millions of dollars each year for the school and for the NCAA, and bowl game revenues in particular are astronomical. And the NCAA and its handmaiden henchmen, sports conferences, have been most instrumental and incredibly successful in helping to secure big-time television revenue for schools that can bring their "A-game" and huge TV audiences on Saturday afternoons in the fall.

"The university presidents, conference commissioners, athletic directors and corporate marketers who attend" sports conferences, like the annual IMG Intercollegiate Sports Forum, "spend very little time mouthing the usual pieties about how the 'student-athlete' comes first," according to New York Times columnist Joe Nocera. "Rather, they gather each year to talk bluntly about making money." IMG, which lists the NCAA as one of its partners, labels the forum on its website a "must attend event for anyone involved in the business of college sports." At its most recent forum, the keynote speaker was none other than the sanctimonious Mark Emmert, NCAA president, giving new meaning to the term "lip service."

On a forum panel devoted to trying to cut sports expenses, "several panelists suggested that the only sure way to cut back on coaches' compensation would be to amend the nation's antitrust laws to allow universities to band together and cap coaches' pay.

"Well, yes, I suppose that's one way of doing it," wrote Nocera. "Another way, of course, would be for college presidents to show some backbone and say no." He then added, "Fat chance."[43]

But if schools truly want to put education ahead of sports, perhaps they should look backward, not forward, for guidance.

In 1892, the same year the school was founded, the University of Chicago started its football program. Three years later, school athletic officials met with seven of their counterparts in the Palmer House in Chicago and discussed starting a sports conference. The following year, six schools returned, and what ultimately was to become the Big Ten conference was inaugurated. The University of Chicago, unquestionably one of the finest schools in the nation, a true intellectual powerhouse that is known more for its record number of Nobel laureates[44] over the years than for its roster of football players today, was a founding member and an early leader of the Big Ten—a fact that may surprise many diehard football fans.

This, by the way, was a decade before the NCAA was founded in 1906.

Not only was the school a charter member of the Big Ten, but it immediately became a football titan. During those early decades, the school won several Big Ten and national football championships, and one of its star players, Jay Berwanger, was the very first recipient of the coveted Heisman Trophy in 1935 and the first college player drafted by the National Football League's inaugural draft.[45] And, the prestigious Maxwell Award, presented annually by the Maxwell Football Club to the nation's best collegiate football player, is named after former University of Chicago guard Robert W. "Tiny" Maxwell.

The team's coach was the legendary Amos Alonzo Stagg, Sr., who was responsible for such innovations as tackling dummies, laterals, the reverse, the man in motion, and even numbered uniforms. The school was a true football leader and gridiron force in numerous ways.*

All that came to a screeching halt in 1939.

The university president at the time, Robert Maynard Hutchins, was determined to eliminate anything that could be a distraction to students and faculty and a high quality education, and he placed football at the top of that hit list. "We shall get rid of an important handicap to education. It is hard for an educational institution to live in a satisfactory way with football, win or lose," he said.[46] Football had become too dominant and too much of an interference on campus, he felt, and something needed to be done to return the school to its primary focus. Knowing that it would be an unpopular decision, he waited until the 1939 Christmas break, when students would be home for the holidays, to shut down the school's football program. Contrast Hutchins's crisis communications skills in the timing of his unpopular announcement to minimize possible backlash and rioting to that of the Penn State board of trustees when faced with its own conundrum. It would be 40 years before football returned to the school, in the form of Division III athletics.[47]

The purpose of schools is education, not sports. Hutchins was, as you would expect, very unpopular on campus for his action and the manner in which he carried it out. But when he thought football was becoming too dominant at the school and was creating too much of a distraction from its foremost goal of academics, he acted decisively; some might say with backbone.[†]

His vision was unclouded, and the school has not suffered; in fact, many would assert that Hutchins's move to so decisively and

----

* The University of Chicago is the only school in the nation whose football team remains undefeated against powerful Notre Dame, with an unblemished 4-0 record—an interesting fact almost certain to win a round of drinks in a bar bet. Reportedly, the "Fighting Irish" have demanded a rematch ever since, which the "Maroons" of UChicago have ignored.

† I am not advocating this policy; I happen to enjoy college football.

demonstrably put education ahead of athletics made the school the academic leader it is today.

The similarities between the University of Chicago then and Penn State today are eerie: both are or were Big Ten schools, both are great and well-known schools with far-reaching reputations, both have or had dominant football programs, both had innovative and legendary coaches, both had a single Heisman Trophy winner (besides Berwanger, Penn State boasted John Cappelletti in 1973), both had fierce football-oriented nicknames (compare UChicago's long-ago moniker, "the Monsters of the Midway," with Penn State's former sobriquet, "the Beast from the East"), and both had powerful presidents.

But, when it comes to getting priorities straight, that's where the similarities end. Graham Spanier couldn't clean Robert Hutchins's boots.

For that matter, neither could Mark Emmert.

In November 2012, the Pennsylvania attorney general announced that Spanier, Curley, and Schultz were being charged with perjury, obstruction of justice, endangering the welfare of children, criminal conspiracy, and failure to report suspected child abuse.

On the heels of the initial revelations in November 2011, Coach Paterno learned that he had advanced lung cancer and did not have long to live. He succumbed on January 23, 2012. He never had the chance to meet with the Freeh commission, although the former FBI director said publicly that he believed Paterno would have done so willingly.

Three days later, a standing-room-only crowd of more than 15,000 people filled the Bryce Jordan Center on campus for a three-hour-long public memorial for Joe Paterno, in remembrance of the man and all he had done for the school—not just for football[48]—for more than 60 years, along with prayers for the victims of Sandusky's crimes.

Lewis Katz, former owner of the New Jersey Nets and a major Penn State donor and supporter, commented, "So sad you do 1,000 things right and you make one bad decision sometimes in a matter of seconds and [a] lifetime of good is eviscerated."[49]

The Associated Press succinctly said: "A half-century in the making, Joe Paterno's impeccable reputation was shattered in a matter of days."[50]

Both quotes are important crisis communications lessons.

Penn State University, an excellent school that excels at so many things, deserves a failing grade for its leaders' response to the crisis (as does its woefully inept board of trustees, which failed to probe when it first learned of Sandusky's improprieties), and especially for its pitiful crisis management and crisis communications efforts following the revelations—then and now.

The Penn State crisis is not some abstract metaphor; it serves as a concrete reminder that crises are inevitable, and even the best organizations are vulnerable. Moreover, it demonstrates how a lack of crisis communications understanding, skill, and preparedness can make a bad situation worse, and can fell a towering giant.

A century and a half in the making, Penn State's impeccable reputation also was shattered in a matter of days.

There is a tear in the eye of the famed Nittany Lion statue—a tear for the victims and for the school that failed to protect them.

Earlier I said that in a crisis of this magnitude, every utterance from all quarters qualifies as crisis communications, and so the question may be asked, was there anyone who did a good job in crisis communications? The answer is yes: Bill O'Brien, Paterno's replacement as head coach.

O'Brien came into this job from the New England Patriots with his eyes open; he knew that sanctions were likely. In interviews he gave following the Freeh report and the NCAA and Big Ten sanctions, O'Brien consistently gave the most upbeat reports about the team's spirits and its chances for the future, rather than cursing his lot for being saddled with sanctions that were not of his making. His blue-sky comments were undoubtedly an attempt to create a perception that most thought more optimistic than the reality, especially given the spate of team defections. Nevertheless, it was refreshing to hear such positive crisis communications messages amidst a sea of negativity. Remember, perception trumps reality.

But in this case, perception and reality were in sync.

Against all odds and expectations, Penn State finished the season with an impressive 8–4 overall record (6–2 in conference play).[51] Equally impressive was O'Brien being named the unanimous choice as 2012 Big Ten Coach of the Year. He also received the prestigious Maxwell Football Club Coach of the Year, ESPN, and "Bear" Bryant Coach of the Year honors.[52]

Finally, following the most turbulent year in the school's long history, with the first year of sanctions successfully under its belt, and the school and the team finally moving on with their lives, it seemed a period of resigned acceptance had at last settled over Happy Valley like early morning dew . . . until another shoe dropped.

Ringing in 2013 like a loud and drunken reveler, the "see no evil–hear no evil–speak no evil" governor of Pennsylvania, Tom Corbett, unilaterally filed suit[53] against the NCAA seeking to overturn the sanctions against Penn State. These were the very same sanctions he—as a member of the board of trustees as well as governor—had publicly proclaimed six months earlier were appropriate and which the school should accept and move on. What was Corbett up to?

Curiously, Penn State was not a party to the action and may not have even known about it. Or did they? How likely is it that the governor would file this type of landmark litigation against a prominent institution like the NCAA without the knowledge and tacit approval of the school? Perhaps the school simply decided to keep quiet since they had signed that consent decree ceding its right to sue or appeal, lest they face the "death penalty." And if Corbett actually did take such an action without consulting Penn State authorities, what kind of message does *that* send about the school's emasculation? It's unclear, but baffling. What *is* clear is that Penn

State did not denounce the suit or ask Corbett to withdraw it. That silence speaks volumes.

And why did Corbett wait six months to file the action? His stated reason was that he didn't want to do anything that might interfere with the football season, conveniently ignoring the fact that there were some six weeks between the announcement of the sanctions and the opening day kickoff in September. But more to the very damning point made by the Freeh report, here was yet one more example of one of the most powerful men in the state putting Penn State football ahead of everything else.

Corbett's jaw-dropping audacity is compounded when you recall that this is the very same man who for three years knew about Sandusky's sick actions and did nothing—*nothing*—to stop it.

But, our role is not to dissect the merits of the case, and its ultimate outcome doesn't even concern us; we are looking at crisis communications lessons from these sad events. If anyone should be suing the NCAA, it's the school, not the governor. While it is usually advantageous to have the government stand by your side during a crisis, this was a blatant case of the governor hijacking the crisis leadership mantle from Penn State. This maneuver sends a clear message that the administration and the board are *still* incapable of properly managing its crisis or its crisis communications.

But the real motive for the governor's grandstanding action is probably more shameless. He is coming up for reelection.

Ending this chapter as I began it, with full disclosure, I was invited to be the guest of newly named Penn State President Rod Erickson in his luxury suite at Beaver Stadium at the October 27, 2012, Penn State–Ohio State football game. I declined.

There is a final macabre irony to this requiem. With Penn State's past 111 football victories vacated going back to 1998, the school's last official victory of the Joe Paterno era was on November 22, 1997, a 35–10 blowout against Wisconsin.

The winning quarterback: Mike McQueary.

14

Dealing with Death: Fatality Communications

■ ■ ■

There is nothing worse than a company crisis involving fatalities. I know; I have managed or otherwise been involved in
a number of crises over the years in which people died. And
worst of all, crises involving the death of children are the most
heart-wrenching.

Suddenly, it becomes very personal, especially if the fatalities
occurred as a result of your product. During the infamous Tylenol
poisonings, I recall being told by crisis management team member
Dave Collins, at the time the vice chairman of Johnson & Johnson's
executive committee, as well as the chairman of McNeil Consumer
Products Company, the J&J subsidiary that actually manufactured
the capsules, how scared he was. He reflected emotionally on how
upset he was when he learned that his daughter's fifth-grade class-
mates taunted her because her daddy worked for a company that
kills people.

"I was afraid of the next phone call," Collins told me one day in his J&J office in New Brunswick, New Jersey. "When the phone rang at home at night, I was almost afraid to answer it; afraid someone would tell me there had been another death. I couldn't sleep.

"It is a terrible responsibility to cause someone to die."[1]

Of course, Collins was not responsible for anyone's death, nor was corporate giant J&J or its McNeil subsidiary. But when someone uses your product as an instrument of death, it becomes very, very personal.

No matter what else happens on your watch—mergers, acquisitions, awards, promotions, or setbacks—*this* is what you will be remembered for; *this* is what will cause you sleepless nights of second-guessing; *this* will be part of your obituary, maybe even the opening line. *Get it right!*

Generally, a crisis involving a fatality means that you, your company, your equipment, or your product is at fault; alternatively, someone or something else is to blame, but you, your company, your product, your equipment, or your personnel are involved.

Whatever the reason, whatever the cause, all eyes will be focused laserlike on you. Your every move and utterance will be picked apart and analyzed ad infinitum. You will be dissected just like that poor frog in your middle school biology class. Regardless of your words and deeds, some people will object vociferously and very publicly to your actions. Life as you once knew it will cease to exist.

There are certain things you can count on.

You will be sued. No matter what you do or don't do, say or don't say, litigation is just around the corner. There are too many hungry and aggressive plaintiff's attorneys out there to just give you a pass. So don't be surprised when you or your attorneys are served.

Because you will be sued, your well-meaning attorneys will advise you not to say anything, since (among other reasons) in some jurisdictions, just saying you're sorry could be construed as an admission of culpability.

My advice: ignore *that* advice. As I've said before, do not go radio silent in a crisis, especially *this* crisis. People need to hear from you.

I typically advise clients that where there is death, the CEO or the highest-ranking executive needs to be the visible spokesperson. Assuming that the CEO is capable of communicating in the language of the people, this is not a job to be staffed out. The head of the company needs to be seen and heard, and she needs to express sympathy, empathy, and compassion as soon as possible. And if you're the head of the company, step up. *This is why you earn the big bucks.*

With a fatality, early facts are usually hard to come by. That's OK; say so. Get out in front of the story as soon as you can. Express your sympathies for the victims. Explain that an investigation (by law enforcement, OSHA, your own internal investigation, or someone else) is being conducted, and as soon as facts are in, you will convey them promptly.

If, for example, this is the first fatal accident in your company's history, say so. Explain how this tragedy is an aberration.

The public wants—nay, *demands!*—to know three things:

1. What happened? (Explain the basic, bare-bones *facts* as you know them, sketchy though they may be. Never speculate; explain *only* what you know to be true and which you are at liberty to disclose.)

2. How did it happen? (Do not go into this, for anything you can say at an early juncture is speculation at best. This is what the lawyers want you to avoid, and on this point, they are right. Your go-to response may be something like, "That is what we/the authorities are trying to determine, and as soon as we have anything to report, we will do so.")

3. What are you doing about it, or what are you doing to prevent it from happening again? (Again, you can

and should say that investigations are underway and promise more information when it becomes available.)

And sometimes you will have to use the "S" word: say you're sorry, just because it is the right thing to do, and you know it in your heart. I have been on crisis management teams involving fatalities or serious injuries, and in preparing a written statement or briefing the CEO for an interview, the question will inevitably be raised. The argument against saying "we're sorry" is usually voiced by an attorney, who posits that an apology complicates litigation and may be construed as an admission of guilt or culpability.

But here's the reality: I've been practicing crisis management for about three decades, and I've never seen a single instance where *not* saying "we're sorry" ever staved off litigation.

In other words, as stated earlier, you are going to be sued.

So why not at least be perceived by your constituents and the public at large as a compassionate company, a company that cares about people, a company that experienced an unfortunate fatality and is expressing remorse? There is always more to a crisis than legal wrangling, and you have to protect the entire company so that after the lawsuits are over, you still have a company to manage. In other words, be a *mensch*.

Steel yourself for what has to be done, take a deep breath, and get out in front of the story.

What you do *not* want is for the media—mainstream or social—to print, broadcast, or post stories denouncing you for stonewalling, for not being available, or for saying "no comment." That makes people suspicious of you and not trust you, and the public's trust and support is what you need in a crisis.

Recently, a midsized agribusiness client suffered the tragic loss of two young workers on its rural property when the workers presumably were overcome by toxic fumes while cleaning a storm drain. Long before this unfortunate accident, this particular client had been very distrustful of the media, and the CEO had never, ever spoken with them in the nearly 20 years the company had been in business, nor had anyone else at the company. The client had experienced some zoning violations over the years and paid whatever fines were assessed, but when the local newspaper and radio and TV stations reported on the events, they always had a negative slant, since no one was presenting the client's point of view. When my firm was brought in following the two deaths, we advocated an immediate reversal of this policy and outlined a proactive approach of addressing the media in a series of one-on-one interviews. This strategy took on even more urgency because the local county board of supervisors had scheduled a vote on the company's continued operations, since it was situated on public land that the client rented. We advocated that the head of the company meet with the supervisors privately to explain the accident and what steps the company was taking to mitigate any future problems or areas of danger.

The client refused to meet with the media and declined the opportunity to meet with the supervisors. Instead, he sent an outside environmental consultant to meet with the five supervisors and lay out the company's case. The consultant reported back to us several days later that it looked as if we had two solid votes in our favor, and possibly a third, which was all the client needed in order to survive.

The night of the monthly supervisors meeting and vote on my client's future, each and every supervisor took great pains to denounce my client publicly, one going so far as to say of the company, "I cannot ever believe anything they say."

The subsequent vote was unanimous: 5–0 to put the company out of business and assess millions of dollars in fines.[2]

And the media delighted in telling the story.

Would a proactive crisis communications strategy, including meeting with the media and the supervisors, have helped? Not to sound flippant, but the results couldn't have been any worse. The outside consultant in whom the client had expressed so much hope was a complete washout. And my sense is that the company struck out because all that the supervisors—and the public, after all—really knew about the client was what the media had been reporting very one-sidedly.

Also, remember that in a crisis involving a fatality, the CEO should be front and center. In this case, the client's staunch belief that the media would report only negative information became a self-fulfilling prophecy.

But when you do face the media in the wake of a fatality crisis, be contrite. Do not be argumentative and rise to the inevitable bait. In a news conference, in particular, some reporters will try to get a rise out of you. Don't fall for it. Maintain your composure, stay on message, promise more information when you have it, and exit gracefully.

Understand one thing: even if you do everything right, you will still have your critics. There always will be gadflies and naysayers who will take the opposite position on whatever is going on. Talking heads on radio and TV have hours of airtime to fill, and they often fill it by stirring whatever pot happens to be handy. If your crisis lands on the front page of the morning newspapers, Tag! You're it!

At the end of every interview and at the end of every day, do a postmortem with your closest advisors. Review what you (and the company) did and communicated that day, examine how it played, and analyze where improvements could be made; then make them. Review and analyze what slings and arrows were sent your way. Were they justified? If not, decide whether a response is required, and, if it is, set about issuing one by the most effective means possible. This, though, is a bit tricky, for while you do not want to let inaccurate slurs go unchallenged, you do not want to get into a tit-for-tat pissing contest with your antagonists. That only gives them more visibility and the satisfaction of knowing that they got a rise out of you.

It's normal to feel anguish. It's normal to internalize every-thing. That's why Dave Collins expressed to me how terrible it is "to cause someone to die," even though he had nothing to do with it. But it was his company and his product, and he took it person-ally, as did the other members of the J&J crisis management team.

If the same emotions run through you in similar circumstances, it's only human nature.

It means you have a heart. Let the world see it.

15

Crisis Communications Strategies

■ ■ ■

Different types of crises require different crisis communications messages and strategies. First, you need to understand exactly what sort of crisis you are in so that you can employ the proper crisis communications strategy.

At first blush, you may find that last sentence obvious, if not simplistic. Beware. Understanding *exactly the sort of crisis* you are experiencing is far more nuanced and is vitally important if you are to mount the most effective crisis communications strategy.

Say your crisis involves product liability. Well, then, what else is there to know, you may ask? But the *sort* of crisis you are experiencing may have more to do with whether or not the liability was your company's fault.

Some years ago, someone wrote a book listing nine types of crises an organization might face, but trying to pigeonhole crises in this way is unrealistic and a waste of time. All crises can be sorted neatly into pair sets, and of these possibilities, from a crisis communications perspective, the most important distinction is whether your crisis is an oppositional crisis or a nonoppositional crisis. Stated more starkly: are you victim or villain? This is how you determine whether 100 percent of the public will be on your side, be completely against you, or fall somewhere in the middle.

So, if your customers, a governmental regulatory body, or the news media allege that you manufactured a faulty product that caused or contributed to injury or death, *regardless of the facts, you are in an oppositional crisis.*

Thus, you know from the outset that your every message will be picked apart and fiercely debated by countless oppositional parties. Be sure you can defend whatever messages you convey. Line up your allies, experts, and defenders early, those who can and will speak on your behalf, if necessary.

Obviously, you need solid facts, and those are often the hardest things to come by early in a crisis. You are handicapped because the opposition forces (for example, angry customers) can and usually do say whatever they want. You are not so fortunate. You can't just make stuff up; you need to speak the truth with conviction. But you already know that if *you* don't have the facts, chances are that neither does your opposition. That might be your strongest argument against a rush to judgment against you.

Oppositional crises are the most difficult to deal with in a crisis communications battle. Steel yourself for the long haul.

When the facts are known (and your team should know them *first*) and it is determined that you do have responsibility, your overall message should be one of explanation and a forward-looking message of how you intend to correct the problem and, if appropriate, make amends to injured parties.

Again, there *will* be litigation. But your crisis communications messages should be intended to put forth the perception that while something untoward may have happened, you are still a good company; the crisis was certainly not intentional, and here's how you are going to move forward.

Naturally, if your crisis occurred because you were victimized somehow, you have more leeway. Assuming that you have a good image in your communities (see the discussion of reservoirs of goodwill in Chapter 21), your constituents are already on your side. They may even feel angered that someone took advantage of you, tried to hurt you, or tried to harm the company where their friends and family members work.

In a nonoppositional crisis, your messages may be similar to those for the oppositional crises (here's what we know, here's how we intend to fix it, here's what we intend to do to help any victims, and so on), but now at least you won't have an army of snipers taking potshots at you. Your constituents, including those affected by your crisis, will be rooting for you to succeed. Often, the livelihoods of others depend on your success.

The main difference between similar messages received in an oppositional or a nonoppositional crisis is that in the former, people will view your comments with some suspicion, and in the latter, they will simply add those words to the already good feelings they have for you.

In either type of crisis, choose your public spokesperson carefully. This individual, in addition to having been crisis media–trained, should be able to convey compassion for victims (if there are any) and should personally be knowledgeable about the situation, if possible.

Be aware as well that in the early days of a crisis, when you are under attack, you may often be perceived as the villain. However, as facts and investigations unfold, the paradigm may shift in your favor. Look for these openings and pounce on them.

There is one other pair of crises you should be aware of: long-fused and short-fused crises. As the categories imply, either you have little or no time to prepare, or you have the luxury of time.

Examples of long-fused crises may be major litigation, where you know months in advance that when your CEO testifies in court, you will need to be prepared with a postcourtroom message strategy. Perhaps your organization is in the midst of labor negotiations, and, should the talks break down, a strike is imminent—that also is a long-fused crisis.

Short-fused crises are anything that gives you little or no time to prepare: it's all reactive. But that's no excuse for not being prepared with a crisis communications strategy and the ability to implement it.

To communicate effectively in any crisis, there are certain things you need to know well in advance, among them the following:

- **With whom do you need to communicate?** Know in advance who your key constituents are for any given crisis. Hopefully, these are not total strangers, meaning that either you know them personally (such as clients) or they have seen and heard from you in the past (such as via social media). Your relationships with your key constituents should be well and regularly maintained.

- **How will you communicate?** Will you use mainstream or social media outlets, or a combination? Are you prepared to post videos on YouTube? Are you effectively monitoring all media sites 24/7 so that you know the instant an "attack blog" gets posted? Do you have a rapid response team or protocol established to deal with such posts? Do you have well-trained spokespersons and surrogates who can fan out across the country and speak on your company's behalf, either in person or via satellite hookups? The time to plan these strategies is *before* the crisis is upon you.

- **Who is going to speak to your constituencies?** This is a fluid question, and the answer determined in large measure by the nature of the crisis. As stated earlier, a crisis involving death requires the CEO (or highest-ranking corporate officer) to be front and center. However, there is no rule that says that there has to be just one spokesperson. If you have suffered a food-related crisis, you may have the head of your quality assurance department available to field applicable food safety questions. You may need outside experts (say, an epidemiologist) to handle questions related to the source and ultimate containment of your crisis. If your industry is one in which you may, at some time, suffer a crisis where an outside expert is required, you should have a good database of such experts already identified and lined up in advance. And, if you use surrogate spokespersons in different regions of the country, are these surrogates crisis media–trained? Do they have specific ties to specific regions, so that they are already well known and (hopefully) liked locally? And are you prepared to ensure that they all speak with one voice?

■ **Will the government stand by your side?** Keeping in mind the importance of perspective, it is hard to argue with government regulators if they say you are wrong. Arguing publicly in those cases gives the perception that not only are you at fault, but you are trying to cow poor overworked and underpaid government workers. But what was your relationship with those who regulate your business *prior* to your crisis? For example, if you are in the restaurant business and your restaurants are regularly inspected by health inspectors, what is your track record? Do you regularly receive "A" grades? And, if so, should you suddenly have an E. coli outbreak that is clearly an aberration, will the local health department stand by your side or issue a public statement attesting to your superlative past record? Do you have good and clear lines of communication with those who regulate your business?

Here's an example demonstrating just how important this is. Recently, I was called into a crisis involving a national seafood importer, and I was brought in late on a Sunday by a lawyer who knew that the situation called for crisis management expertise in addition to her own considerable legal prowess in the import-export field. All we knew Sunday night was that one person in the Midwest had died, that the preliminary allegation was that he had died from contracting cholera by eating the client's product, and that the FDA was mandating a Class 1 nationwide recall first thing Monday morning. We had our work cut out for us and little time to do it.

While I dispatched my FDA team Sunday night to begin prepping for a recall the next morning, I simultaneously dispatched my public health team to look into the death. The lawyer and I had the same thought: on the surface, there did not seem to be enough evidence to support such a recall, and we couldn't understand the FDA's dictum. One lone individual—whom we soon determined had a long history of health-related issues—had died, and there was not a single hospital report anywhere in the region or the state that even hinted at any other patients with cholera or even choleralike symptoms. Moreover, the victim's wife had cooked and eaten the same food from the same package, and she was perfectly fine. We needed to determine what in the world had led the FDA to its conclusion, and we needed to do it fast. Of course, while we were doing that, we also needed to prepare for a recall in the event that the FDA still held that conviction on Monday morning.

Fortunately, the attorney dealt with the FDA on a regular basis and had good contacts and good working relationships with those regulators in Los Angeles, Chicago, and Annapolis, Maryland. As it turned out, the FDA had been responding to preliminary hospital lab results (*which were wrong!*), and when confronted by the attorney, the agency agreed that it needed to do its own testing. The problem, though, was timing. The test for cholera takes anywhere from 48 to 72 hours for the incubation period to yield results, and if no recall was issued and the tests came back positive for cholera, there would be panic and possibly more deaths.

Luck was on our side in one respect: the suspected product came from just one store. We had the product removed from the shelves of that store and shipped back to the distributor's warehouses so that no one else would be exposed, assuming that there was anything to be exposed to. Also, we were then able to begin our own independent testing on the suspect product.

We needed the FDA to give us a directive. If it said "recall," we were prepared to move immediately; my team was in place and ready to spring into action the next morning.

In short order, the agency backed down on the recall notice; days later, it confirmed what our own independent labs had reported: no cholera strain was found. In fact, the FDA even went so far as to say publicly that it was safe to put the product back on the store shelves. (We declined to do that, though.)

Also on our side was the fact that the FDA knew the client and knew that it had never been cited for *anything* in its 50-some years in business—a remarkable and enviable record, to be sure, and one that we used to our advantage in compiling our crisis communications strategies.

So ask yourself this candid question: if it is your crisis, will the government stand by your side? If not, you have your work cut out for you.

And there are other questions to ask, too:

- **What are your key message points?** There should be few, perhaps three, and they should be easily digestible by the media and your constituents in the form of sound bites. They should be compelling, and they should be repeated over and over so that they sink in. Obviously, there will be details to be imparted, but not all the details have to be imparted at once, especially if there is a chance that the complexity of the details might overwhelm the essence of the message points. There will be time to convey the details, but in the rush to provide proper perspective, focus on key message points.

- **Keep coming back to the same message points** regardless of the reporter's question (within reason). But when you do your daily postmortem, ask yourself if you need to change any of your message points.
- **Anticipate the questions** that you will be asked, and create your message points accordingly.
- **Keep your message and your message points specific**, narrow, and focused. Don't be all over the map. Don't "birdwalk."
- **Keep your language understandable** at all times, but especially if you have a technical crisis. Speak in the language of the people you are trying to reach. Avoid technical words and phrases (unless they are essential to the story) that merely confuse or frighten people. Avoid needless jargon.
- **Whatever you say must be honest, provable, and supportable** with rock-solid facts. Know that *everything* you say will be picked apart by scores of others—some media, some lawyers, some just plain old pains in the ass who have nothing more useful to do. Nothing is worse than being caught in a lie or a sloppy "fact." This is one time where the cliché "close enough for government work" just won't cut it.
- **What is your takeaway message?** As you prepare your list of message points, do they flow together to tell the story you want to tell? What do you want people to remember when you leave the stage or when the story airs? You should know in advance what you want your takeaway message to be, and then examine your message points to see if you have accomplished that goal.
- **Use relatable examples.** When you give examples, try to use ones that people can relate to, and use colorful examples to make your point. I may not know the size of something, but if you put it in terms of football fields, I can get a good picture of it (for example: as long as two football fields, as tall as the Empire State Building, could fill the

Rose Bowl, and so on). The everyman imagery helps make your point.

- **Finally, what do you do if you are the story, you are the crisis?** You need to handle it like any other crisis. Your one key decision early on is whether you personally should be the spokesperson or whether you should designate someone to speak for you. There are too many variables to be able to provide a concrete answer to this question. However, the same rules cited earlier apply, with this caveat: if the subject of your personal crisis has to do with moral turpitude of any kind, *you* should be the spokesperson—either to use message points to explain why the story is false or to issue your resignation.

Remember, your message points—made early and often—will help shape the perception of your crisis.

The Good, the Bad, the News Media—or, Juggling Chain Saws

■ ■ ■

Would you willingly walk into a lion's den unarmed and unprepared? Of course not. So why would you willingly agree to sit down with a ferocious reporter who wants to feed on your bones for dinner?

Mark Twain never lived to see a modern chain saw, so for his metaphor of the interview process, he likened it to a cyclone. In a treatise he penned around 1890 called "Concerning the 'Interview,'" he wrote:

> No one likes to be interviewed, & yet no one likes to say no;
> for interviewers are courteous and gentle-mannered, even
> when they come to destroy. I must not be understood to

mean that they ever come consciously to destroy or are aware afterward that they have destroyed; no, I think their attitude is more that of the cyclone, which comes with the gracious purpose of cooling off a sweltering village, & is not aware, afterward, that it has done that village anything but a favor. The interviewer scatters you all over creation, but he does not conceive that you can look upon that as a disadvantage.[1]

To those who are not experienced in speaking with reporters, that may be how it seems, but it doesn't have to be that way. Let's see if we can level the playing field *now* while things are calm and before there is a crisis, so that you are somewhat armed and better prepared when your crisis does hit.

In a crisis, you do not have to grant *every* interview request that comes along, as long as you are making yourself available to a sufficient number of news outlets so that it does not appear that you are in hiding or in the witness protection program. Of course, the bigger the crisis (and especially if fatalities, serious injuries, or massive damage has occurred), the more you'll have to address your publics—to meet the press, or your cyclones, as it were. The power of social media means that if you want to communicate with your constituents during your crisis, you can do so directly. Just understand that whatever you say or post on your Twitter feed, the mainstream media will pick it up and report on it. Nevertheless, as long as conventional newspapers, newsmagazines, and TV and radio news outlets still survive, you can and should be prepared to speak with at least some of them.

When working proactively with clients to train them to prepare for the inevitability of a crisis, we practice "crisis inoculation" exercises. Usually, this includes practice media sessions designed to give the members of the management team a sample in advance of the stress they will experience when they are under media fire. This helps build up their immunity, much as when a doctor administers an inoculation to a youngster, he is giving a small, harmless sample of the virus so that the patient can build natural antibodies. Moreover, by practicing on a regular basis, you'll avoid being stale on "game day."

Your communications department or outside public relations firm can help you here, but I would take it one step further and suggest that you meet with some actual reporters in an informal setting, maybe over lunch. Don't be surprised or offended if the reporter insists on paying, or at least paying for herself. It's a common practice designed to prevent any hint that you are currying favor with reporters by "bribing" them with lunch.

Regardless of who pays, developing personal relationships with reporters is important for several reasons: seeing and meeting a reporter off the record (and more on *that* phrase momentarily) helps the inoculation process; there may come a time when you want to meet with a friendly reporter in a noncrisis environment, perhaps to advance a story that is important to your business or give a business reporter a heads-up on a new product you are working on, and now you have a rapport with one or more newspeople; the reporter could be an ally if you are looking for a reliable way to correct a damaging and erroneous story that someone else has written or aired; and, during an actual crisis, having this kind of personal relationship will help you immensely at the moment when you do have to sit down with the press and discuss or disclose troubling information.

Just because you have a relationship with one or two reporters, however, don't think that those reporters will necessarily "go easy" on you during a crisis. Reporters are not and never will be your friends. Assume that they are always working. They are always on the clock, so assume that anything you say in their presence is fair game. *Anything.*

When I lecture on crisis communications, I often tell the story about well-known *60 Minutes* correspondent Lesley Stahl, who once was taping an interview with a company CEO. The precise subject of the interview is irrelevant, except that it had to do with a lawsuit against the company filed by a fired female worker. After some 10 minutes or so, the interview had to be halted while new tape was loaded into the camera. During that brief downtime, as the reporter and her subject were sitting knee-to-knee in classic *60 Minutes* style, the CEO leaned over and, in a conspiratorial voice, whispered to Stahl—his new best friend, so he thought—some very disparaging comments about the terminated worker, alleging that she had mental issues and so on, which was what was really behind her accusations and her lawsuit. Naturally, he didn't want to disclose this on the air. What he was trying to do was stack the deck, to make the reporter sympathetic to the company's side of the allegations in what he deemed a casual and off-the-record setting, but he certainly did not want to be caught saying any of those things on camera and publicly tarnishing the poor girl's reputation.

But Lesley Stahl didn't get to where she is by being anyone's fool. She listened politely until they were back on camera—and then she let him have it! She very publicly exposed what he had said and what he had tried to do, concluding by scolding him: *"We're not your pals; we're reporters!"*

Remember that. You heard it from Lesley Stahl.

However, while they may not be my *friends*, I consider the media to be important *allies* in a crisis, and so should you. The clout of the mainstream media may have been diminished over the years, but as long as they are still around, they do have influence—influence that I want on my side during a crisis.

In the midst of a client's potential public health crisis that was just unfolding in the Midwest, in which rumors were everywhere, but hard facts were like hens' teeth, a local Fox TV station posted on its website what I considered to be inaccurate—or at least troublingly outdated—information that was severely damaging to my client. The news director immediately took my call, and, because we had already established a good working partnership (we both wanted to protect the public), after I calmly explained my concern and told him where and how the story on the site was in error, the entire website went dark almost before I hung up. Badgering the reporter would have antagonized him and accomplished nothing; the rapport we had already established gave me an edge.

If the reporter has developed a sense of you as a direct and honest broker, she may tend to give you the benefit of the doubt on a story that could tilt either way—as long as you don't burn her by taking advantage of your "relationship" and lying or misleading her. Also, with the right kind of relationship, it is possible to get reporters to work for you, in a sense. I have had reporters call me to tip me off to a story because they were seeking a reactive comment. And sometimes that "heads-up" has proved extremely beneficial in planning a crisis communications strategy. Or sometimes a reporter will tell me what he has heard because he wants to use me as a sounding board to help him determine the validity of the information. I am always happy to oblige and keep those channels of communication open. It is definitely a two-way street.

Your communications department should already be doing all of these things on their own, developing relationships with reporters, just as reporters use your communications people to develop and cultivate news sources. I am not suggesting that you supplant these activities; just dip your toe in the water so that the idea of meeting with and talking to reporters is not completely alien to you.

However, because of budget cuts in mainstream media outlets touched on earlier, news staffs are a lot leaner and far busier than ever before— they are stretched thin and there are fewer people doing more work. That simply means that they may not have the luxury of being able to have a leisurely three-hour lunch with you, unless they're working on a story. So, don't waste their time.

And when you meet with reporters, whether during a crisis or not, understand and practice the rules of engagement so that you don't get burned.

As stated before (but it's important enough to repeat), "no comment" translates into "guilty as charged." It's flip; it's arrogant; it's desperate. It connotes, "I don't want to speak with you because the accusations against me/the company are true," or "I'm better than you, and I don't have time to waste talking to peons," or "I'm too stupid to think of anything else to say."

It is always possible to engage in a conversation with a reporter without actually saying anything that will get you into trouble. If you really *cannot* comment, as opposed to *will not* comment, take the time to explain why. Phrases such as these accomplish the same thing as "no comment," but without making you look as if you have something to hide: "I'd like to answer that question, but as you know, the judge has directed all parties not to speak publicly until the trial has concluded," or, "I'm not sure I can give you a complete answer to that question now, since we are still working on the issue, and I'd prefer not to give you a less than complete response." These suggested responses say nothing of substance and should not get you into trouble, but in a more palatable and less arrogant way than "no comment." These are merely loose guidelines to demonstrate how you can achieve "no comment" without looking or sounding guilty.

There may be times when you want to convey information to a reporter, but you don't want the information to be used in the story. In such instances, you may want to use that well-worn cliché "off the record."

Don't!

That shopworn phrase is supposed to mean, "What I am about to tell you cannot be used in your story." The problem is, it can be, and therefore it can embarrass or hurt you if you don't know what you are doing. It's akin to playing with a hand grenade. A reporter may respect that *you* said it was off the record, but if the information is really good or juicy, she can always try to obtain the same information from another source, now that she knows what she's looking for and maybe even where to look. So, the old adage, "Don't say anything to a reporter that you wouldn't want to see in the morning newspaper, or see or hear on TV or radio" still holds. Consult with your communications department or an outside firm for guidance.

If you *do* want something reported, but you want to protect *your* identity as the source, you can say: "This is not for attribution." The reporter is then free to use the information any way he wants, but without naming you as the source.

Who hasn't seen countless news stories citing an "unnamed source"? Sometimes a reporter will ask how he should identify you, the source: "According to an unnamed member of senior management"? "According to someone who is not authorized to speak on the record"? A recent news story in the *Washington Post*, reporting on allegations that the United States and Israel had jointly developed the computer virus called Flame and aimed it at Iran to gather intelligence designed to slow that country's ability to develop a nuclear weapon, cited as a source "Western officials with knowledge of the effort."[2] For all you know, that could be the president of the United States.

One former secretary of state was notorious for often leaking tantalizing but unquotable information to selected reporters, then instructing the reporter to credit "someone familiar with the secretary's thinking."

There are a couple of additional layers to this delicate onion. Speaking to a reporter "on background" means different things to different reporters, so before you go out on this limb and assume that it means not for attribution, confirm it with the reporter.

And "deep background" is essentially the same; don't try to split hairs.

But these qualifiers can be tricky, especially if you and the reporter don't agree on your terms before you blurt something out. It's hard to say something and then add as an afterthought, "That was off the record." Some reporters may give you a break, but others won't. For that reason, I usually tell clients that when they are talking to a reporter or are anywhere in a reporter's earshot, they should assume that everything they say is on the record. If you want information conveyed "off the record," leave it in the hands of professional communicators, who are simply more accustomed to the various nuances and more accustomed to dealing with reporters.

If you are going to meet with reporters during a crisis, how should you do it? Should you have a long string of one-on-one interviews, or should you get it all over with in one fell swoop with a news conference?

I dislike news conferences unless they are absolutely necessary (and sometimes they are). They can turn into zoos and screaming matches. This is not like making a speech to a friendly audience, and forget about the sort of decorum you are accustomed to seeing at presidential news conferences from the White House; you will be facing a brash, brusque horde of reporters, most of them on deadline, shouting questions at you and challenging nearly everything you say after "Good morning." In such confrontational situations, it is far too easy to get rattled and forget the message points you wanted to convey. You will feel compelled to answer every question, and before you can complete your answer, someone else will be jumping up and shouting a new question.

Of course, you could convene the news media and merely read a statement without taking questions, but that is generally ineffectual and leads to anger and frustration on the part of the media, which will be passed along to the general public by the way the media slant the story about your refusal to answer questions. In such situtations, the release of a written prepared statement may serve you better.

In cases of dire emergencies (for example, your nuclear power plant had "an event"), it is crucial to get the CEO or someone with knowledge and authority front and center to explain what happened and what is being done to fix it. However, in today's digital age, there are many other ways to communicate that emergency message faster and to a wider audience. And, during your news conference, there will be reporters sitting mere feet away from you who will be tweeting about the proceedings in real time. But still, it's a zoo.

So, if I can have my clients avoid the group grope nature of a news conference, I prefer one-on-one interviews, since they are so much more manageable. There's more give-and-take, you can cherry-pick who is granted an interview, and the back-and-forth is more conversational and certainly less adversarial (at least on the surface). Also, clients are more comfortable in these interviews because it is simply a more famiar setting than a news conference.

How do you give a good interview?

First, how do you define a "good" interview? Is it one that goes completely your way? In an oppositional crisis, fair reporters will give the other side a chance to be heard in the same story, and consequently, you will like only half the story that ultimately appears—if that.

Know in advance what you want to say, the message or messages you want to convey.

Develop a workable number of message points: the points that are most important to your overall message. Practice using your message points to give answers to questions regardless of what is asked.

Know your overarching theme. In preparing for a noncrisis interview, you should *develop a compelling message* that you want to get across. During a crisis, the compelling message must be what is being done to manage the crisis. That message must be conveyed in a manner that speaks to management's handle on events, and thus conveys the crisis communications perception that the situation either is under control or soon will be.

You need to *be strategic about the interview*. Have an agenda, and one that is supported by your message points. Time permitting (something that is not always true during an acute crisis), practice with your communicators.

Tough or sticky questions. Suppose a reporter asks you a question that you'd rather not answer, or at least not answer until you've laid a proper foundation. You might say, "I think a better way to look at that issue would be . . ." and trot out your applicable message point. This is known as "blocking."

Other examples—and if you pay attention, you will see skilled interviewees, such as politicians, using this technique all the time—might include saying, "I think what you are really asking is . . . ," and then recasting the question to your advantage; or saying, "The most important thing to remember is . . . ," and then laying it out for the reporter; or saying, "That question speaks to the bigger issue, which is . . . ," and explaining what you believe that bigger issue to be. In other words, be an *active* participant in your own interview, not a passive one, and feel free to ask yourself the questions you want to answer.

One phrase I used in the preceding paragraph, *the most important thing to remember*, is pivotal, and you should use it often. When the reporter and her editors are working on the story, that phrase will jump out at them. It's easy to highlight what you feel is the most important point, but years ago other ruses had to be employed. One of the classics involved the late U.S. senator from South Carolina, Strom Thurmond. Whenever Thurmond was giving an important speech, he would pause and take a sip of water just before he got to his most important point. And then he'd say, "What I'd like the president to know is . . . ." Why the sip of water? When the analog tape of his speech was reviewed, and TV news editors were looking for a good sound bite, they could fast-forward until they saw the senator take that drink and locate the important point immediately.

You don't have to resort to such tactics, but you should still signal to a reporter what *you* consider the most important point. With luck, and practice, he may even agree with you.

Don't be afraid to say the three magic words that will get you out of most tough situations: "I don't know."

I have seen many interviews implode because the subject felt that she *had* to answer every question, perhaps imagining that failure to answer constitutes weakness or lack of knowledge or inability to manage the crisis. I've actually had clients tell me during crisis media exercises that they felt that the interview was like a high school or college test, and that every nonanswer was a mark against them. Nonsense. When you start speculating or making stuff up, that's when trouble happens. Of course, if you can add to "I don't know" the qualifier "but I'll find out," so much the better.

Never lie to a reporter.

Respect a reporter's deadline. If you say you'll get back to him by a certain time, try your level best to honor that commitment, and if later in the day you realize you can't, either you or someone else should call the reporter and tell him so he's not left hanging. Being lax with a reporter's deadline is equivalent to stonewalling. Remember, you want reporters to be your allies in a crisis; missing their deadline does not endear you to them. In fact, it downright pisses them off.

Everyone at our clients' offices who answers phones (such as receptionists, switchboard operators, personal assistants, and secretaries) is instructed to ask *every* reporter if she is on deadline, and if so, when her deadline is. This is done right after establishing the media outlet the reporter represents.

Don't get defensive with a reporter. First, if he sees that he's hit a nerve, he will come back for more. (What, you thought he'd just go away? *Hah!*) Try to remain cool and calm. Sometimes your mannerisms convey as much information as your words, if not more.

If a reporter gets an important fact wrong, correct it. Or, at least go on record as having tried to correct it, and memorialize your attempt in writing. (This may prove useful if litigation ensues.) You don't have the right to see the story or your quotes before the story runs, but you do have the right—and, in fact, the obligation—to correct errors of fact.

Many times a print reporter will interview me, and the story will first appear online. If I see that there is an error or if I think that I or my client has been misquoted, I will call and point out the problem; often, the correction will be made online immediately, which ensures accuracy in tomorrow's newspaper. I have even called reporters after giving a quote, offering a better, stronger quote than the one I saw online ... and the reporter agreed and made the change. That kind of dynamic is possible only if you have a good relationship with the news media.

Never answer a negatively charged question without first turning it around into a positive, and never repeat the negative phrasing. It's often said that no one remembers the question, only the answer. So don't be foolish enough to have negatively charged phrases coming out of your mouth. If you are asked, "Why did you lay off so many workers?" your response might be something like, "If you are asking did we make some hard, strategic decisions to save the company from going under and help 1,000 other workers keep their jobs, the answer is yes."

A reporter generally will ask about a problem (by definition a negative); you should answer by talking about solutions (a positive).

Practice giving responses in sound bites; avoid long, rambling responses, which will be edited. If you keep your responses short, you have better control over which of your words will be used.

And when you are finished, *shut up!* Reporters often remain completely mute after your response, hoping that you will fill the awkward silence with more of an answer, which leads to rambling, which leads to trouble. Don't fall victim to this ploy. Say your piece and shut up.

If the reporter says nothing for what you consider a prolonged period of time, or if she does this repeatedly, simply say, "Well, if you have no more questions ... ," and then make like the interview has ended and start to get up.

Do your homework on the reporter and the media outlet he works for *before* the interview. Trust me, he will do his homework on *you!* What kind of stories does he write? Does he know your industry or your company? Does he understand the complicated, technical issues that involve your business? Does he do "hatchet jobs"? Which way does he or his paper lean politically?

Try not to take it personally. (I know that's hard.) The toughest questions will be asked. If you are in a crisis involving public health or the safety of the community, tough questions *must* be asked. The reporter is doing her job.

Walk reporters through complicated responses—something that's easier to do with print reporters than with broadcast reporters—to make sure they understand the situation fully. Offer to review the technical parts of the story—not the entire story—to make sure they've got it right. If it's wrong, you can ask for a correction, which reporters do not like. Therefore, I usually find reporters receptive to my offer to review a small chunk of a larger story just for accuracy, technical or otherwise.

Always make yourself or someone on your staff available for follow-up technical questions. This is key. You may not like the reporter (for whatever the reason), but if she's going to write about your company, it is your obligation to help make the story accurate.

And as all of this is going on, do not neglect the constituents with whom you connect via social media. For example, if we suspect one of our clients is going to be slammed in tomorrow's newspaper, we might break the news ourselves to those who are most important to us (our clients): our loyal customers who "like" us on Facebook, follow us on Twitter, and so on. Perhaps we might record a video of the CEO breaking the bad news himself and post it on YouTube, rather than allow the newspaper to herald the story.

It's a different media world out there from what it was just a few years ago, and the rules have changed. You need to have a healthy mix of mainstream and social media outlets on call so that you can develop and put into play an effective crisis communications strategy.

Perhaps one of the most important things to remember is simply this: reporters are smarter than you are, and they always have the last word.

17

Senior Management: Your Own Worst Enemy?

■   ■   ■

very once in a while, I get a call from a company with an unusual request. The company either is in a crisis or sees one on the horizon, and the relevant managers know exactly what needs to be done, but they can't persuade the CEO or other appropriate members of senior management to take action. Or, sometimes there is no actual crisis, but the managers have seen how other companies have suffered during crises, and they feel that their business needs crisis management and crisis communications plans, teams, and training before it's too late. They feel that, because of my experience, if I have a meeting with the reluctant individuals, I can somehow persuade them that action is required.

Often I succeed; other times it's the proverbial case of that well-known horse and some water. But you don't always need me to make the case for you. Especially if yours is a publicly traded company, you can use widely available public information to demonstrate to your senior management how the reputations and the stock prices of other companies have suffered during a crisis. If any of those companies happen to be in your industry group, so much the better for making your case—a case that there but for the grace of God . . . .

In fact, whenever a company in its industry suffers a crisis, smart managers look inward and ask, "How would we have fared if that had been *our* crisis?"

Case in point: soon after the landmark Alaska oil spill, when the tanker *Exxon Valdez* ran aground in Prince William Sound and created what was then the worst oil spill in U.S. history, I was asked by the *New York Times* to write a by-lined piece for its Sunday business forum on how Exxon was managing the crisis. At the time, Exxon's then CEO, Lawrence Rawl, was being roundly vilified for failing to fly to the far-off wilderness of Valdez and the even more remote Prince William Sound to manage the crisis personally. In my view, had he done that, he would have lacked the capacity to obtain and disseminate information easily, and he would not have been properly situated to manage the crisis.

In my article, in which I took Rawl to task for his lack of crisis communications, I wrote, "[T]hose who say Mr. Rawl should have gone to faraway Valdez just because 'it is the right thing to do in these types of crises' are overly concerned with symbolism and naïve about the exigencies of crisis communications and management." And later in the same piece, "In the Alaskan disaster, the problem was not where Mr. Rawl spoke from, but rather that he was slow to speak at all. He was right to stay put but wrong to stay silent."[1]

So his travel instincts were right, but his radio silence was wrong.

The penultimate paragraph carried this message, which is even truer today than it was at that time: "A chief executive must also decide what messages are to be presented and determine how and when to present them most effectively, striking a delicate balance between symbolism and substance, perception and reality. He must act with all deliberate speed to let the public know that he is in charge and that the crisis-management process—and the company—is firmly under control. In all these areas, Exxon's performance fell short."[2]

That article generated a lot of attention, but nowhere more than from the oil industry itself. On Monday morning, the day after the piece appeared, my phone was ringing off the hook when I got to work. I had calls from nine of the biggest oil companies in the world. Some of the calls were from members of the senior management team, and one or two were from the CEO personally. All had essentially the same request (paraphrased): "We don't need help responding to a spill; we feel confident we can handle that. But in the event of a crisis, we don't want our CEO coming across (or *I* don't want to come across) as poorly as Larry Rawl."

I applaud these companies and countless others like them that recognize the inevitability of a crisis and take proactive steps to deal with it. I learned that some of these companies compiled information, including my article and information gained through meetings with me, as well as stock declines, and made compelling cases to their top senior management for the need for proactive crisis management and crisis communications training and preparation.

(Disclosure: BP was one of the companies that contacted me, and we flew to its U.S. corporate offices to meet with its senior management. Ultimately, we did not represent the company, and I recall that this was BP's choice. I also do not believe that BP hired anyone else for this task, leaving one to wonder what might have been.)

You might think that especially today, no company would have to be sold on the need for being prepared for a crisis, but you'd be surprised. I see it on occasion in cases of companies with strong, up-by-their-bootstraps owners who feel that since they built the company "from scratch," they can handle any curveball that's thrown at them. Sadly, sometimes the machismo of the CEO is such that no amount of reasoning will get through to him. That's when your CEO or senior management winds up being the company's own worst enemy. In cases like that, all you can do is make and document your best case. Don't fall on your sword, though. If you feel that your company is at risk for a crisis and you can't get your senior management to see reason, perhaps it's time to pull a LeBron James move and take your talents elsewhere.

There is, however, a silver lining. If you make a compelling enough argument, the CEO will often turn it back on you and give you the responsibility for assembling the right team of people, insiders and outsiders, and preparing the company for a crisis. You are now in a position of power with a seat at the table should a crisis hit. This could be the moment you've been waiting for.

Earlier in the book, in describing the four stages of a crisis, I mentioned that the chronic stage is also the risk and reward stage. If your crisis planning has saved the company from disaster or reputational damage, this could get you elevated to the corner office.

Take Your Own Pulse—or, What Were They Thinking?

■   ■   ■

Before leaving the subject of senior management completely, I believe it would be a good idea for those in charge of instituting new company policies to run those ideas past professional crisis communicators *first*, before unleashing them on an unsuspecting public. Simply put, ideas that look good on paper, as well as on the bottom line, sometimes backfire. And any ideas that originated during happy hour should usually be revisited after the buzz wears off.

Ask your company's crisis communications guru how the new idea is likely to play in the marketplace and with your constituents, try to determine whether a new policy might cause a crisis backlash, and govern yourself accordingly. Crises will find you without your help; why put out the welcome mat?

Here are a few examples of otherwise good companies that simply blew it because they tried to ramrod new ideas down their customers' throats without considering the obvious consequences, and had to backpedal fast on their crisis communications bicycles.

Just a short trip down memory lane and we stumble upon the Coke debacle of some years ago, in which marketing geniuses decided that the world's leading soft drink needed a new taste. Apparently never having become acquainted with the phrase "If it ain't broke, don't fix it," Coke abandoned its legendary century-old formula, introduced so-called New Coke, and brought down upon its massive shoulders one of the biggest self-inflicted crises in the annals of American business. Consumers rejected the new taste in droves and widely lambasted the company for its bizarre move.

Pepsi, its archrival, trumpeted "The Other Guy Just Blinked" in full-page ads nationwide, and even declared a one-day holiday for all workers. Coke had to scramble fast to bring back the original formula, under the new name Classic Coke.

Of more recent vintage, Instagram, the popular photo sharing app recently acquired by Facebook for a cool $1 billion, executed one of the fastest U-turns in history. Unveiling its new "terms of agreement" that users had to accept in order to continue using the site, it stated that, among other things, the company claimed ownership of all of a user's photos, which they could sell to third party companies to appear in online ads—all without the user's knowledge or approval. As a tidal wave of angry users began deleting their accounts, Instagram's founder, Kevin Systrom, had a change of heart and reversed course . . . sort of. Rather than come right out and say they were wrong, Instagram instead claimed their message was misunderstood. No, it was understood just fine, and people weren't happy about it. But users are watching Instagram for its next move to try to make money.

Recently, Netflix, too, shot itself in the foot. Twice.

In the summer of 2011, Netflix angered its customers by imposing a whopping 60 percent price increase by charging separately

for receiving DVD movies by mail in those popular red envelopes
and for streaming movies online or on TV. But even before the dust
had settled on that crisis, the company announced that fall that it
was splitting itself into two completely separate companies with
two different names: Qwikster for the DVDs by mail and Netflix
for streaming. And subscribers would get two separate charges on
their monthly credit card statements.

To be clear, sometimes radical change is required, but this was
not one of those times. It is obvious that no competent crisis communicator had ever reviewed and passed on this decision. So who
was the brain trust that pulled the trigger? Apparently, it was none
other than Reed Hastings, cofounder and CEO of Netflix.

Hastings disclosed that one night, while sharing a hot tub with
a friend (similar to a happy hour), he revealed his still-secret plan
to divide the company into two: Netflix and Qwikster.

> "That is awful," the friend, who was also a Netflix subscriber,
> told him. . . . "I don't want to deal with two accounts."
>
> Mr. Hastings ignored the warning, believing that chief
> executives should generally discount what their friends say.
>
> He has since regretted it. Subscribers revolted and many
> dropped the service. The plan further tarnished a once
> widely respected service that had already been wounded by
> an unpopular price increase in the summer. Mr. Hastings
> was forced to reverse the planned split—but not the price
> increase—three weeks later and apologized.[1]

The company lost more than 800,000 angry subscribers in one
fell swoop, and a lot of goodwill, too.

In September of that year, a chastised Hastings, with his hat in
his hand and his tail between his legs, sent an e-mail apology to all
Netflix subscribers. The letter began:

> I messed up. I owe you an explanation.
>
> It is clear from the feedback over the past two months
> that many members felt we lacked respect and humility in the

way we announced the separation of DVD and streaming and
the price changes. That was certainly not our intent, and I
offer my sincere apology. Let me explain what we are doing. [2]

I offer credit to Hastings for his apology letter— up to a point.
It is a good example of effective crisis communications. He laid
it on the line. He took full responsibility—*personally*. ("I messed
up.") He offered an unqualified apology. ("I offer my sincere apology.") And he provided a full explanation of what happened, why,
and what he was planning on doing about it. ("Let me explain
what we are doing.")

In the interest of accuracy, I should note that his apology
letter also went into great detail about Qwikster, but that ill-
conceived scheme also was abandoned following the reaction to
the rest of the apology letter. So, while Hastings was on the right
track at the outset of his apology letter, it just didn't go far enough
with the second half of his poorly thought-out scheme. Also, after
the announcement of how many members had defected, the company's stock plummeted 27 percent in after-hours trading.

Chief executives might discount what their friends say, but
they should consult crisis communicators and ask, "What, in your
expert opinion, if anything, will be the result of such-and-such new
policy?" before it is too late.

Also in the fall of 2011, Bank of America—already much reviled,
along with every other bank in the world, simply because of how
banks contributed to the financial crisis this country suffered for
years beginning in 2008—came up with what it thought was a nifty
way to squeeze even more money from its financially beleaguered
customers. The bank decided to charge customers a fee of $5 per
month just to use their own debit cards, which, as you know, give
you access to *your own money*. How well do you think that went
over? If you recall, earlier I asked whether the government would
be on your side in a crisis. BofA didn't have to ask.

"After setting off a firestorm of criticism from consumers, Capitol Hill, and the White House, Bank of America is rethinking elements of its plan to charge customers $5 a month to use their debit cards," wrote Nelson Schwartz in the *New York Times*. Schwartz quoted President Obama as scolding that customers should not be "mistreated" in pursuit of profit, Vice President Joe Biden as calling BofA "incredibly tone deaf," and Illinois Senator Richard Durbin as taking "the unusual step of denouncing the bank on the Senate floor, urging customers, 'Vote with your feet. Get the heck out of that bank.'"[3]

As a Jamaican cabdriver I once had in New York City sagely observed after turning the wrong way down a very busy one-way street, "This not good, mon."

Days later, BofA abandoned its ill-conceived plan, as did Wells Fargo and JPMorgan Chase. The latter two banks let BofA take the bulk of the flak while they went to school on their competitors' crisis.

> "We have listened to our customers very closely over the last few weeks and recognize their concern with our proposed debit usage fee," David Darnell, co-chief operating officer at Bank of America, said in a statement. "As a result, we are not currently charging the fee and will not be moving forward with any additional plans to do so."
>
> "The revenue the bank expected to raise from the debit card fee was not worth the damage to its reputation," according to a bank official.[4]

Someone at BofA came up with what she thought was a unique way to increase profits without running the concept past a crisis communicator for his assessment. The bank could have run it past my Jamaican cabdriver and gotten better advice.

Another misguided attempt to gouge customers came from Verizon, which in late 2011 tried to sneak past a holiday-weary public a scheme to charge customers $2.00 to pay their bills. Your read that correctly: some Verizon mastermind decided that it wasn't enough to charge you for using the company's services; if you wanted to pay your monthly bill, you would have to pay a fee to do so. Overcome by a nationwide torrent of criticism, the plan was dropped like a hot potato after just one day. And you can almost bet that as the wireless giant knuckled under to this very vocal crisis backlash from its otherwise loyal customers, more than one of them said, "Can you hear me now?"

The 2012 U.S. Olympic Committee demonstrated its crisis obtuseness when it proudly unveiled the all-American, red-white-and-blue outfits that the U.S. athletes would wear at the opening ceremonies of the 2012 London Olympics. Designed and produced by iconic clothier Ralph Lauren/Polo, according to the labels on every garment, the clothes were all manufactured in China, as originally revealed by ABC News.

The public and government officials were not pleased, to put it mildly. Senate Majority Leader Harry Reid called for the clothes to be collected, put into a big pile, and burned.

Ralph Lauren, which also had the contract to outfit the U.S. athletes for the 2014 winter games, quickly apologized and said that it would not make that same mistake twice.

The next story underscores quite clearly that no organization is bulletproof when it comes to crises and the importance of proactive and reactive crisis communications, not even high-profile, do-good charities. I refer to Susan G. Komen for the Cure, a highly successful fund-raising charity presumably dedicated to finding a cure for breast cancer, with a mission to put a pink ribbon on everyone's lapel.

Not since the March of Dimes campaign to fight polio or the Jerry Lewis Labor Day telethons to raise money for muscular dystrophy has a medical-related charity gained such prominence in the American psyche as Susan G. Komen for the Cure. It seems that almost every time you turn around there is another 5K or 10K "Walk for the Cure," threatening to blind bystanders with a tidal wave of hot pink.

And then, in early 2012, the charity announced that it would no longer contribute funding to Planned Parenthood, and a full-on nationwide crisis erupted immediately.

Why did the charity do it? When it comes to crises, "why" is a luxury question.

Even though the funding to Planned Parenthood paid for breast cancer screening for women, which was in full lockstep with Komen's stated mission, it seems apparent that strong antiabortion elements within the breast cancer charity opposed Planned Parenthood's mission of supporting and funding a woman's right to choose.

Caught flat-footed and completely by surprise by the huge public outcry over its action, the Komen group tried to explain its "new policy" as one that does not allow funding for any group that is under local, state, or federal investigation, and cited a federal investigation of Planned Parenthood led by an antiabortion Republican congressman, Cliff Stearns, as the reason for the cutback. This argument quickly fell apart when it was widely pointed out that Komen funded breast cancer research at Penn State's Milton S. Hershey Medical School. Penn State at the time was under federal investigation for possible violations of the Clery Act,[5] for reasons elaborated upon in an earlier chapter.

The facts on the ground led to a different conclusion: a year earlier, Susan G. Komen for the Cure had hired Karen Handel, a failed Republican candidate for governor of Georgia and an outspoken opponent of Planned Parenthood, as its new vice president for policy. As a gubernatorial candidate in 2010, one of the planks in her platform had been to eliminate government funding for Planned Parenthood. In her new policy role at the charity, she was one of the senior leaders who persuaded the board to reverse its long-established course and abandon Planned Parenthood, cutting off some $700,000 of annual funding. The Penn State funding, which was not touched, was $7.5 million.

Komen's founder, Nancy Brinker, who started the charity in memory of her sister, is a major Republican donor, as was her late husband. She also served as ambassador to Hungary in the George W. Bush administration, and later served for two years as Bush's chief protocol officer. Opposition to abortion is a major tenet of GOP doctrine.

Antiabortion protestors had put pressure on Komen for years to distance itself from groups like Planned Parenthood. Catholic bishops in Ohio called upon parishioners to boycott Komen walks and races because in addition to Planned Parenthood, Komen also gives money to medical centers that are engaged in stem cell research.

Those who supported Planned Parenthood called for their followers to stop giving money to the Komen organization, and supporters of the cancer charity did the same in reverse.

Brinker tried desperately to save the foundering ship, but as a crisis communicator, she has a lot to learn. She held a press conference to declare that politics or abortion never entered into the charity's decision, but one of her own board members who was also a Washington lobbyist, John D. Raffaelli, swiftly contradicted her. He told a reporter that the change was made specifically to end the charity's relationship with Planned Parenthood.[6]

Remember, when communicating in a crisis, speak with one voice.

The decision so outraged New York City Mayor Michael Bloomberg that he wrote a personal check for $250,000 to help make up the Planned Parenthood shortfall. "Politics has no place in healthcare," he said.[7] (An interesting choice of words, considering the fierce national debate surrounding "Obamacare." But that is not our subject today.)

There was the predictable huge backlash on numerous social media outlets: Facebook, Twitter, and Tumblr chief among them. "It demonstrated again how social media can change the national conversation with head-snapping speed."[8]

Within days of the debacle, the Susan G. Komen for the Cure group reversed itself and rescinded its decision to cut off funding to Planned Parenthood, which was flooded with some $400,000 in additional contributions as a result of losing its funding from Komen. At the same time, Handel, the charity's new policy vice president and the lightning rod for the storm, resigned.

Usually in an oppositional crisis, one side or the other is against you. But in its tone-deaf handling of this self-inflicted crisis, Komen managed to anger supporters on *both* sides of the issue: first it angered pro-choice supporters by eliminating funding, then it angered pro-life supporters when it reversed itself. A fierce anti-Komen social media campaign called #takebackthepink, initiated on Twitter and launched on Super Bowl Sunday, urged people to abandon Komen and pointed them to other breast cancer charities that they could support.

"Komen's board members and senior leaders did not anticipate the public outcry over their decision to cut funding to Planned Parenthood," wrote one reporter.[9]

But how could they *not* have anticipated it? The ill-advised decision may have been vetted by certain board and senior staff members, but it is difficult to believe that any competent crisis communicator could have blessed this decision. No matter which side of the argument you support, you have to consider the red state–blue state nation in which we live and the wide chasm that exists between the two sides. In other words, how could rational, objective-thinking people not be able to predict the public outcry that resulted?

Not only could a skilled crisis communicator—had she only been consulted in advance—have predicted what the reaction would be, but if she had been unable to talk the charity off the ledge, at least she could have made preparations to deal with the predictable firestorm so that people would at least have their stories straight. It is always a sign of fouled crisis communications when the CEO is saying one thing and a prominent board member is saying something else.

In accepting Handel's resignation, Brinker said, "We have made mistakes in how we have handled recent decisions."[10] Gee, do you think?

And lastly, we come to the bizarre self-inflicted Chick-fil-A crisis saga, led by company president Dan Cathy. Treading carefully so as not to be accused of taking sides, the basic facts are that Cathy and a foundation that he and his family control, which is largely funded by Chick-fil-A profits, publicly and loudly oppose same-sex marriage. Cathy makes no apologies for his beliefs, and the foundation donates money to antigay groups.

This is a country founded on freedom of speech, and Cathy has a right to his views. But when he involved his company, he created a crisis management and crisis communications nightmare. Stores were picketed and boycotted, and the nation was further divided. The reaction—which involved everything from a "Mike Huckabee-orchestrated 'Chick-fil-A Appreciation Day,' to the 'Same-Sex Kiss Day' that came after, the talking heads, the relentless stream of articles and opinion pieces on the controversy, the thousands upon thousands of online comments, the vitriolic tweets, impulsive Facebook statuses, and equally tart replies, the strained friendships, heated arguments with family members, all of it—began when . . . Cathy said in an interview with the *Baptist Press* that *the company* was 'guilty as charged' when it came to endorsing the biblical view of traditional marriage."[11] (Emphasis added.)

Note that he didn't say that *he* was guilty as charged; he said that *the company* was guilty as charged.

You can be sure that no competent crisis communicator was ever consulted on any of the issues cited in this chapter.

But you may rightly ask, why should a crisis communicator be consulted? And my response is: why shouldn't he be? How long would it take to do so? In the midst of the nation's worst financial meltdown since the Great Depression—and as bank and Wall Street executives were being burned in effigy and "occupied" for excessive salaries and bonuses—how dense do you have to be to figure out that charging people money to gain access to *their own* money is just not going to fly, and will create a needless crisis for the companies involved?

The moral of the story for Chick-fil-A, Susan G. Komen for the Cure, and *you* is this: unless your business is politics, keep politics out of your business.

Get in the habit of taking your own pulse, asking yourself or your crisis communicator: if I were a consumer of my own company, how would I react to this idea or this comment? Is it good for my company and its employees and shareholders?

You can avoid a lot of needless and easily avoidable trouble by doing so.

19

Internal Crisis Communications

■ ■ ■

I n a crisis, will your employees be your allies or your enemies? If you said your allies, how do you know?

We were retained some years ago by a large multinational consumer products company to put together a proactive comprehensive crisis management and crisis communications program. In meeting with senior management and outlining our proposed plan of attack, we discussed conducting benchmark interviews with large swaths of employees in various locations and across many job descriptions, from the shop floor up to the executive suite. Senior management balked, saying that this was a waste of time. We countered with a compromise proposal: let us at least begin, and if the interviews yield no results, we will abandon the rest of them.

There were several things we wanted to know, and chief among them was what prodromes or potential crises *the employees* saw looming and how they felt about the company as a whole. The pre-liminary results were startling.

To begin, the employees had unique vantage points that were not readily available to senior management. They talked to people in other companies in much the same way that servants of old in big households talked to other servants in other big households, with the result that the lowest members of the household staffs often knew more about what was going on in their residences than the landed gentry upstairs who employed them.

Without trying, people on the shipping dock who engaged in day-to-day casual discussions with the people they dealt with often learned which of the company's competitors was laying people off or cutting back or beefing up orders of raw material, who was talk-ing about tasting samples of new, not-yet-announced products, and so on.

After a few days of interviews, among the several eye-opening revelations we discovered was that a major competitor was getting ready to make major incursions into some of our client's most lucra-tive territory. We also learned that a long-standing sponsorship of the local Major League Baseball team, which had been exclusively our client's for some 20 years, was going to be challenged by this competitor, who was preparing to make the team an offer that would be difficult for it to pass up.

Senior management was unaware of any of these things.

We were given the green light to proceed with the rest of the interviews as originally planned. And, by the way, both of those events occurred within six months, but now our client was pre-pared to deal with both situations successfully.

The point here should be obvious: to truly understand a com-pany, *all* perspectives should be considered.

But more illumination was yet to come. During the interviews, we wanted to know how the employees felt about the company and its management. More than one said that they felt like mush-rooms—"kept in the dark and fed shit all day long."

Moreover, there was a general consensus that the way they learned what was going on in their own company was by talking to their peers in *other* companies.

Management was shocked by this. Prior to these interviews, the managers had told us that they had a group of good workers all across the board. That may have been true, but that is not the same thing as having workers that are active allies in a crisis.

When I talk about your constituents, your employees *at all levels* are an important part of this group. Overlook them at your own peril.

You should proactively make your employees ad hoc members of your crisis communications team. Make sure they are among the first to know of important announcements. Nothing can anger a worker more than learning something that affects his job or his company by hearing it from someone else or reading about it in the morning newspaper. Instead, your employees should hear the news—good or bad—from you or senior management *first*. After all, they are on the front lines. If false rumors are rampant, who better to squelch them than someone on the inside who is talking to a friend or family member on the outside? Part of your crisis communications strategy should be to arm your employees with facts—even fact sheets—so that they not only have a clear and honest understanding of the situation, but can talk intelligently about it should someone ask.

I am a big advocate of the company in a crisis having its spokespersons speak with one voice. To that end, we are usually very careful in selecting who can speak with the media. But the reality is that your employees will talk—among themselves, certainly to their friends and family outside of the company, and maybe even to reporters. Wouldn't you want them to at least speak truth and not rumor, fact and not fiction?

In these situations, we will often send word via company department heads that no one is authorized to talk "on the record" with a reporter, "but here are the salient facts of the situation, so that in case you hear anything to the contrary, you can correct mis-information."

Speaking of talking "on the record," in a big crisis, the media will find and target your employees to try to ferret out information. Despite your best efforts, some employees will talk.

You will always have the occasional disgruntled worker with an axe to grind, or someone who is just looking for her 15 min-utes of "fame." This just goes with the territory, and if it is only an isolated instance, it is easy to deal with. But what do you do if a siz-able chorus of employees sings the same or a similar public refrain that throws the company and the management under the bus?

While every crisis is different and it is difficult to apply a one-size-fits-all response to this dilemma, don't ignore it; address it in much the same way we have been talking about addressing other issues. Try to get out in front of the grievances before you are over-whelmed by them.

"Stuff" happens to good companies all the time. Be sure that your employees understand what is going on. This is not hard to do, and it avoids wild speculation.

Avery Dennison, a Fortune company and a client at the time, suffered a well-publicized episode of international economic espi-onage some years ago. A scientist at the company, who had worked there for 11 years, had been stealing the company's most valuable trade secrets and selling them to a Taiwanese competitor, Four Pillars. The employee was a naturalized U.S. citizen at the time and had been educated in the United States, but had been born and raised in Taiwan.

Working closely with the FBI in a closely choreographed sting operation, we knew exactly when the arrests were to be made. We also knew when the FBI was planning on holding a news confer-ence, and it was big news, since it was about to become the first case to go to trial after the passage of the landmark Economic Espionage Act. The last thing we wanted was to have the company's more than 15,000 employees worldwide hear about this on the news or read about it in the papers, especially since this particular employee had been fairly well known and liked within the company.

Therefore, we prepared a worldwide internal employee voice mail and e-mail blast, timed to be released simultaneously with the FBI's press conference. The message came from the then-chairman and CEO. It was candid and pointed, and it discussed the shock and disappointment felt at this betrayal. It requested employees not to talk to the media—they were given guidelines on how to refer any media inquiries to the worldwide communications department in California—but it also provided them with *facts* in case any of their customers wanted to discuss it, or so that if anyone had misinformation, they could set that person straight. The message made sure to get across the fact that the company was all right and would continue to be despite the theft.

When the flood of questions came, the employees around the world were our first line of defense in calming any jitters from customers, since they already knew the salient facts of the story.

A crisis will hit, and when it does, you will have your hands full dealing with the mainstream media and social media. Why add to your already heavy burden by also having your employees against you? Before they become enemies, and well before any crisis hits, part of your proactive strategy should be to embrace your countless employees as visible and vocal allies in your crisis communications battle.

Rally the troops early. It will pay big dividends when the chips are down.

20

External Crisis Communications

■ ■ ■

Before you start communicating with the outside world, it is important to know whether you are immersed in an oppositional or a nonoppositional crisis. I touched on this earlier, but it is important to reinforce the critical nature of this element.

At its root level, the difference has to do with whether your company is responsible for the crisis, or whether someone else is and your company is merely suffering from the fallout. Knowing and understanding this distinction drives your entire crisis communications strategy. If you are in the midst of a major acute crisis—lives have been lost, the environment has been damaged, a threat still looms, or something similar—the world is either with you or against you.

If you are a victim, one crisis communications strategy I have observed is to let others speak on your behalf. The apparent rationale here is that, first, if others speak on your behalf, you won't say anything on the record that can bite you later, and second, it keeps your hands clean.

Sorry, I don't buy it.

There is no one who can speak more effectively for you and your company than you, and if you are in a crisis—and most especially if you are the victim in a crisis—your constituents need to hear your voice. Failure to make yourself heard in a crisis is a very risky move, almost as much as failure to communicate at all.

Some years ago, the Pepsi-Cola Company was dogged by a ridiculous—and completely false—rumor that somehow syringes were being found (and presumably placed) in cans of Pepsi. The allegations never passed the "smell test," but nevertheless they spread like wildfire. An initial report out of Tacoma, Washington, was broadcast on a local TV news show, and that seemed to unleash an avalanche of identical, copycat claims in half the country in a matter of some 48 hours. The FDA issued an early warning in five surrounding states, instructing people not to drink Pepsi from cans, but instead to first pour the soda into a glass and examine the contents—not exactly a vote of confidence in the product.

Each report seemed to have *scam* and *hoax* writ large upon it, but still the allegations poured in. In that regard, there were similarities to the Wendy's finger-in-the-chili fraud discussed earlier, where the perpetrators were looking for a fast payday. But like Wendy's, Pepsi didn't rise to its own defense effectively, or at least not sufficiently. Instead, it had no less a personage than former FDA commissioner David Kessler trying to put out fires on the company's behalf, appearing on *Nightline* and numerous other TV shows to defend the company's production process. Pepsi North America CEO Craig Weatherup did make an appearance, but throughout the crisis, Pepsi never seemed to mount an effective counter to the claims. It seemed as if its executives were thrown back on their heels, busy trying to put out fires while new ones erupted without warning throughout the country. As ludicrous as they may have believed the claims to be, they seemed stymied as to how to quiet the accusations with proof positive that the charges were baseless.

Earlier, if you recall, I asked, will the government stand by your side in a crisis? The situation here gave the appearance that the company was standing by the government's side, rather than the other way around. It seemed to be Kessler in the forefront, but even he was not enough, and the overall perception was that Pepsi was willing to allow the FDA chief to speak for the company. I recall some colleagues at the time wondering aloud whether the lawyers had issued a companywide gag order. Meanwhile, more claims of syringes found in Pepsi cans were reported throughout the country.

I have spoken with people at Pepsi who were involved in managing that crisis, and they pat themselves on the back and think they did a great job. I disagree with their myopic view of the bigger picture. If they had, indeed, done a great job, this crisis never would have gotten off the ground in the first place. Let me explain.

Five days after the crisis erupted, Pepsi at last released much-needed footage of the can line portion of its manufacturing process, which clearly showed empty cans on a high-speed conveyor line being washed clean by high-pressure water jets, then turned completely upside down to let the water drain completely; the cans were then turned upright again, filled with Pepsi, and sealed. All this happened in a matter of seconds on an automated, high-speed line. There was no way anyone could get a syringe into a can on that line, which turned over the cleaned-out cans a split second before they were filled and sealed. Once this footage was released, and the public saw how baseless the syringe claims had to be, the crisis ended because the public could clearly see with their own eyes that there was no validity to the claims. This was crisis communications gold. There were no more complaints, and those who had filed claims earlier either withdrew them or were charged with a crime by local law enforcement. Some went to prison.

Had that footage been released earlier, the crisis never would have gained traction. So why wasn't it?

Because it didn't exist until then. It took Pepsi five long days to figure out how to use effective crisis communications to put an end to a crisis that never should have gained traction in the first place. And it wasn't until the footage was released to the world that the company really spoke effectively to its constituents and conveyed the critical crisis communications message: *it is safe to drink Pepsi.* Mere words were inadequate—even from the FDA Commissioner—to squelch a crisis that had gripped the nation—or at least that portion of the nation that drinks Pepsi—with fear and uncertainty.

Meanwhile, the company lost between $25 and $35 million in sales as a result of the hoax.

When putting together proactive crisis management and crisis communications plans for our manufacturing clients, we always recommend shooting "B" roll (silent) footage of the entire manufacturing process. We lock it up somewhere, ready to be appropriately edited and trotted out, if need be, to bolster a critical crisis communications message. You never know when it might be needed, so we try to err on the side of caution and preparedness.

Even absent this footage, Pepsi should have been front and center defending itself and its manufacturing process. Pepsi could have walked reporters through the can line to show them how incredibly unlikely it was that anyone could insert anything into those cans. Even without the footage, and even when you are clearly being reactive, look for ways to be proactive.

The reality was that Pepsi was safe; the perception was otherwise. Pepsi's mission should have been to devise an effective and strategic crisis communications message that brought perception and reality into alignment. It took the company five long days to figure out how to do that, which is why I do not give it high marks for its handling of the crisis. In a crisis, speed is of the essence, and five days is an eternity.

So how did this crisis get started in the first place?

A diabetic relative visiting in the house from which the first report emanated discarded a used insulin syringe in an empty can of Pepsi, placed the can on the kitchen counter, and then left the house before the syringe was discovered. It was innocent. The homeowners, however, contacted their lawyer, who contacted the local TV station, and—well, the rest is history. And another innocent company suffered a crisis caused by others, and suffered more because of a lack of prompt, adequate, and effective crisis communications. It can happen to you.

The safe bet is that there will come a time when it is essential for you to take your critical message to your constituents.

Who exactly *are* your key publics? Do you know? They probably fall into one or more of several categories, including, but not limited to, customers, clients, employees, families of employees, board members, shareholders, government regulators, politicians (local, state, and federal), community and religious leaders wherever you have operations, residential and commercial neighbors, foreign dignitaries or officials, business associates, competitors, vendors, lenders, partners, analysts, union leaders, suppliers, distributors, retirees and pensioners, and Facebook friends and Twitter followers (who may also be in one or more of the other categories).

And, oh, yes, the mainstream news media in general, and those that cover your company or industry in particular.

By definition, everyone other than current employees is "external," and you need to have an external communications strategy for reaching each and every group, individually or collectively. In a crisis that requires you to get the word out as widely as possible, even if you can do so via the news media, you *still* need to reach out to your key constituents and let them know what's going on, how they are affected (or not), and your plans or your timetable for returning to normal. Your various publics will appreciate the personal touch. It will also give them a chance to ask questions, which you should encourage. Those who reach out should be well briefed on not only what to say but what questions might arise and how those questions should be answered so that the *entire* company is speaking with a single voice.

Also, understand that each group of constituents will have different concerns; therefore, targeted messages need to be drafted for each group. And in doing so, take an accurate picture of the reality of the situation and the current perception. If the reality is actually better than is being reported, and the perception is skewed negatively, the thrust of each of your communications messages should be designed to improve that perception.

And, how will you reach your publics, and how long will it take you to do so? And no matter what you answer in your own mind to that question, answer this one: How do you know? Have you ever tested your crisis communications plans?

A client, a nationwide food importer and distributor, had a scare recently when it thought it would have to order a nationwide recall of one of its products. As we were waiting for lab results and a government decision on the recall, I asked if the company was prepared to notify all of its distributors and retail outlets that one particular item needed to be removed from public use, if necessary. I was told that the company could issue the appropriate recall in under two hours. But that was wrong. Very wrong.

The system had never been tested. And when the system had first been established—many, many years earlier—the company was smaller, so a notification of this kind (which was never needed) was a simpler task. Fortunately, no recall was needed, but the company learned an important lesson about proper preparations for external crisis communications.

Make certain you are prepared, too. For in the midst of your crisis, if you cannot communicate with your publics swiftly and effectively, you will be held responsible for that lapse in addition to everything else that's going on. Plus, your opposition will seize on your delay as an opportunity to get their message out there first.

Finally, what procedures are in place to allow for and even encourage feedback? If you want to learn instantly how you're doing and how your crisis is being perceived by your publics, listen; they will tell you loud and clear. Do not discount their comments and posts. Even a single blogger with a large following can tip the scales for or against you.

I have been in the center of numerous crisis storms over the years, and when you are under siege day and night, it is easy to take a Ptolemaic view of the world, in which it seems as if everything is revolving around you. It's not. There is life beyond your crisis bubble, and much of it involves your constituents. Listen to them, and make sure they are listening to you.

Remember, even if you *think* you have things under control, if the perception from your publics is that you don't, they're right; you're wrong.

Fix it.

21

Reputation Management and Reservoirs of Goodwill

■ ■ ■

What do people think of your company and its management? How do you know?

Now, before a crisis hits, what do your clients or your customers think of you? What do media outlets, both social and mainstream, think of you? What do your key publics think of you?

Perhaps most important, what do you *want* them to think of you? And, does the reality match your wishes?

I can't begin to tell you how many companies find religion while they're going through a crisis. There are a lot of things that happen in a crisis over which you have no control; your reputation shouldn't be one of them. What are your strengths, and what are your weaknesses? If your reputation today is not everything you'd like it to be, do something about it, for in a crisis, a good reputation sometimes buys you a pass or some much-needed time to regroup.

There's an old military expression that during a war, there are no atheists in foxholes. Once you're hunkered down in a crisis foxhole, you may find religion, but it will be too late to use it to rebuild your reputation.

We often use the phrase *reservoirs of goodwill* with our clients, and part of your proactive crisis management and crisis communications strategies should be to measure the depth of your goodwill reservoir and see what you can do to increase it. The more goodwill you have in the bank or reservoir, the more your public will tend to trust you and believe you when your crisis hits, and the more you can draw on it to tide you over. This is critical in a crisis in which the accusations or the facts are horrendous. If they are untrue, and your reputation is intact, you have the benefit of the doubt going into the arena.

When you Google yourself and your company, what do you find? Chances are there will be news stories that may stretch back many years. Read them. Analyze them. Categorize them.

Are they generally positive, negative, or neutral? Are they accurate? Are stories missing that you feel would cast your company in a better light? Is there incorrect, inflammatory information that can be corrected?

This is subjective, of course, so you may want to solicit the views of coworkers or outside objective parties who have read the same stories and then compare notes. A consensus generally will form. Not only is this an important crisis communications learning exercise, but if your reputation is negative or questionable, it will probably cost you new or recurring business, as well as employees—some who no longer want to work for a company like yours and others who'd rather not join your shop in the first place.

Of course, what you are reading are news stories, presumably objective, that were written by reporters who covered a story or a news event. What do *real people* think of you?

Are you listed in *Fortune* magazine's "Best 100 Companies to Work For"? If your company is not large enough to be included in that list, how do people in your industry measure you against your competitors? Are you the "hot shop" that everyone wants to work for, or are people leaving your firm to work for one or two of your biggest competitors? Why? What can your human resources people tell you about how prospective new hires think of you?

Companies often hire outside consultants to take confidential surveys of their employees to answer just such questions. As mentioned earlier, your employees are one of your first lines of defense in a crisis. However, if you do this, make sure the surveyors know what they're doing. A manager in charge of executive compensation at a major utility company told me a horror story recently having to do with just such a survey. After listening in on a conference call in which employees were openly critical of the company and its management, the consultants collected the names of those employees and decided to make them the focal point of their survey. Talk about skewed results!

What do people in the community think of you? (This question applies to wherever you have facilities.) Are you considered a good corporate citizen? Or, are you the town's biggest polluter? Years ago, we represented a large Fortune company that operated a manufacturing plant in a small town not far from its corporate office near Los Angeles. This one plant, which was saddled with old furnaces, was always cited in the annual list of "Top 10 Polluters" in the local media for its high release of reactive hydrocarbons.

The truth was that this company was a good corporate citizen by any measure and operated on a global scale with a workforce of upwards of 20,000 people, but the CEO was irked when his luncheon partners at his private dining club needled him each year for being such a big polluter. He wanted the problem fixed and the company's reputation restored. That was true, but what he also wanted was to eat in peace without being teased by his CEO peers.

Fixing the actual problem—the reality—was accomplished by replacing the aging furnaces. This helped fix the reality and the perception, but we also arranged for the company to be given a city council proclamation for extraordinary measures designed to improve the environment and the local air quality.

The company was never again mentioned in a list of local polluters, and the CEO—proud of his company's new achievement and civic commendation—ate his lunch without indigestion.

Here's a basic pop-culture analogy that will demonstrate the importance of reputation versus notoriety.

When a celebrity is involved in any type of altercation or situation that involves the police and/or a mug shot, one of the first questions the media examine is whether this was a first offense. When former U.S. commerce secretary John Bryson was involved in two separate Southern California auto accidents in a matter of minutes, the first one actually giving the appearance of being a hit and run, it was an aberration given his lack of previous similar incidents, and it flew in the face of his reputation as a community leader and former CEO of Southern California Edison. It turned out that Bryson had suffered a seizure, which caused the erratic driving episode. (He later resigned his cabinet post to seek medical treatment.)

Now, if actress Lindsay Lohan is involved in a traffic accident, what is your *first* thought? She was drinking? She was high on drugs? She was speeding?

Before you even know the facts, you are going to form an opinion—maybe even an opinion that you have trouble changing in the face of facts to the contrary. Is this fair? Actually, it doesn't matter whether or not it's fair; it's human nature. Her long and unfortunate history of traffic incidents and DUIs helps form your first impression when you see any similar story that concerns her and an auto mishap or other erratic behavior. In fact, a recent story that concerned her missing work on a movie set one day had a kind of "here we go again" tone; in reality, she had been working so hard each day on the set that she just overslept one morning. But it is unlikely that *that* was the general consensus of first opinions.

Now, what if you heard a story that Oprah Winfrey was involved in a traffic accident. She may not even drive her own car, but work with me here. What would be your *first* thought? Drinking? Drugs? Hit and run? I seriously doubt it. Ms. Winfrey's reservoirs of goodwill—from her on-air persona and her charitable work in starting a tuition-free "leadership academy" for deserving girls in South Africa—are so deep in her vast communities that she has earned the benefit of the doubt if such an occurrence were to cross your news feed.

So, which are you or your company? Lindsay Lohan or Oprah Winfrey?

There is a third alternative: *nothing*. We refer to this as "the Rorschach phenomenon," and it's dangerous.

You are probably familiar with the famous Rorschach inkblots. That's essentially what your company is if it has not taken the time to establish reservoirs of goodwill: an inkblot. And everybody will see something different when they look at it. The good news is that if it's currently an amorphous shape, you have time to mold it into whatever you want people to see. The bad news is that if it remains amorphous when a crisis erupts, your adversaries have an excellent chance to shape it *their* way, since there is no impression to the contrary. Put in stark terms, your reputation and your future are in your own hands. And, if your adversaries begin to give form to the inkblot (read: shape a negative message about you or your company) *first*, you will have an uphill battle on your hands.

Rumors are also something that needs attention, even those that at first blush seem preposterous. If they are allowed to grow unchecked, rumors have a way of planting just enough seeds of doubt that you need to deal with them before they escalate into crisis mode. When you have deep reservoirs of goodwill, a highly specious rumor will have trouble gaining strength or traction.

Reputation management should be an ongoing process, and your public relations department or outside public relations firm should already have been given this important responsibility.

Wherever you are perceived as weak, play to your strengths and devise a strategy to bolster your image. Do this in deeds, not just in words. If your research and your own gut instinct tell you that your key publics already hold you in high esteem, keep at it. People who rest on their laurels are wearing them in the wrong place.

Improving your reputation is good for business in general, but in a crisis it can spell the difference between success and failure.

Think of a crisis as gains or losses on a football field. When the fourth quarter—the crisis—starts, are you deep in your own end zone facing a blitz, or have you already made so much progress that you have a good chance of scoring a touchdown? If you have a better than average reputation and deep reservoirs of goodwill, that perception of you and your company will help better position you on the crisis gridiron when the whistle blows to start the action.

22

Issues Management

■ ■ ■

Many companies have issues that they are advocating, one way or the other. This advocacy may be in the guise of civic involvement, but you actually may have a deeper, vested interest in the outcome of the public debate or the city council vote. To further your interests, your public relations department or outside firm has developed an "issues management" campaign designed to enlist support for your way of thinking. Perhaps you have a lobbyist on retainer.

There's nothing new here; it happens all the time.

But "issues" have a nasty way of turning into full-blown crises if they are not managed properly. Prepare yourself.

Almost by definition, if an issue exists, chances are that there are two sides to it. That means that whenever your side is gaining traction, the other side is digging in its heels and calculating what strategies it can employ to derail your efforts or undermine your public credibility. To prepare for the crisis that may befall you, and to be ready to mount an effective crisis communications counter-argument, you should engage in "opposition research."

This phrase is more widely associated with political campaigns, where one camp assigns a team to find out everything it can about its opponents. At times, someone may be given the task of "being the other guy," putting herself in the place of the opposition and trying to figure out what she might do or say next. During political debate practice, someone plays the other candidate and answers questions the way the opponent might. This is neither new nor news.

What I suggest is that as part of your broader issues management strategy, you proactively try to determine in what form and from what corners the attacks against you, your company, and your ideas will come. For they *will* come.

As you do this, it is important to develop specific messages targeted for specific groups. Note: this does not mean talking out of both sides of your mouth. It simply means that if you have different points to make in support of your issue, you need to understand which publics would be most interested in which points and shape your messages for the various interest groups in a strategic and targeted way that will maximize your crisis communications messages and minimize backlash.

For example, if your issue has to do with controversial zoning variances that would enable you to build or expand a facility, who would benefit from (1) the expansion, (2) the increased taxes you'd wind up paying as a result of the expansion, (3) the increased jobs that would be created, and so on? There will be a whole host of special interest groups popping up to either support or oppose your issue.

The biggest advantage that you have—or should have—is that an issues management campaign does not run the risk of turning into a public crisis until it becomes public. Typically, the issues and the communications strategies designed to support them are formulated behind closed doors, away from public scrutiny. In forward-thinking companies that engage in strategic planning, the communications department should be given the luxury of developing the messages and the means of delivery in a relatively calm, noncrisis environment. Embrace this gift and make the most of it.

When you have a clear vision of your issue and your messages, you should also have a good idea of your friends and your foes. Who are your natural allies? Who might you enlist to become an ally? Who will speak on behalf of your issue? Who will speak about the merits of your issue and the accumulated benefits to the community? Will the government stand by your side? Will religious and civic groups support you? Work with them; develop joint strategies.

Who is likely to oppose your issue? Understand the issue from *their* point of view. Determine whether their likely arguments have any validity, and develop messages in advance that address and refute likely attacks. What is *their* agenda? Who benefits or profits if their arguments triumph and your issue is defeated?

If you plan your crisis communications arguments strategically, you can prevail. And nowhere is this more evident than when you examine the single greatest issues management campaign in the past couple of hundred years: the Declaration of Independence.

Contrary to what you may have been taught in school, the primary target audience for the Declaration of Independence was not King George III, nor was it the British Parliament. No. Thomas Jefferson, in his infinite genius, wrote the document as an issues management campaign—*an argument*—to persuade those in the colonies who were still loyal to the Crown that independence was the right move, and that it was an *issue* that was worth fighting—and dying—for ("We mutually pledge to each other our Lives, our Fortunes, and our sacred Honor"). He also was writing to other nations, letting them know why we were declaring our independence and going to war, and soliciting either their support or their neutrality.

This was classic issues management, and the issue was independence. A careful reading of the document shows how Jefferson, in his skillful writing, crafted a logical and persuasive argument for independence. ("The history of the present King of Great Britain is a history of repeated injuries and usurpations, all having in direct object the establishment of an absolute Tyranny over these States. To prove this, let Facts be submitted to a candid world.") And then Jefferson let loose with more than two dozen specific and provable charges of abuse and tyranny by the Crown for the colonial loyalists and other nations of "a candid world" to read, coupled with arguments as to why we deserved to be free from such well-documented oppressive and despotic rule. It was a well reasoned and persuasive argument.

Yes, we went to war (the crisis), but the successful management of the issue (crisis communications) ensured that we had an army of volunteers to fight.

23

Crisis Communications for Publicly Traded Companies

■ ■ ■

Every publicly traded company has either an investor relations
department or an outside firm filling the same role. It would be
wise to consider investor relations—maintaining and sustain-
ing two-way communications with the investment community—as
proactive crisis communications.

Reactive crisis communications is investor relations on steroids.

Most crises play out over a period of time. When a crisis arises,
a publicly traded company, regardless of whatever is going on in
the actual management of the crisis, is not as fortunate. There is
an additional and immediate crisis involving the stock market and
maybe the SEC, and it plays out with every rise and fall of your
stock price. Every day, Monday through Friday, from the opening

bell to the closing bell, when the stock market is open, your constituents are sending you loud and clear messages about how they think your company is managing its crisis. As with so many other situations, it doesn't matter whether you have the crisis well in hand; if your shareholders doubt you and desert you, the perception *and* the reality are aligned: you have a crisis.

Compound this with the fact that the financial media, as well as online blogs, will write about your travails and speculate about your future survival. The right perception can maintain or raise your stock price; the wrong perception will lower it. But in this instance, reality and perception must be in sync. If senior management has the crisis under control, and the crisis communications team is on top of its myriad audiences, the investor relations team needs to get that message out to its spirited audience in a well-choreographed pas de deux.

Failure to treat your investment community as hair triggers during a crisis may create a crisis where one need not exist, or overly prolong one that should have been retired long ago.

24

Crisis Litigation

■　■　■

t is the safest of bets that one of the end products of your crisis
will be litigation. Plan on it; prepare for it.

Even though the acute stage of your crisis may have ended
quite some time ago, welcome to the chronic stage, the third and
most protracted of the four crisis stages discussed earlier. You may
have successfully capped that runaway oil well and saved the environment; you may have successfully stemmed the threatened run
on your bank, prevented the Feds from seizing control, and saved
thousands of jobs; you may have solved the product liability problem that was suspected of having been responsible for several fatalities. But you are far from out of the woods.

As a result of your crisis, you have been sued, big time, maybe
even class action big time. And the public is probably watching
intently.

Who is your opponent? If you've been sued by the government, there are two things to keep in mind. First, the public is very probably against you. You and the government can be at odds all you want behind closed doors, but in the light of day, if the government says you did something wrong, it's a good bet that the public agrees with it, and that the obvious perception is that you are somehow evil. Deal with it.

The second thing is, if you have been sued by government lawyers, you have an excellent chance of beating them. How many times has the government brought a high-profile civil case (criminal cases are a little different) against a defendant where the preponderance of the disclosed evidence seems to be stacked against the defendants, and yet the government loses and the defendants walk? Why is that?

Economics, plain and simple.

Big law firms that represent big clients, and that pay first-year associates buckets of money, recruit from the top of the classes at America's finest law schools. It's economics: money attracts talent, and talent goes where the money is.

Those big law firms then spend countless hours and perhaps tens of thousands of dollars to further train future lawyers in such things as courtroom demeanor, how to close a deal, and so on. In other words, firms like Philadelphia's white-shoe law firm Drinker Biddle & Reath actually have formal programs in which they take top law school graduates and train them in how to actually become lawyers. This type of training is commonplace at big firms. The government offers nothing equivalent.[1]

This is embarrassing for the government. I once had the excruciatingly painful experience of watching one of the Justice Department's alleged "top lawyers" almost single-handedly lose a landmark case when he was unable to properly introduce key evidence at a major trial. Don't they teach this stuff in law schools?

The government attorney was taking a whistle-blower witness through his testimony, and every time he tried to introduce a key document into evidence, the defense counsel (from a top, very expensive Washington, DC, law firm) objected; usually it was because a proper foundation had not yet been laid. As the judge sustained each objection, the hapless DOJ attorney tried again using different wording, but to no avail. Time and again, his own ineptitude and rattled nerves thwarted his efforts. Even the judge tried to coach him at one point; no luck. The more times he failed, the more flustered he became. He finally sat down without introducing numerous crucial documents into evidence, and most of the case fell apart.[2]

And there are other well-known examples, such as the failure of government lawyers to secure convictions in the trials of John Edwards and Roger Clemens—two very public cases with mountains of evidence and eyewitnesses on the government's side.

But there is a double-edged sword here: people may feel that when the government sues a private company that is involved in, say, a public safety–related crisis, the government is trying to protect them. Beating up on the government and beating it in court doesn't always translate into a boost for your public likability factor. Almost overnight, your name and the phrase "must've pulled a fast one in court" may start popping up a lot in the same sentence.

(Note: it is not my intention to engage in a political debate with some in this country who feel that government is too big and shouldn't be meddling in our lives in *any* way, litigation ostensibly designed for our protection included. I'm just pointing out that even if you win a lawsuit against the government, you may have a larger perception problem that needs to be addressed.)

If you are being sued by individuals or in a class action suit, you have a similar problem. If you win, some people will judge you for using slick, high-powered attorneys, getting off on a loophole, or something else that will allow them to continue to beat that incessant drum that says you are evil.

When your lawyers are closing up their briefcases and considering the case closed, the crisis usually is far from over. And one of the mistakes I've seen occur is that the crisis communicators think their jobs, as well as the lawyers', are over. You still need to gauge the public perception of your company and respond accordingly. See how much you have drained from your reservoirs of goodwill.

If you are being sued by widows and orphans or other indisputable victims, consult with your attorneys and consider settling out of court. (But *really* out of court, not the way Penn State very publicly and shamelessly broadcast its intention of paying child sex abuse victims, as cited in an earlier chapter.) The longer such victims remain in the public eye, the more likely it is that your vilification will continue unabated. I say "consider" because it is impossible to make a blanket general recommendation about how to handle litigation without the facts, but my concern is how you are being perceived by your key constituents.

When you are a plaintiff in public litigation, your crisis communications messages must be clear, articulate, easy to understand, and pointed. You need to use the Thomas Jefferson approach to crafting your arguments and, in fact, structure your arguments in such a way that you have cut off as many possible means of reasonable rebuttal as possible. These messages need to be proactive, and you need to understand that the first message is like the first move in a chess game: there *will* be a response. If your initial arguments are sound, there is a greater chance that counterarguments will ring hollow and that you will have gained the high ground. Nevertheless, you should try to determine and plan for likely responses.

Attorneys for plaintiffs are generally more open with their proactive communications. They and their clients feel that they have the moral and legal high ground (why else would they sue?), and they are not at all shy about sharing this belief with the rest of the world.

In any communications "battle," as stated earlier but worth repeating, it is always better to play offense than defense, and crisis communications when you are the plaintiff is no exception.

When you are the defendant in crisis litigation, your position is different. Chances are that your attorneys will not want to comment for fear of revealing a strategy that they'd prefer to unveil in court or during deposition. This is a very valid point. But, as mentioned before, if you go completely radio-silent, you are giving your opponents an open field to do and say as they please, and shape the message to their liking. It may not win them the case, but they will have a better chance than you at winning the perception battle. So, what to do?

Compromise.

I respect your attorney's point of view—it has much validity—but especially in matters of complex litigation, there is always the possibility that you can pluck one or even two attack points and turn them around online or with a reporter to demonstrate the fallacy of your opponent's argument. My comment to a reporter might therefore be structured along these lines: "As you know, it is very difficult to comment on pending litigation, but let me give you just one or two brief examples of why this suit against us is without merit." Then, lay out the best argument you can make—using the Jeffersonian model for arguments—so that the other side has little chance for effective rebuttal.

You might then say, "Obviously, I cannot get into other areas of the case, especially as it is so complex, but we are fully prepared to refute each and every baseless claim against us in court the same way."

Note: tread carefully if the plaintiffs opposing you are widows and orphans who earned their unfortunate status as a result of your product's defects. You still need to defend your position publicly, but not at the cost of looking like an unfeeling ogre.

There will be cases where you really can't offer any comment, such as in cases involving an employee's termination. For one thing, there is the matter of privacy to be considered. But take the time to explain what you can, and also explain why you cannot comment on confidential employee matters.

One of the most frustrating cases I ever worked on, where our hands were really tied, involved the UCLA School of Medicine's famed Neuropsychiatric Insititute. The Institute and one of the staff psychiatrists were sued by a former patient, who alleged that as a teenager he had been put into an experimental drug treatment program without proper informed consent. He and his family made the litigation very public, proactively participating in media interview after media interview to drum up publicity for their case. Our clients were naturally asked for comment and wanted to refute the allegations, but could not do so due to doctor-patient confidentiality. This was disappointing because we felt we had an important and persuasive counter message. One national television network even went so far as to try to get the patient and his father to sign a waiver giving the doctors permission to discuss the young man's case publicly. The physician in question even wrote to the American Psychiatric Association looking for guidance, as well as a clearance, and was told emphatically by the AMA that regardless of any waivers, he would be jeopardizing his medical license if he even acknowledged the young man had been a patient.

Also, always respect a gag order. If the judge orders attorneys not to discuss a case with the media, that order usually broadly covers others who are involved in the case (that is, plaintiffs, defendants, and their agents), even those who are involved only tangentially, such as communicators. A gag order does not prevent the media from speculating, however, and at times such public rumination can be even more damaging than the facts. You've seen it many times on TV: the media talk to "legal experts"—lawyers who know little more than you do, except that they've been to law school—who pontificate about what is likely to happen. Often their track record compares with those of psychics and tea leaf readers, but that doesn't stop them from speculating on the air about you, your crisis, and your legal case. Often, such speculation takes on a life of its own.

What can you do?

If you have a good working relationship with the media, encourage them to share with you what they've "heard" or what they intend to write so that you can at least wave them off if they're about to make public something that is completely wrong. This is a tricky maneuver, but it can work to your advantage as well as the reporter's. A smart reporter can ferret out the right path to pursue just by your roadblocks, which can help him avoid retractions later on, and you haven't violated the gag order. Note: do not intentionally mislead a reporter by heading him off a story line that is damaging to your side, but essentially true. You will have lost his trust.

Someday, you may be accused of some wrongdoing by a public prosecutor.

The ballet very rarely changes: you protest your innocence, the district attorney says very little (unless it's an election year), and the public has the perception that you are guilty. A grand jury is convened (unless one already is sitting), and you make your required appearance.

Since grand jury testimony is confidential and sometimes sealed, there is little you can do directly after the fact. But if you've been constantly increasing the levels in your reservoirs of good-will, *this* is where and when it starts to pay off. You may just catch a break and be given the benefit of the doubt because of your outstanding reputation.

The better and more positive the public's perception of you is, the greater the likelihood that you can regain and retain your reputation when the grand jury is finished with you—unless, of course, you are indicted.

You should listen to and consider very carefully the advice of your attorneys—and then consider whether following their advice strictly would help or hurt you and your firm in the long run. Then, make an informed decision concerning what you can say, to whom, and under what circumstances.

Depending upon the nature of your business, one day you may be invited to testify before Congress. Whether you wanted to or not, you are about to engage in crisis communications writ large, and you had better be well prepared.

Typically, there are two parts to your crisis communications strategy, which coincide with the two parts of your congressional testimony: your opening statement and the always-fun Q&A session that follows. You should make a point of meeting personally with your executioners—sorry, questioners—before D-Day, and your DC lobbying firm will help arrange this. It won't necessarily change the tone or the intensity of the questions, but it may give you some insight into the directions from which the attacks will come. These hearings are usually highly coordinated affairs. Moreover, when you see the representatives on their elevated bench staring down at you, having met them earlier in a more relaxed and presumably informal setting may help to remove some of the intimidation factor that, along with the setting, gives them home court advantage.

In addition to having your attorney by your side at the witness table, you should have your crisis communications chief close behind. He will want you to meet with reporters following your testimony to put your "spin" on the session. Do it. This is a chance to say what you meant to say inside the hearing room but forgot to say or were blocked from saying, or to correct a misstatement that you may have uttered or offer a more reasoned rebuttal to a congressman's full-throated accusations. Your testimony will be scripted; your Q&A session will not be, although it should be practiced, with your communications people and attorneys firing questions at you and evaluating your responses.

Litigation, depositions, and courtroom or congressional testimony are all forms of crisis communications, just in different packaging. Don't let the fancy wrapping and pretty-colored ribbons throw you off.

25

How to Break Bad News

■　■　■

There will come a time in your crisis when you may have to convey bad news. For most people, this is not easy, yet it has to be done. If women readers will forgive me, the phrase that springs to mind is, "Man up!"

As a World War II history buff, I have always been impressed that prior to rolling the dice on D-Day, the very risky Allied invasion of Normandy that proved to be the pivotal turning point in the war, General Dwight D. Eisenhower handwrote a note taking full blame for the defeat! If the invasion had failed, if we had not been able to gain a toehold in Europe, and if he had been killed, the supreme allied commander of the European theater of operation wanted to make sure that the world knew who had made the critical decision during that crisis point, and who was to blame. Thus, the night before the invasion, and fearing the very real possibility of a failure, Ike penned this note:

> Our landings in the Cherbourg-Havre area have failed to gain
> a satisfactory foothold and I have withdrawn the troops. My

decision to attack at this time and place was based on the best information available. The troops, the air and the Navy did all that bravery and devotion to duty could do. If any blame or fault attaches to the attempt, it is mine alone.

I have counseled the CEOs and senior management of companies for many years, and I have seen the struggles some of these individuals have gone through and know the sleepless nights they have suffered.

The advice that follows will not necessarily make what you have to do any easier, but it will help get you through it.

First, it is probably better to read from a script of note cards rather than ad lib. You don't want to forget anyone or anything under the stress you are experiencing.

There are four basic things to keep in mind. You should communicate bad news:

- **Calmly.** It will serve no one's interest if your anxiety, your nervousness, your uncertainty, or your perspiration show through.
- **Honestly.** More than ever, tell it like it is. There is little worse than being caught in a lie when you are already conveying bad news. Why would you want to run the risk of compounding the severity of what you are saying with a falsehood?
- **Succinctly.** Don't elaborate unless it is called for, and don't speculate. Say what you have to say and leave the stage, unless you are prepared to answer some questions. On occasion, we have arranged the conveyance of bad news in two or more stages. First, the manager reads an announcement to the assembled workers. Perhaps a written handout is provided that repeats the announcement. Later that day, after people have had a chance to process the news, the managers

reassemble the workers in small groups for a candid Q&A session.

- **Factually.** Make certain that whatever you say is factually true and (if appropriate) provable. Giving wrong information, even inadvertently, is counterproductive to your goals.

As you convey the bad news, provide data-based statements and give a realistic and honest estimate of the situation.

One of the most effective methods for conveying bad news is the "sandwich technique." It is quite simple to explain and utilize, and it is very effective when delivered properly. There are three basic steps:

First, provide a positive statement about progress being made.

Second, deliver the bad news.

Third, provide a positive statement and assessment about solutions going forward.

With this method of delivery, you have fulfilled your basic requirement (delivering the bad news to your targeted audience), but you have softened the blow somewhat by sandwiching it between two positive statements.

Finally, I always tell my clients that recognizing "bad" news as a prodrome can actually turn into "good" news. It's all a matter of perspective and perception.

26

The Blame Game

∎ ∎ ∎

Don't point fingers in a crisis. It's a tempting knee-jerk reaction, especially when you are in the right. Nevertheless, it is a risky move and a huge crisis communications error.

Rather, try to take the high ground. If you find yourself in a debate—whether an actual debate or a pseudodebate via the news media or social media outlets—try to explain your argument in a compelling and positive light, letting the audience draw its own conclusions. Look for examples in the Jeffersonian model of arguments: state your position so that there is no possible conclusion other than the one you are drawing.

This has the same effect as pointing a finger, but without actually doing it.

If this is a public health or safety issue, a better strategy is to bring people to your side of the crisis and enlist them as allies. The early days of any crisis are typically murky—facts need to be sifted and events have to be analyzed. But the public has a right to know what is being done to protect it. That now becomes your job.

Earlier in the book, in describing the E. coli outbreak at the Pat & Oscar's restaurant chain, we knew the brand name of the packaged product and the outside supplier who delivered the contaminated lettuce very early on. Despite pleadings from the news media, *we* never disclosed the name of the supplier (a name, by the way, that would have been meaningless to the restaurant patrons and the public at large). We did, however, state that we had provided the name of the supplier to the state and county departments of health, lest anyone think that we were trying to shield the supplier. The media could try to obtain the name from health officials, not from us.

The crisis communications message we conveyed was that we had determined that the problem had been caused by an outside supplier who had been identified and replaced. And, in the future, even though the lettuce was triple-washed before it reached our kitchens, we intended to hand-wash it one more time before serving it. When we held a media day, that was what we wanted the public to see. That was the message that we wanted to convey via our crisis communications activities: a new supplier and new safety measures. Laying blame would have served no purpose. That was for the lawyers to duke out later.

Your publics will stand behind you if they think you're standing behind them.

27

Crisis-Induced Stress

■ ■ ■

C risis management is vigilant decision making under stress.

In the next chapter, we will explore exactly what vigilant decisions are, how to make them, and how they can help you, but first let's talk about the stress you will feel when you are in a crisis and how that affects you and your communications. As Dr. Hans Selye, the father of modern stress management, once famously observed, "It's not the stress that kills us, it's our reaction to it."

Stress during a crisis not only is normal, but should be welcome. The by now well-known performance/stress curve (see Figure 27-1), which I displayed previously in my crisis management book, demonstrates that while too much stress, or a hyperarousal level, is bad for you and results in poor performance, too *little* stress, or too low an arousal level, has the same effect. What is required for optimum decision making during a crisis is a *moderate* stress response.

If you are too stressed, you will not be able to make vigilant decisions; conversely, with too little stress, your attitude may be the wildly inappropriate, "Who cares?"

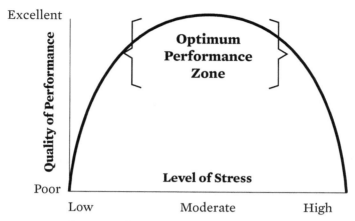

Figure 27.1 Performance/stress curve

In managing both your crisis and your crisis communications messages, it is appropriate and helpful to feel some stress. Don't fight it. That's counterproductive.

"In order to be effective under stress," said psychologist and author Dr. Harriet Braiker, "in order to heighten your own natural ability to achieve and make sound decisions during times of crises, the mind needs to be placed in a vigilant state."[1]

The best way to achieve moderate stress levels is to engage in crisis inoculation exercises. In other words: practice, practice, practice.

If you have a general sense of what is going on even before you get involved, let alone immersed, in the crisis, you will begin to feel some stress because you know what is coming and what is required of you. If you have never been through a crisis, you may feel a sense of panic and abject terror, fear of the unknown, or concern over your own vulnerability. But if you have been through a crisis or a crisis simulation, you will be better prepared to perform because you and your psychological and physiological selves know what to expect. Psychologists sometimes refer to this as *schemas*, "packets of knowledge that provide expectations about the activities we do [that] help us comprehend new situations with familiar details."[2]

Beilock, mentioned earlier, gives an example of someone entering a new restaurant for the first time. Even though she's never been to that restaurant before, she knows generally what to expect: a hostess will seat her, menus will be provided, food will be ordered, dinner will be served and eaten, and a check will be presented. This is a schema—the general knowledge of what to expect even in a brand-new restaurant you've never before visited.

But someone who has never been to *any* restaurant before—someone who lacks the schema—might feel so much stress in the new environment that he might just walk past the hostess and into the kitchen and start cooking his own meal.

Your crisis and the messages you need to convey are far more weighty issues than ordering a meal in a restaurant, but the analogy is apt. If you have a sense of the general schema of a crisis and of your communications requirements, you will not be overstressed.

A lack of this foreknowledge creates fear of the unknown, which can lead to panic and poor decisions. If that happens, you are likely to err not only in the management of the crisis but in the crisis communications component as well. You may feel challenged and threatened by every question that comes along and by every message that you need to convey.

You should also be alert for any signs of what I call a "bunker mentality," in which the senior executive retreats to a "bunker"—sometimes behind his locked office door; sometimes out of the office and unreachable—and is unable or unwilling to face the unfolding crisis. This is almost always a direct result of crisis-induced stress.

There are other negative effects of stress, such as analysis paralysis, where an issue is considered and considered and considered with no action. This serves no useful purpose; eventually you *must* act. If you delay, you are imperiling your management of the crisis.

This further complicates the job of the crisis communicator and may even call for a change in crisis management leadership.

Are you prepared to step up?

28

Making *Defensible* Decisions: Decision Making Under Crisis-Induced Stress

■ ■ ■

Vigilant decision making ensures that the best-quality decisions are made under stress, and vigilant decisions are *defensible decisions*.

If there is a possibility that you will at some time be called upon to communicate your company's crisis decisions one way or the other, knowing that you can demonstrate that a defensible decision was made in the heat of the acute crisis is crisis communications gold. It will be hard for your opponents to lay a glove on you.

The goal is to make decisions that will withstand second-guessing, withering cross-examination, courtroom testimony, government hearings, and media investigations. It also includes decisions that will pass muster with the public and be supported by your key constituents, once you have explained these decisions to them.

Important note: this does not mean you necessarily made the *right* decision, which is a stark, draconian measure of an absolute: right *or* wrong. It means that you made the *best* decision possible at the time, given the circumstances and the available information. And if you can demonstrate that, you can defend it.

A vigilant decision is one that is highly adaptive to the realities of the crisis; it is achieved by objectively collecting all available information, weighing the pros and cons, searching for other possible alternatives, and—most important—actually making a decision.

If you do this, you have the best chance of vigilantly reaching a sound, defensible decision that allows for updates based on the fluid situation in which you find yourself. Such decisions should not be made in isolation, but rather in a group (the crisis management group), and include the following seven steps:

1. Identify the problem, the crisis, as a decision that has to be made.
2. Brainstorm *all* possible ideas and alternative solutions.
3. Collect all available data within a reasonable time frame.
4. Weigh the pros and cons of *each* possible solution.
5. Select the best solution (or the least undesirable alternative).
6. Implement the decision.
7. Identify new problems as decisions that have to be made—in other words, start again at number 1 with updated information.

Here's why this is so important, not just in the management of the crisis, but in the crisis communications aspect as well. At some point, you are going to have to explain what you did and why—that is, why did you make such a controversial decision in the heat of the crisis? Anytime you are asked that question, the person asking it is not your friend. It is a highly charged question, and you are being put on the defensive. The person will want to know, for example, whether you panicked or whether you thought through the consequences of your actions.

If your response begins with an explanation of your vigilant decision-making process, and you can justify it, it is hard to be faulted. For example, in responding to a particular question, you can begin by saying something like, "That decision had to be made by 3:00 p.m. on the Friday in question. On that day, we had a fully staffed and qualified team of managers, technical people, and quality assurance people sitting with me at our crisis management table. Collectively, we represented more than 225 years of experience in the field. We considered the following five options, which were the only options open to us at the time." Then you list the options and explain why you rejected four of them. Then you say, "We therefore concluded that Option 5 was the most viable option that would address the problem as we knew it at that time, and with the information we had at the critical time, at 3:00 p.m. on that Friday.

"Now, on Monday morning, with new facts in hand, someone could come along and say we should have done something else. But we didn't have the luxury of waiting until Monday, and we certainly didn't have any unconsidered facts when the decision was due. We had to act on Friday, three days earlier."

This, as presented, is considered a defensible decision. Your explanation shows that it was not a hypervigilant (knee-jerk) reaction to events, but a well-thought-out, properly analyzed, and carefully considered response. Someone can always come along and play Monday-morning quarterback, but during game time—Friday, when *your* ass was on the line and decisive action was required—you and your team made the best decision available.

Moreover, through the information you laid out in this sample response, you demonstrated that you solicited and considered other options. You did not rush to judgment, you did not make the decision in isolation, and, once the decision was made, you implemented it before the required deadline. If you can do that either in litigation or in an interview, you are essentially bulletproof.

Also, what did you actually do on Monday when new information was available? Did you modify your decision? Good; that shows that even though you had previously decided and acted, you still were open to alternative solutions as new information became available and was appropriately considered by the crisis management team.

You want to try to avoid falling into any of the following four maladaptive decision-making models:

- **Unconflicted inertia.** A refusal to consider any alternatives, opting instead to just go on as though it is business as usual.
- **Unconflicted change.** Just following the last idea that was said or suggested.
- **Defensive avoidance.** Evasion and unwillingness to accept reality, looking for the path of least resistance and highest acceptance.
- **Hypervigilance.** A knee-jerk reaction, running from pillar to post. People in crisis who are said to be "running around like a chicken with its head cut off" are in this mode.

In making decisions, and especially in trying to determine the best course of action, it is perfectly all right, if not advantageous, to approach each possible decision with a healthy dose of skepticism. In so doing, you are in effect serving notice that you want whoever is advocating a particular position to convince you of why *it* is the most desirable alternative.

At the University of Chicago, a school that prides itself on teaching students to be skeptical, a distinguished professor once observed, "Commitment without skepticism perpetuates mediocrity; but skepticism without commitment is paralysis."[1]

29

Apologies: Shakespeare—
Still Right After
All These Years

■ ■ ■

To apologize or not to apologize . . . that is a question?

When you do something wrong or you accidentally hurt someone, you say you're sorry. Didn't your mother teach you that? Why, then, does it seem that companies are reluctant to do the same when their crisis causes injuries, damages, or pain?

First, I think things are improving. It seems that more companies today understand the importance of demonstrating compassion to the public during times of crisis, and for that I applaud them. But typically, in my experience, well-meaning attorneys sometimes throw up roadblocks that prevent a company from saying, "We're sorry" or expressing any degree of remorse.

We touched on this briefly earlier, but depending upon how an apology is worded, it can be construed as an admission of wrongdoing, and that's the last thing your lawyer wants you to do. Such an admission would have an excellent chance of resulting in a substantial increase in the amount of any damages you may have to pay, should you be found liable in litigation.

But here's where I part companies with unbudging lawyers: I am not proposing that you fall on your sword at the first opportunity, but if your company is involved in a crisis, and people have been injured as a result of the crisis, as a crisis communications strategy if nothing else, you owe it to your public to demonstrate that you have a heart, that you are caring and not just a cold, unfeeling corporate entity. You need to demonstrate compassion. You need to express some empathy, if not actual sympathy. You need to express some remorse that this tragedy occurred. You can express all of these things without admitting or even suggesting culpability.

The problem is that when you say nothing, you come across as unfeeling and unsympathetic to the suffering that people are experiencing. Giving you the benefit of the doubt that this is not an accurate portrayal of who you really are, why would you want people to think it is?

As stated before, if people want to sue you, you will be sued. Expressing regret that an accident happened is not going to get you sued, nor is not saying anything going to prevent litigation. If you accept that, why wouldn't you want to go out of your way to let your myriad publics know that what happened was an aberration and you are saddened by it?

In the E. coli outbreak at the restaurant chain discussed earlier, the full-page ad we placed said, "WE'RE SORRY" in big, bold letters. But it said that we were sorry that people got sick in our restaurant, even though it wasn't our fault. That was sincere; company management did indeed feel sorry that some people had been taken ill and required medical treatment. People knew that it wasn't the chain's fault. No lawsuits resulted because the company said it was sorry.

When you are in a crisis, if you have assembled a diverse crisis management team to assist and advise you, you may find yourself being subjected to varied points of view depending upon the speakers and their specific training. But you need to decide what is best for the company, its employees, and its stakeholders and then act accordingly.

The best marching orders I ever received from a client as I was about to take over the management of a full-blown crisis came from Chuck Boppell, at the time chairman and CEO of Worldwide Restaurants, Inc., owner of the Pat & Oscar's restaurant chain, which was going through that E. coli outbreak. On a conference call with executives and a slew of in-house and outside attorneys, at the end of the call, Boppell said to me for all to hear, "Take charge, and don't let the lawyers run the show!"

And while there was discussion and debate about the ad's wording, no one held up a stop sign, and the crisis was successfully resolved; business was not only restored but significantly increased, and the chain's reputation in the community was stronger than ever.

There are certain essential elements of a "good" apology, and you should be aware of them.

If you are going to issue an apology, it is better to do it early, while it still looks like it was your idea and, therefore, is sincere. If the public thinks an apology is called for and you are slow to the gate, it will look as if you were shamed into it, and your credibility will be diminished by your delay. That's almost as bad as saying nothing.

You need to choose the language of your apology carefully. An effective apology requires strategic thinking, reservoirs of goodwill, and communications skills.

A good apology:

- Is not self-serving.
- Is directed at the injured parties.
- Is accompanied by reparations or a cessation of the conduct that made the apology necessary in the first place.

Keeping these factors in mind may explain why Rupert Murdoch's full-page apology in the wake of News Corporation's phone-hacking crisis was considered disingenuous, at best.

As you may recall, in 2011 it was finally revealed how Murdoch's media empire, especially the British tabloid *News of the World*, had been able to score such tremendous news scoops. The editors and reporters cheated. Well, actually, they committed criminal acts by illegally hacking into private telephone conversations, including some by Prince Charles and the late Princess Diana. As the Brits might say, this wasn't cricket, nor was it remotely legal.

Murdoch and his news media empire—which includes the *Times* (London), the *Wall Street Journal*, and many others—were brought to their knees when their misdeeds were revealed. Editor after editor denied knowledge of any hacking, and then were soon terminated or charged with a crime for their role in the scandal when the truth was ultimately revealed. In an effort to show how sincere he was about reforming, Murdoch made the unprecedented decision to shutter the *News of the World* (the 160-year-old paper that was at the center of the crisis), thereby putting hundreds of innocent people out of work—the many paying for the sins of a few.

Murdoch and company, including his son and heir apparent James and longtime editor and close Murdoch associate Rebekah Brooks, continually denied involvement of any kind, including initially denying that such a thing had ever taken place. For a bizarrely long stretch of time, the two Murdochs seemed to go out of their way to defend Brooks. A humiliated Murdoch and his son James were both forced to testify before Parliament. And when Murdoch was asked pointedly by MP Jim Sheridan, "Mr. Murdoch, do you accept that ultimately you are responsible for this whole fiasco?,"[1] Murdoch said tersely, "No."

But, of course, they were; the world knew it, and ultimately someone said that they needed to apologize. And so on July 27, 2011, Murdoch took out full-page ads in all of his British papers that, under a large, bold headline, read as follows:

We are sorry.

The *News of the World* was in the business of holding others to account.

It failed when it came to itself.

We are sorry for the wrongdoing that occurred.

We are deeply sorry for the hurt suffered by the individuals affected.

We regret not acting faster to sort things out.

I realise [British spelling] that simply apologizing is not enough.

Our business was founded on the idea that a free and open press should be a positive force in society. We need to live up to this.

In the coming days, as we take further concrete steps to resolve these issues and make amends for the damage they have caused, you will hear more from us.

Sincerely,

/s/

Rupert Murdoch

It was well crafted, but it was generally dismissed as too self-serving and not at all sincere. An apology ad that douses itself in a bath of humility fails after so many boisterous denials of involvement, let alone knowledge and complicity. Plus, it was very late in coming, and it gave the feeling that it was being trotted out simply because other strategies had failed. In short, people didn't buy it.

Contrast Murdoch's apology with David Letterman's after the late night talk show host went on the air in 2009 and proactively revealed his affair with a female assistant—an affair which he had reason to believe was about to be disclosed publicly by a failed blackmailer who had gained access to Letterman's e-mails and demanded money to keep quiet. Letterman instead blew the whistle on himself, and after disclosing the affair, said:

> My wife, Regina, she has been horribly hurt by my behavior. And when something happens like that, if you hurt a person and it's your responsibility, you try to fix it. At that point there is [sic] only two things that can happen: Either you are going to make some progress and get it fixed, or you're gonna fall short and perhaps not get it fixed. So let me tell you folks, I got my work cut out for me.[2]

Letterman's comments meet all three of the criteria cited earlier for a good apology: it was not self-serving, it was aimed at the injured party, and it included a promise of cessation of such behavior in the future.

In the same vein, U.S. Senator Michael Crapo, a Republican from Idaho, was stopped by police after running a red light in Washington, DC, in December 2012. Having failed a field sobriety test, he was promptly arrested and taken to jail, where he posted a nominal bail and was released in less than five hours. Before the next sun set, he released this statement:

> I am deeply sorry for the actions that resulted in this circumstance. I made a mistake for which I apologize to my family, my Idaho constituents and any others who have put their trust in me. I accept total responsibility and will deal with whatever penalty comes my way in this matter. I will also undertake measures to ensure that this circumstance is never repeated.

It is a sad commentary on today's society that such incidents are so commonplace today that the only surprise would have been if this exact statement had *not* been issued. Crapo certainly had plenty of examples to emulate. But the good Senator has other problems that also will require some apologies: he is a devout Mormon, the religion that forbids its members from drinking alcohol (among other restrictions), and Crapo has said publicly in the past that he does not drink.

The social media site Tumblr went dark for several hours in late 2012, resulting in a loss of use and a loss of some 100 million views. When service was restored, here's what Tumblr posted to its users and staff. See if you think this is a good apology:

> Our engineering processes seriously failed this afternoon and cost you and your blogs nearly 4 hours of downtime and almost 100 views.
>
> Painfully, this isn't the first time this winter [we've] had to give you similar news.
>
> When incidents like this happen, our entire engineering team comes online to support the recovery as needed. Immediately, we begin taking every measure to protect from the uncovered issue in the future.
>
> We are constantly working to shore up our processes and solidify the stability of this quickly growing network, even more so as we've fallen behind in the last few weeks.
>
> Tumblr's success is supporting your success, and we take this mission very seriously.[3]

So, if you were Tumblr's crisis communicator, how would you rate this offering? Plenty of rhetoric, but how does it measure up as an apology?

Give yourself an A if you gave Tumblr an F.

Simply stated, there is no apology here. It is nothing more than a self-serving statement of "how great we are" . . . except this time. And the previous time it happened, their offering was equally wanting. What Tumblr said would have been much better if it had included two simple words: I'm sorry.

In *The Iliad,* Homer wrote, "There is strength in the union even of very sorry men."

With that thought in mind, I have long maintained that a timely and effective apology would have saved Nixon's presidency. That's something to think about when you are in a crisis involving your company and you contemplate an apology.

30

Crisis Advertising: Does It Work?

■ ■ ■

Paid advertising has a place in crisis communications, but perhaps not the one you think. If it is used properly, it can be an effective part of a much bigger crisis communications strategy.

The public today is a lot smarter than ever and knows that since you are paying for your own ad, you have complete editorial control over its content. Try to avoid making the ad seem self-serving. This is not the place to assign or suggest blame.

Essentially, there are only two reasons for a paid ad in the midst of a crisis: first, as an expression of compassion for those who have been injured, and second, as a source of information (for example, here's how we're going to fix the problem or here's whom to call to file a claim). You've probably seen these in newspapers, often written in the form of a letter and signed by the CEO, or on TV, featuring the CEO. These can be effective if done properly.

If your crisis is ongoing (say, an environmental cleanup), a series of paid ads or TV spots would be an effective way to talk about your progress. However, in this situation, social media can be even more effective, to say nothing of much cheaper. YouTube, in particular, gives you the ability not only to bring numerous updates to your publics, but to do so from a series of spokespersons, perhaps selected based on their areas of responsibilities, their expertise, or their geographical locations.

Take these messages directly and unfiltered to the key constituencies that you have established through conventional and social media means. This is where all those thousands of posts and thousands of followers you've been cultivating for so long begin to pay off. Remember, what you tweet can be retweeted, thereby adding more punch to your message because your words are now being shared on a peer-to-peer network.

Plus, if your message is newsworthy, which is likely during a crisis, the mainstream media, which monitor social media 24/7, may pick up on it as well. This will further increase your reach and present your message as "news," rather than merely a "post"—or at least that will be the perception. This helps the gravitas of your message because it is likely that someone who is discussing the crisis with a friend or colleague might easily say, "I saw the story in the *Chicago Tribune*," or, "I heard the CEO on NBC News," instead of "I saw this on YouTube" or on so-and-so's Twitter feed.

31

Crisis Communications Plans

■   ■   ■

t should come as no surprise to readers of this book that I am an
advocate of written crisis communications plans, but that recommendation comes with a number of caveats.

When I am working with new clients on proactive crisis management and crisis communications assignments, I generally ask to
review any current plans, and some common flaws that I often discover are worth noting.

Many of these plans are simply too big and cumbersome. At
some point, the writer of the plan decided to err on the side of all-
inclusiveness and thought that adding the kitchen sink was better
than omitting it. In a crisis, where speed is of the essence, having
to thumb though the Manhattan phone book is counterproductive. Rather, people and their backups should be trained and tested
with simulations, and written plans should be merely a thin outline
of assignments, phone numbers, some basic strategy, and a mission statement. Rely more on your people. Good people, if they are

properly trained, tend to make good decisions during periods of crisis-induced stress; if untrained, they can flounder.

Many plans that I review are outdated. Depending on the size of your company, you may have an annual employee attrition rate north of 10 to 15 percent. If Joe Johnson is listed as a member of your team by virtue of his position within the company (say, director of quality assurance at a food company), and he is transferred or leaves the company altogether, has the plan been updated to identify his replacement? How many other Joe Johnsons are there at your company in different divisions? And who has the responsibility for making certain that the plan is updated? We usually have a client's human resources department put a flag on the employee's payroll or employee record. If the status of someone who is on the team changes, HR is usually in the loop. The flag tells HR to notify *someone.*

Many people at large companies, I have found, are simply unaware. Does everyone on the team know that she is *on* the team? Using the example in the preceding paragraph, if Joe Johnson's replacement is named, does the replacement know that she's also on a crisis management or crisis communications team with added duties and responsibilities? Has anyone ever given her a copy of the plan? Has she been trained? Whose job is it to make sure that these things are done?

Many plans have never been tested. An untested plan is like a fire extinguisher that's never been tested or refilled. Testing the plan on a regular basis affords you the opportunity to train and educate the new people who previously never knew that they had additional responsibilities. This avoids the very real problem of finding your fire extinguisher empty when the flames start licking at your heels.

By definition, a crisis communications plan will be thinner than a crisis management plan; it may be as light as a single page or a small computer file. That file should be readily accessible to all concerned. When I first began in crisis management, members of a corporate crisis management team needed to keep multiple hard copies of a crisis management binder at work, at home, at their vacation homes, and anywhere else they might be. Digital communications have simplified that. If you work for a company that gives you access to the server 24/7, you can access the plan anywhere that you have an Internet connection. Smaller companies might want to put plans on apps like Dropbox, which can automatically update any changes in a plan to all devices: computers, laptops, smartphones, tablets, and so on. As a result, if a new replacement with new contact information is hired, one change to the master file on *any* Dropbox device will automatically update that information to everyone at the same time.

During a crisis, the responsibility of the crisis communications team is to craft and disseminate messages that explain the crisis, bringing perception and reality into sync. Presumably, during the calm period, you have been actively creating and cultivating your key constituents, building a database of followers and favorable bloggers, and also mainstream media reporters, community and religious leaders, opinion makers, legislative representatives, government regulators, law enforcement officials, and other such groups. Your portion of the crisis communications plan may just be a comprehensive list of audiences that you need to reach and the best ways to reach them. It need not be fancy, but it needs to be checked for accuracy periodically and updated accordingly.

During a crisis, your time is better spent shaping and disseminating the series of messages that will be required.

There is another benefit to a written plan: simply that it's written down, and that is always a good idea. All teams should have backups, and if your backup has to fill in for you, a written plan will prove most useful to him. Also, if the person in charge of crisis communications leaves (or dies), his successor has a good handle on things from day one.

Finally, one weakness I have noticed in some crisis communications plans is the communications approval process. How many people need to sign off on a message before it's communicated? The bigger the crisis, the more layers of approval are likely to be needed. When speed counts—and speed *always* counts in a crisis—this may cause a time-consuming roadblock.

I recommend that the approval process for messages be memorialized in writing in the plan, so that there is no confusion, and I recommend that it be streamlined. Here's whose approvals are usually essential:

The CEO, who should review messages for content and tone.

The corporate counsel, who should review messages for legal issues.

The head of corporate communications, also for content, tone, and message points.

Plus, anyone whose specific duties and training are relevant to the crisis at hand. For example, for an industrial accident, you might include your head of health and safety; for an environmental crisis, the head of your environmental sciences department should be consulted; for a food-related crisis, your director of quality assurance and food safety should be in the loop. These people should be asked to review crisis communications messages for accuracy in their respective areas.

The point is, keep the review of key messages as simple and as facile as possible so that you can be nimble on your crisis communications feet.

32

The Failure
of Business Schools

■   ■   ■

Our nation's business schools are failing their students.

While some, although certainly far from all, offer a course in crisis management, these seem to be mostly classes on theories, case studies, or academic treatises, or that offer guest speakers (like me). Interesting though these may be, they have little or no utilitarian value in the real world. None of these schools actually teaches its MBA students the hands-on skills they will need to manage a crisis should one befall them at their new company after graduation.

And this, in my view, is a great failing that should be remedied.

When I subtitled my earlier book on crisis management "Planning for the Inevitable," I wasn't being flip, just prescient. Finding a company that has never suffered a crisis is as rare as spotting the Abominable Snowman.

This point was first driven home to me some years ago by the late Gene Webb, associate dean and professor at the Stanford University Graduate School of Business when we first met. Gene had just read *Crisis Management* and was anxious to meet me when he learned that we had a mutual friend in common. He asked our friend to arrange a meeting in Los Angeles; Gene flew down, and we met for a very enjoyable lunch.

At the time of my book's publication, crisis management was still a new field, but Gene saw the importance of the topic and immediately saw the benefit of teaching the subject to his graduate students. He asked if I would help him put together what ultimately became the first crisis management curriculum ever offered in a business school, and I agreed. When the first class was set to convene the following fall, Gene called again and said in so many words, "Well, now that you've helped create the beast, you've got to come up here and help me teach it." And I did. This was a very pragmatic curriculum, designed to impart tried-and-true real-world methodologies to the class, to give students not only theoretical knowledge (Gene's forte) but actual real-world skills (my specialty) that they could take with them after graduation.

Unfortunately, Gene died within a few years, and the class died with him. Occasionally, over the years, I have tried to interest other business schools in offering a *pragmatic* crisis management class to second-year graduate students, but while I have seen a great deal of interest (or at least lip service), I have found that if it isn't a topic that the dean or another leading professor has a personal interest in, the discussions are merely cordial conversations that have no effect.

The Harvard Business School, which enjoys a very fine reputation, is known for its case study approach to subjects, but all the case studies in the world will not prepare a Harvard MBA for being a member of a crisis management team, let alone assuming a leadership position during an actual crisis. This is not a slight against

Harvard, for I could make the same statement about most other business schools, too.

When I used to interview newly minted MBA graduates as prospective candidates for employment at Lexicon Communications Corp., and they told me that they had studied crisis management or crisis communications at such-and-such graduate school of business—and even used my *Crisis Management* book as a text!—I would ask one or two probing questions, and soon discover that they had nothing to contribute to helping to manage a crisis. I don't mean that they lacked experience (after all, what newly-minted college or business school graduate has any real-world experience?), but that they lacked even relevant intern experience or any pragmatic knowledge of the exigencies of a crisis. In short, I never hired a business school graduate as a prospective member of a crisis management or crisis communications team for us or for any of my clients. When companies in crisis come to my firm for assistance, they are seeking solid experience and a proven track record in crisis management and crisis communications; they will not sit still for academic theories that don't even come close to addressing the actual crisis at hand.

A professor I know at a leading university that I will not mention taught crisis management to graduate students until recently. He has a background in sociology, and he approached the subject of crisis management with that particular bias.

One day over lunch some years ago at his faculty club, he allowed as how he had been reviewing the original Tylenol crisis, trying to figure out the mindset of the perpetrator who had put cyanide into the capsules, especially since no legitimate ransom demand had ever been received and no culprit was ever caught. His obsession seemed to be the total inability to offer a plausible explanation for the killings. And since he knew that I knew members of the J&J crisis management team, he wanted to float his latest theory past me in hopes that I would pass it along. In his view, the person who had laced Tylenol capsules with cyanide and killed seven people had been weaned off his mother's breast at too young an age, and the poisonings were his way of lashing out. (I'm not making this up; as I said back in Chapter 1, you *can't* make this stuff up.) This was the way in which he approached the broad subject and the way he was teaching crisis management to his unsuspecting students.

Setting aside any discussion of the merits (or absence thereof) of his theory, the question is simply: What in the world does this have to do with crisis management? Is there an FBI database of premature breast weaners in the Chicago area that could be consulted in a desperate search for suspects? Or, perhaps he thought that J&J's human resources department had such a database of its employees. And when one of this educator's former students is out in the workforce and is asked to serve on a crisis management team, what might his contributions be, or how would he be received by his peers, if this is what he has as a crisis management foundation, or worse, offers up as a suggestion?

Remember what I said in discussing the Wendy's crisis: the company's job is to manage the crisis, and law enforcement's job is to catch the culprit. Whether this educator's theory was sound or not, it was not the company's issue to ponder.

Business and communication schools that offer *only* academic or theory-based curricula on crisis management or crisis communications are doing a grave disservice to their students. Those schools are graduating students who think they are prepared for crisis work, and they most decidedly are not.

I feel strongly that the nation's business and communications schools, especially at the graduate level, should think outside academia and bring in real crisis management practitioners—people who have actually managed business crises or crisis communications—and have those people teach crisis management and crisis communications *skills* to students as a way to prepare them for the day when the company they're working for suddenly suffers a megacrisis and the CEO is looking for knowledgeable people to help join or even one day lead a crisis team. Give the students real-world crisis simulations to manage, and let them make mistakes, but learn from those mistakes from practitioners, not academicians or theorists. Let the students handle the crisis communications for a major crisis in a simulation. See how they do when they have to face the media and deliver essential messages in a life-or-death situation.

Business schools are supposed to teach tomorrow's business leaders, and the leading business schools are teaching those who someday soon will become CEOs of the nation's leading businesses.

We have already seen the ill effects of business leaders who are clueless about crisis management and crisis communications. Isn't it about time that our business schools set out to rectify this obvious shortcoming? This gross deficiency is why I maintain today's graduate business and communications schools are failing their students.

One more point about business schools. *New York Times* technology columnist David Pogue relates an experience he had when he was teaching a class at Columbia University's Business School. He was lecturing on consumer tech success and disaster stories, and he zeroed in on how many tech companies rush unfinished products full of bugs to market, creating crises in the marketplace because of unhappy customers and bad press. Pogue said that he had hoped to convert the students to the "doing what's right" school of thought "before they became corrupted by the corporate world."

> But it was too late.
> To my astonishment, hands shot up all over the room. These budding chief executives wound up telling me, politely, that I was wrong. That there's a solid business case for shipping half-finished software. "You get the revenue

flowing," one young lady told me. "You don't want to let your investors down, right? You can always fix the software later."

You can always fix the software later. Wow.

That's right. Use your customers as beta testers. Don't worry about burning them. Don't worry about souring them on your company name forever. [See Chapter 11, "Protecting Your Brand."] There will always be more customers where those came from, right? That "ignore the customer" approach hasn't worked out so well for Hewlett-Packard, Netflix and Cisco. All three suffered enormous public black eyes. All three looked like they had no idea what they were doing.

Maybe all those M.B.A.'s pouring into the workplace know something we don't. Maybe there's actually a shrewd master plan that the common folk can't even fathom.

But maybe, too, there's a solid business case to be made for factoring public reaction and the customer's interest into big business decisions.[1]

Just as there's a case for factoring in crisis management and crisis communications, too.

33

Speed Is of the Essence

■ ■ ■

few years ago, a large, global insurance company that often
taps us to represent its policyholders in crises contacted us on
behalf of one of its clients, a national hotel chain.

We are one of a small handful of crisis management firms on
this insurance company's crisis panel. Some of its policyholders
have a crisis rider that allows them immediate access to a crisis
firm, without having to take valuable time to sign contracts. This
gives us the opportunity to hit the ground running in the event of
a crisis with any of the insurance company's policyholders. This is
critical, since, as this chapter discusses, in a crisis, speed is of the
essence.

In this instance, a female guest at the hotel had accused one
of the staff maintenance workers of "inappropriate behavior"
toward her during her stay, which had taken place some weeks earlier. She never stated or even implied that anything inappropriate
had actually happened between her and the worker, and she had
not reported this alleged behavior while she was still a guest at the

hotel, but through her attorney she accused the hotel worker of being, well, *forward*. Her lawyer never filed suit and had not at that time reported the issue to law enforcement. He just sent a demand letter for $20 million(!), or else he was going to hold a news conference in 72 hours and denounce the hotel publicly.

Some people might describe this as attempted extortion, not the typical actions of an upstanding member of the bar.

On the morning we got involved, the primary client contact—a young woman who served as the company's risk manager—arranged a large conference call, which she asked me to run. Our purpose was to get everyone on the same page with what was being alleged and what the worker said when he was interviewed, and to determine our best crisis strategies. There were more than a dozen people on the call, mostly lawyers, plus the client, the insurance company's crisis management supervisor, and me and some of my staff. There were only two people on the call who had ever been involved in a crisis before: the insurance supervisor and me.

As we were getting the fast rundown, it was obvious that the claimant's story was full of holes. For example, her lawyer claimed that she was so frightened that she had locked herself in her room in the afternoon and never came out until morning. However, her electronic keycard record told a different story. She had been in and out of her room multiple times during the afternoon, evening, and night, and she had even logged on to the hotel's public access computer in the middle of the night to chat online with her boyfriend in Hungary. It was obvious to everyone that this was a bogus claim, but the hotel chain wanted us to shut the story down before anything happened, and certainly before any news conference or any news of the claim leaked out, even though we counseled it on the unlikelihood of that actually taking place or of such a demonstrably false story getting any "play" in Los Angeles. For example, while it was a well-known national chain, it was not a high-end hotel in Beverly Hills, and the alleged victim was not a celebrity of any kind. There just wasn't anything to interest the Los Angeles media, in our opinion.

During the conference call, I was quickly asking questions and giving assignments to those who could contribute to the management of the crisis, and I must have been going pretty fast. These situations are akin to triage in a hospital emergency room, which if you've never been there before can seem overwhelming your first time, but if you have some experience, you have a better understanding of what's happening.

Suddenly, the young risk manager—our main client contact—called out in a loud and panicked voice: "Stop! Stop! It's all going too fast! Can't we slow this whole thing down?"

I suddenly felt sorry for her. It was clear that she was in way over her head and was getting dizzy, especially from the way the insurance crisis manager and I were talking in rapid bursts, sort of shorthand, having done this sort of thing so many times in the past.

I then explained to her, slowly and I trust patiently, that in a crisis, speed is of the essence. I certainly was not trying to "talk down to her"; I was, however, explaining that we could accomplish exactly what we were being asked to do, but we had to move swiftly. In this particular crisis, there was a clock ticking, and we needed to be mindful of that. We didn't set the agenda, and we didn't start the clock, but if her company wanted this crisis resolved, before the threatened news conference was held, we needed to move fast. In short, even if we had wanted to, we couldn't stop.

She soon recovered her composure and allowed us to get back to our jobs.

The bottom line was that the crisis was resolved successfully by the end of the week. Total payout to the hotel guest and the blackmailing lawyer? Zero.

Had we dragged our feet, we might not have been so fortunate.

Had we dragged our feet, the much-feared negativity might have gotten some traction.

In a crisis, speed is of the essence.

34

Rising to the Occasion

■ ■ ■

There is a tide in the affairs of men
Which, taken at the flood, leads on to fortune;
Omitted, all the voyage of their life
Is bound in shallows and in miseries.
On such a full sea are we now afloat,
And we must take the current when it serves,
Or lose our ventures.[1]

In the late 1980s and early 1990s, I represented the giant defense contractor Northrop Corp., prior to its merger with Grumman. The company's crisis at that time was exceedingly public and well covered by the national media, so I can mention it here. Northrop was the target of at least five Justice Department investigations and faced a litany of more than 140 charges alleging that the company had falsified test data on the MX missile, falsified test data on the Marine Corps' Harrier jet gyroscopes, overcharged the government on the cutting-edge B-2 stealth bomber, and bribed officials of the South Korean government to secure military contracts. To compound matters, the company's stock was tanking, and there was speculation that the company might not survive the myriad of crises confronting it. I was on the crisis management team, in charge of crisis communications, and there was little positive news no matter where we looked.

The crisis management and crisis communications teams consisted of just a small handful of men. One day, when things looked particularly bleak, we met in the company's corporate boardroom. We had been seated for several minutes when Northrop's then-executive vice president and team leader, Les Daly, walked in and took his place at the head of the table. The room was silent, and Daly did not speak for several minutes. Many of those present expected him to throw in the towel and announce that the company was going to declare bankruptcy, be taken over, or worse. And then, after looking around the room and making eye contact with each of us individually, he began to quote the end of one of Shakespeare's most famous soliloquies, the St. Crispin's Day speech (more commonly known today as the "Band of Brothers" speech) from *King Henry V*. It was dawn, just before the pivotal battle of Agincourt in 1415, as the Bard wrote it, when Henry's beleaguered and badly outnumbered English soldiers had no reason to hope that they would live out the day against a superior and well-rested French army. Seeing the bloodied and forlorn faces of his men, Henry rallied his troops in a stirring speech, saying, among other things, that he would not wish for one man more to fight on their side, and the fewer of us who fight the battle, the greater our share of honor when we prevail:

> *We few, we happy few, we band of brothers;*
> *For he today that sheds his blood with me*
> *Shall be my brother. . . .*[2]

Henry had imbued his men with the will to go on against impossible odds, and that spirit helped lead them on to win the day. Les Daly's speech had the same effect, and the besieged company overcame incredible odds and, despite some legal setbacks at the time and a very large fine, Northrop Grumman today is one of the world's leading defense contractors.

When dealing with a client's crisis, I often think back to Les Daly and how his leadership helped motivate his beleaguered company and his crisis management team to battle on despite the steep odds and the clamorous naysayers.

The one thing that is always needed in any crisis situation, and that sometimes is in critically short supply, is leadership—bold, decisive leadership. And in the absence of an in-control leader, trying to formulate and implement an effective crisis management plan or crisis communications strategy becomes problematic when the ship is rudderless.

One of the biggest mistakes that companies that are in a crisis make is inaction. Sometimes it's inertia caused by fear, denial, analysis paralysis, or wishful thinking that the problem will simply go away. The reasons don't matter as much as the calamitous result. You can't manage a crisis by just sitting there on the sidelines as a passive observer. The situation is not going to improve on its own, and the longer you delay, not only will the crisis grow, but so, too, will the voices of your critics, which will become louder and more firmly entrenched.

The stakes in a crisis are often so enormous that fear—fear of the unknown, fear of making a mistake, fear of losing the company—can be palpable, especially when so many people are taking potshots at you from so many different positions. At those times, take solace from Winston Churchill's wisdom: "Nothing in life is so exhilarating as to be shot at without result."

There are ample opportunities for individual leadership in a crisis, and not just from the top. Nowhere is this more true than in the crisis communications aspect of the event. While the CEO may turn out to be the primary spokesperson, the person who crafts and manages the communications messages during a crisis is involved in all aspects of the crisis and will interact with all the key players, especially the CEO. This is a chance to be looked upon and relied upon as an effective team player, one who can think outside of the box when necessary and help keep everyone on message. It is a central, pivotal role in a crisis, for it helps shape perception. Most of all, it is a chance to shine.

When the seas are calm and everyone on the crew simply goes about his job, no one person really stands out. That's fine. But when a crisis hits, and emotions and sometimes panic run high, *this* is where someone back in the pack has a chance to surge ahead. *This* is where reputations are made. *This* can be the fast track to the corner office.

This is the rising tide that can lead on to fortune.

Don't hesitate. Rise to the occasion and take charge of your crisis with confidence, conviction, and character.

However, as we've seen with poor crisis performers, like BP's Tony Hayward, this also is when reputations of the *other* kind are made.

In virtually any crisis, it is difficult to overcome blatant lying, hypocrisy, and lack of credibility. But you have it within your power to choose to sidestep these minefields by your words and by your deeds.

In some 30 years of helping clients in all sorts of crisis situations, I've seen it all—virtually every conceivable sort of crisis and every type of crisis manager. I can report that Virgil had it right: fortune does, indeed, favor the bold.

Be bold, and may your biggest crisis be an embarrassment of riches.

Notes

■ ■ ■

PREFACE

1. A geobyte is a 1 followed by 30 digits and is equal to about 1,000 bron-tobytes, which is approximately 1,000 yottabytes, which is about 1,000 zettabytes, which is about 1,000 exabytes, which is about 1,000 petabytes, which is about 1,000 terabytes, which is about 1,000 giga-bytes ... or just think of it as the digital equivalent of a barrel of ink.

2. Trying to learn from crisis *successes* is misleading and sometimes dangerous. Many companies that wish to better their chances of surviving a crisis mistakenly focus on trying to copy the success of others. Since no two crises are identical, it is unlikely that yours will be an exact duplicate of someone else's. So, trying to emulate what one company did in its crisis might be akin to pounding that proverbial square peg into the round hole. However, in my experience, there are more chances that pitfalls similar to those that tripped up a company will be strewn in your path, so studying the mistakes and failures of companies in crisis offers you a better chance to learn what to avoid.

CHAPTER 1

1. Tony Hayward, speaking to a group of TV and print reporters on May 30, 2010, on the Gulf of Mexico shore. The insensitive and ill-considered quote was widely reported, including in Jad Mouawad and Clifford Krauss, "Another Torrent BP Works to Stem: Its CEO," *New York Times*, June 3, 2010. An NBC-TV News video clip of the quote may be viewed at http://www.youtube.com/watch?v=MTdKa9eWNFw.

2. Brett Clanton, "New Tactic Might Seal Leaking Well Sooner, BP CEO Says," *Houston Chronicle*, May 5, 2010.
3. Skye News interview, May 18, 2010, that was widely reported, including in Rowena Mason, "Gulf of Mexico Oil Spill: BP Insists Oil Spill Impact 'Very Modest,'" *Telegraph*, May 18, 2010. See the video clip at http://www.youtube.com/watch?v=dseMhu5IjHo.
4. Tim Webb, "BP Boss Admits Job on the Line Over Gulf Oil Spill," *Guardian*, May 14, 2010.
5. Bettina Boxall, "Oil Spill Size Near Upper Range of Earlier Estimates," *Los Angeles Times*, August 3, 2010.
6. "BP's CEO Testifies Before Congress," June 27, 2010, http://www.cnnstudentnews.cnn.com/TRANSCRIPTS/1006/17/qmb.01.html.
7. Hayward's testimony before Congress, and as reported online by Michael Newman, *Slate.com*, http://www.slate.com/articles/news_and_politics/politics/2010/06/thejoe_and_tony_show.html, and the CNN hearing transcripts, "BP's CEO Testifies Before Congress," June 17, 2010.
8. John M. Broder, "BP's Chief Offers Answers, but Not to Liking of House Committee," *New York Times*, June 17, 2010.
9. Ibid.
10. Stanley Reed, "Series of Write-Downs Leads to a Loss at BP," *New York Times*, July 31, 2012.
11. Monica Langley, "Hayward Defends Tenure, BP's Spill Response," *Wall Street Journal*, July 30, 2010.
12. Julia Werdigier, "Hayward Defends BP's Safety Record," *New York Times*, September 15, 2010
13. "BP Settles with U.S. for $4.5 Billion in Gulf Spill," Associated Press, November 15, 2012.

CHAPTER 2

1. The Chinese word for crisis, *wei-ji*, is made up of the two syllables and characters for "danger" and "opportunity," thus graphically establishing that a crisis is, indeed, a turning point for better or worse, simultaneously containing the key elements of both danger *and* opportunity (see figure). However, in fairness to opposing points of view, regardless of how myopically wrongheaded they are, at least one Ivy League academic who specializes in Asian languages and civilizations, and who seemingly has way too much time on his hands, takes issue publicly with this fairly well-established concept. He writes that rather than "opportunity," the second Chinese character denotes "an incipient moment; crucial point (when something begins or changes)." He may be enlightened to learn that in the *real* (as opposed to the *academic*) world, a "crucial point" is, in fact, a crossroads, a turning point,

where a company that is in crisis or is about to be immersed in one has the chance to seize and master that "incipient moment" and turn the tide in its favor to secure a favorable outcome. We refer to this as "opportunity," and it is largely determined by the manner in which the crisis is managed. He also lectures his suffering readers that those who believe that opportunity can emerge from crisis "are engaging in muddled thinking that is a danger to society, for it lulls people into welcoming crises as unstable situations from which they can benefit. Adopting a feel-good attitude toward adversity may not be the most rational, realistic approach to its solution." This argument is absurd. As someone who has practiced crisis management in the real world for more than 30 years, I can say two things with absolute certainty. First, no one I know of (and none of my clients, for sure) ever goes *looking* for a crisis, and no one I know of has ever been accused of "welcoming crises." (Actively looking for a *potential* crisis—called a prodrome— with the goal of averting an acute crisis down the road is another matter and a sound business practice of a well-managed company.) The goal of effective proactive crisis management is to be prepared to manage a crisis successfully if and when one occurs. No one ever advocated going out to seek a crisis in hopes of some favorable roll of the celestial dice. Second, it *is* possible to find the opportunity in a crisis and emerge a stronger and more respected company, with newer and/or stronger leadership, management, and direction. For this particular professor to suggest otherwise is a woefully transparent display of supreme business-world naïveté, ivory tower cabin fever, and pedantic academic hubris. http://www.pinyin.info/chinese/crisis.html.

2. Andrew Goldman, "Cornel West Flunks the President," *New York Times Magazine*, July 22, 2011.
3. CBS News, *Face the Nation*, August 8, 2010.
4. John M. Penrose, "The Role of Perception in Crisis Planning," *Public Relations Review* 26(2), summer 2000, pp. 155–171.
5. Ibid.
6. Ibid.

CHAPTER 4

1. Fiona Lee, Christopher Peterson, and Larissa Z. Tiedens, "Mea Culpas: Predicting Stock Prices from Organizational Attributions," *Personality and Social Psychology Bulletin* 30(12), 2004, pp. 1636–1649.
2. Ibid.

CHAPTER 5

1. Peter S. Goodman, "In Case of Emergency: What Not to Do," *New York Times*, August 21, 2010.
2. "Toyota Sinks, Ford Rises, Porsche Tops in J.D. Power Quality List," *USAToday.com*, June 17, 2010.
3. Doug Mills, "In Case of Emergency, What Not to Do," *New York Times*, August 21, 2010.
4. "Toyota Still Doesn't Get It," editorial, *New York Times*, July 24, 2010.

CHAPTER 6

1. To this day, the Tylenol terrorist has never been apprehended, and the FBI says that the case still remains "an ongoing criminal investigation." At the time of the crisis, a man named James Lewis attempted to extort $1 million from J&J to "stop the killings." Although he was caught and convicted of extortion, he was never charged with the poisonings. He was released in 1995 after having served 13 years in a federal prison. In 2009, the FBI raided Lewis's Cambridge, Massachusetts, home after it discovered "new leads" resulting from advances in scientific technology that did not exist 30 years ago, and in 2010, Lewis was forced to give a DNA sample to the FBI.
2. A detailed explanation of this crisis forecasting model, including instructions for actually plotting your potential crisis on a grid and determining your crisis impact value (how big will the bang be?) and crisis probability factor (what are the chances it actually will occur?), can be found in Steven Fink, "Crisis Forecasting," Chapter 5 in *Crisis Management: Planning for the Inevitable* (Lincoln, NE: Author's Guild Backinprint Edition, 1986, 2002). This will help you determine whether you're about to experience a crisis and what steps you need to take to deal with it.
3. For more details, see Fink, "Anatomy of a Crisis," Chapter 3 in *Crisis Management*.

CHAPTER 7

1. Chapter 10 will explain how we prevailed on this point and with this client in particular.
2. Restaurants in California and elsewhere in the country receive letter grades (A for Excellent, and so on) following regular inspections by the local county health department. And restaurants are required by law to prominently display their large, blue letter grade on placards on the outside of the establishment so that all patrons can see it.
3. Obviously, this was not the actual telephone number we used.

CHAPTER 8

1. Felicia Sonmez, "Mitt Romney: Wife Ann Drives 'a Couple of Cadillacs,'" *Washington Post*, February 24, 2012, http://www.washingtonpost.com/blogs/election-2012/post/mitt-romney-wife-ann-drives-a-couple-of-cadillacs/2012/02/24/gIQAMBz6XR_blog.html.
2. In fairness to Romney, he later said that he was misquoted in some of these gaffes and tried to correct the record, but the damage was done.
3. On July 25, 1956, the *Andrea Doria* collided with the MS *Stockholm*, a Swedish vessel, off the coast of Nantucket, Massachusetts, killing 56 passengers. The *Stockholm*, now renamed the MS *Athena*, still carries passengers.
4. As of this writing, 30 bodies were recovered, but 2 more passengers were still unaccounted for and presumed drowned, which would bring the death total to 32.
5. Jennifer Booton, "Carnival Fails Crisis 101 in Failed Costa Response," *FoxBusiness.com*, January 27, 2012.

CHAPTER 9

1. The social media landscape changes every day—nay, virtually every hour!—so trying to publish a comprehensive list of social media outlets now would be pointless, since such an inventory would be obsolete by the time this book is published.
2. I really have no specific source citation for this tongue-in-cheek list. It is readily available in various iterations on the Internet. Just search: Social Media Explained.
3. Thomas Friedman, "A Theory of Everything (Sort Of)," *New York Times,* August 13, 2011.
4. The disturbing 29-minute KONY 2012 video can be viewed at http://www.youtube.com/watch?v=Y4MnpzG5Sqc.
5. For more on this, see Jenna Wortham, "Messaging App Grows with Street Protests," *New York Times*, October 12, 2011.
6. Robert Faturechi and Andrew Blankstein, "The Game's Tweet Leaves Police Asking How to Call Foul," *Los Angeles Times*, August 16, 2011.
7. Ibid.
8. James Rainey, "Jon Fleischman's FlashReport Is Little Read but Much Feared," *Los Angeles Times*, March 13, 2012.
9. Kathleen Parker, "Haley Rumor Run Amok," reprinted in *JS Online*, the online outlet for the *Milwaukee Journal Sentinel*, April 12, 2012.
10. Ibid.
11. Ibid.
12. Maria La Ganga and Lee Romney, "Two Steps Forward," *Los Angeles Times*, January 19, 2011.

13. Michael Muskal, "Teen Tweeter 1, Kansas Governor 0," *Los Angeles Times*, November 28, 2011.
14. Ibid.
15. Ibid.
16. Ibid.
17. The question and my answer are paraphrased according to my best recollection.
18. Michael Walsh, "Siblings' Campaign to Get a Family Dog Draws 2.6 Million Likes on Facebook," *Daily News*, January 18, 2013, and on the web at http://www.nydailynews.com/news/national/siblings-bid -dog-draws-2-6m-facebook-likes-article-1.1242196.

CHAPTER 10

1. *San Diego Navy Federal Credit Union v. Cumis Insurance Society, Inc.*, 162 Cal. App. 3rd 358 (1984).
2. *Dynamic Concept, Inc. v. Truck Insurance Exchange,* 61 Cal. App. 4th 999, as cited in Barry Ostrager and Thomas Newman, eds., "Reservation of Rights," in *Handbook on Insurance Coverage Disputes*, 15th ed., Vol. 1 (Austin: Wolters Kluwer Law & Business, Aspen Publishers, 2010), p. 82.
3. Ibid., p. 83.
4. There was, nevertheless, massive litigation and numerous cross-complaints involving Jack in the Box, the Von's Supermarket chain, and several Texas cattle slaughterhouses. At one point, much time and attention was taken up with the question of whether Jack in the Box had ever apologized, and whether remorsefulness in and of itself was tantamount to saying, "I'm sorry." Full disclosure: I represented Jack in the Box during this phase of the crisis and served as a crisis management expert witness for the company during the lengthy legal proceedings.

CHAPTER 11

1. Randall Stross, "Goodbye to Windows Live (and Whatever It Meant)," *New York Times*, May 26, 2012.

CHAPTER 12

1. Emma Wheeler Wilcox, "The Winds of Fate."
2. E. Scott Reckard, "Japan, Fukushima: Tepco, Fukushima Nuclear Plant's Owner, Is Slammed for Lacking Candor," *Los Angeles Times*, March 21, 2011.
3. Ibid. The professor quoted is Najmedin Meshkati.
4. Ibid.
5. Michael J. De La Merced, "Yahoo's Chief Said to Tell Executives He Never Submitted a Resume," *New York Times*, May 10, 2012.

6. James B. Stewart, "In the Undoing of a C.E.O., a Puzzle," *New York Times*, May 18, 2012.
7. Ibid.
8. Jennifer Booton, "Is CEO Vetting Tough Enough? Yahoo Scandal Fuels Doubt," *FoxBusiness.com*, May 8, 2012.
9. Ibid.
10. Marie Szaniszlo, "Yahoo CEO Could Be Next to Go," *Boston Herald*, May 9, 2012.
11. Booton, "Is CEO Vetting Tough Enough?"
12. Ibid.
13. ABC News, June 6, 2011, http://abcnews.go.com/Politics/rep-anthony-weiner-picture/story?id=13774605#.T8_KhZlYvKE.
14. "Weiner's Fate," editorial, *Los Angeles Times*, June 8, 2011.
15. Sian Beilock, *Choke: What the Secrets of the Brain Reveal About Getting It Right When You Have To*, (New York: Free Press, 2010), p. 7.
16. Mark Dowie, "How Ford Put Two Million Fire Traps on Wheels," *Business and Society Review* 23, Fall 1977, pp. 46–55. © *Mother Jones* magazine, San Francisco.
17. Steven Fink, "Dow Corning's Moral Evasions," *New York Times*, February 16, 1992.
18. Dan Ariely, "Why We Lie," *Wall Street Journal*, May 26–27, 2012, adapted from his book, *The (Honest) Truth about Dishonesty: How We Lie to Everyone—Especially Ourselves* (New York: Harper, 2012).
19. Fiona Lee, Christopher Peterson, and Larissa Z. Tiedens, "Mea Culpas: Predicting Stock Prices from Organizational Attributions," *Personality and Social Psychology Bulletin* 30(12), 2004, pp. 1636–1649.

CHAPTER 13

1. This phrase reportedly was originally uttered during the infamous Chicago "Black Sox" sports scandal. Eight players from the Chicago White Sox were accused, and ultimately found guilty, of throwing the 1919 World Series in favor of the Cincinnati Reds. According to probably apocryphal legend, as star outfielder and local baseball hero "Shoeless" Joe Jackson emerged from the Chicago courthouse, a young boy in the crowd cried out plaintively, "Say it ain't so, Joe!" Many fans of Joe Paterno could identify with that young boy.
2. In addition to Paterno and Spanier, also out or on administrative leave were Tim Curley, the school's athletic director, and Gary Schultz, a vice president for administration, who oversaw the campus police department. Both men were initially charged with perjury (lying to a grand jury) and failure to report child abuse charges; more charges followed.
3. George Vecsey, "Far from the Coach We Knew," Sports of the Times, *New York Times*, November 10, 2011.

4. Jo Becker, "Paterno Won Sweeter Deal Even as Scandal Played Out," *New York Times,* July 14, 2012.

5. Pete Thamel and Mark Viera, "Penn State Trustees Recall Painful Decision to Fire Paterno," *New York Times*, January 18, 2012.

6. Letter from Penn State President Rodney A. Erickson to a high school senior in Penn Valley, Pennsylvania, November 22, 2011. The student had recently been sent an acceptance letter from the school. Despite Erickson's entreaty, this particular student rejected Penn State's offer and enrolled in another university in Boston.

7. Stephanie Gallman, "Despite Sandusky Scandal, Penn State Draws $208.7 Million in Donations," CNN, July 9, 2012, http://www.cnn .com/2012/07/09/us/pennsylvania-penn-state-donations/index .html?iid=article_sidebar.

8. "Report of the Special Investigative Counsel Regarding the Actions of the Pennsylvania State University Related to the Child Sexual Abuse Committed by Gerald A. Sandusky," July 12, 2012, http://thefreeh reportonpsu.com/.

9. John Ziegler, "How the Media May Have Framed Joe Paterno," http://www.johnziegler.com/editorials_details.asp?editorial=220.

10. Undated letter of Graham Spanier to "The Members of the Board of Trustees," as released by Spanier's attorneys and reported on ESPN.go.com. See http://espn.go.com/pdf/2012/0723/espn_otl_ spanierletter.pdf.

11. "Ex-PSU Prez Says He Was Never Told of Abuse," ESPN.com, July 10, 2012.

12. Jeffrey Toobin, "Former Penn State President Graham Spanier Speaks," *The New Yorker*, August 22, 2012, and at http://www.newyorker.com/ online/blogs/newsdesk/2012/08/graham-spanier-interview-on -sandusky-scandal.html.

13. Undated letter of Graham Spanier.

14. Ibid.

15. Ibid.

16. Sara Ganim, "Special Report: Penn State Counsel Cynthia Baldwin's Role before Grand Jury Could Affect Tim Curley and Gary Schultz's Perjury Case, Experts Say," *The (Harrisburg) Patriot-News*, February 2, 2012. http://www.pennlive.com/midstate/index.ssf/2012/02/ penn_state_legal_counsel_cynth.html.

17. Undated letter of Graham Spanier.

18. Statement and press release of former FBI director Louis Freeh, July 12, 2012, http://thefreehreportonpsu.com/.

19. Ibid.

20. "Report of the Special Investigative Counsel," p. 65, http://thefreeh reportonpsu.com/.

21. Corbett previously had been appointed attorney general by then-governor Tom Ridge to fill the 1995–1997 unexpired term of the previous attorney general, Earnest Preate, following Preate's indictment. Preate later pleaded guilty to a charge of mail fraud and spent a year in federal prison.
22. Dominique Debucquoy-Dodley, "Penn State Insurer Seeks to Deny Coverage," CNN, July 26, 2012, http://www.cnn.com/2012/07/25/us/pennsylvania-penn-state-insurer/index.html?eref=mrss_igoogle_cnn.
23. A Message from President Rodney Erickson, "Trial Verdict," June 23, 2012.
24. Ibid.
25. The 2009 Hawaii Bowl. The SMU Mustangs defeated the University of Nevada Wolf Pack, 45–10.
26. "SMU Ends Drought, Accepts Hawaii Bowl Invite," ESPN.go.com, December 1, 2009.
27. Pete Thamel, "N.C.A.A. Gives Penn State $60 Million Fine and Bowl Ban," New York Times, July 23, 2012.
28. As of this writing, that distinction goes to Grambling State University's late coach Eddie Robinson with the Division I record of 408, and Bobby Bowden of Florida State University with 377 and the major college record. Bowden amassed 377 wins before he retired in 2009, not counting the dozen that were stripped from *him* following an academic cheating scandal involving his Seminole players. Paterno dropped from 409 to 298 official wins.
29. In addition to Redd, defectors in 2012, and the schools that embraced them, were: receiver Justin Brown (Oklahoma), kicker Anthony Fera (Texas), backup tight end Kevin Haplea (Florida State), linebacker Khairi Fortt (Cal), offensive lineman Ryan Nowicki (Illinois), defensive tackle Jamil Pollard (Rutgers), safety Tim Buckley (NC State), and quarterback Rob Bolden (LSU). Bolden had actually made the decision to leave prior to the sanctions since he had been passed over as the Penn State starting quarterback, but now he could play immediately.
30. Bush voluntarily relinquished his Heisman Trophy.
31. David Wharton and Baxter Holmes, "Secretive NCAA Is Pulled into the Spotlight," Los Angeles Times, December 24, 2012.
32. For the record, it should be noted that Judge Frederick Shaller is a USC alumnus, by which I am implying nothing.
33. Baxter and Holmes, "Secretive NCAA Is Pulled into the Spotlight."
34. Dan Van Natta, Jr., "Penn State Faced Four Year Death Penalty," ESPN.com, July 25, 2012, http://espn.go.com/espn/otl/story/_/id/8199905/

penn-state-nittany-lions-rodney-erickson-said-school-faced-4-year
-death-penalty.

35. Jon Saraceno, "Penn State Trustee: School 'Rolled Over and Played Dead' to NCAA," *USA Today*, July 24, 2012.

36. Ibid.

37. Ibid.

38. Associated Press, "AP Source: Penn State Trustees to Meet on NCAA Sanctions," *New York Times*, July 25, 2012.

39. Pete Thamel, "N.C.A.A. Gives Penn State $60 Million Fine and Bowl Ban," *New York Times*, July 23, 2012.

40. "Penn State in Perspective," editorial, *Los Angeles Times*, July 24, 2012.

41. Ibid.

42. According to figures released in 2011 for students enrolled in 2001–2004, the most recent data available on the NCAA website. For more information, see http://fs.ncaa.org/Docs/newmedia/public/rates/index.html and http://www.gopsusports.com/sports/m-footbl/spec-rel/110211aaa.html. Additionally, forty active players on the 2010 Nittany Lion squad earned GPAs of at least 3.0, and 15 made the Dean's List with a 3.5 GPA or higher.

43. Joe Nocera, "Show Me the Money," *New York Times*, December 10, 2012.

44. The University of Chicago boasts 87 Nobel Prize winners, in Chemistry, Economic Sciences, Physics, Literature, and Peace, as of 2012, far more than any other university in the world. See http://www.uchicago.edu/about/accolades/nobel/ for names and dates and for more information.

45. Jay Berwanger died in 2002 at the age of 88, http://www.news.uchicago.edu/releases/02/020627.berwanger.shtml. Berwanger was drafted by the Philadelphia Eagles, then traded to the Chicago Bears, but ultimately decided to walk away from what would have been a lucrative football career and went into business instead.

46. Jon Greenberg, "Heisman: First Is Last in Chicago," ESPN Chicago, http://espn.go.com/chicago/ncf/story/_/page/heisman-chicago-week1/jay-berwanger.

47. Since the university had no further athletic use for its football stadium, the University of Chicago's legendary physics professor, Enrico Fermi, used a squash court facility located deep under the empty gridiron, by then called Stagg Field Stadium, to set off the world's first self-sustaining nuclear chain reaction on December 2, 1942, as part of the Manhattan Project. This controlled release of nuclear energy has been lauded as the single most important scientific event in the development of atomic power. It ultimately led to the creation of Little Boy and Fat Man, the two atomic bombs detonated over the Japanese cit-

ies of Hiroshima and Nagasaki, respectively, in 1945, which ended World War II.

48. Joe and Sue Paterno donated more than $4 million to the school's library, which was subsequently renamed in their honor, and endowed a program for undergraduates called "Paterno Fellows." Altruistic actions such as these also were highlighted during the memorial service.

49. Sidebar of notable quotes, Sport section, *Los Angeles Times*, July 24, 2012.

50. Associated Press, "Scandal Leaves Paterno's Reputation in Tatters," *New York Times,* November 19, 2011.

51. Meanwhile, USC—the team that Penn State's star running back Silas Redd defected to, and which was the preseason favorite to play for and win the national championship, and whose quarterback, Matt Barkley, was the all-but-crowned Heisman Trophy winner as the season started—finished the year with a dismal (for them) 7–5 record. Barkley never even made it to the Heisman finals.

52. The Maxwell Club also paid tribute to the 31 seniors on the football squad by awarding them the Thomas Brookshier Spirit Award for their leadership and commitment in holding the rest of the team together in this challenging season, a feat Maxwell Club president Ron Jaworski called "astonishing." And, ironically, the very first winner of the "Bear" Bryant Coach of the Year honors in 1986: Joe Paterno.

53. The suit, Commonwealth of Pennsylvania, Thomas W. Corbett, Jr., Governor, v. National Collegiate Athletic Association, may be read here: http://i.usatoday.net/sports/college/2013-01-02-pennsylvania -ncaa-lawsuit.pdf.

CHAPTER 14

1. Steven Fink, personal interview with David E. Collins, in *Crisis Management: Planning for the Inevitable* (New York: AMACOM, 1986).

2. As of this writing, the client is still in business. It sued to get the ruling overturned, and the case is wending its way through the courts.

CHAPTER 16

1. Mark Twain, "Concerning the 'Interview,'" *Microfilm Edition of Mark Twain's Literary Manuscripts Available in the Mark Twain Papers,* Vol. 25 (Berkeley: Bancroft Library, University of California, Berkeley, 2001).

2. Ellen Nakashima, Greg Miller, and Julie Tate, "U.S., Israel Developed Computer Virus to Slow Iranian Nuclear Efforts, Officials Say," *Washington Post,* June 19, 2012.

CHAPTER 17

1. Steven Fink, "Learning from Exxon: Prepare for Crisis, It's Part of Business," *New York Times*, March 4, 1989. Also available at http://www.crisismanagement.com/learning.html.
2. Ibid.

CHAPTER 18

1. Nick Wingfield and Brian Stelter, "How Netflix Lost 800,000 Members, and Good Will," *New York Times*, October 24, 2011.
2. September 19, 2011, letter from Reed Hastings to Netlfix customers.
3. Nelson D. Schwartz, "Bank of America Rethinking Debit Card Fee," *New York Times*, October 28, 2011.
4. Tara Siegel Bernard, "In Retreat, Bank of America Cancels Debit Card Fee," *New York Times*, November 1, 2011.
5. According to the Clery Center for Security on Campus website, "The Jeanne Clery Disclosure of Campus Security Police and Campus Crime Statistics Act is the landmark federal law, originally known as the Campus Security Act, that requires colleges and universities across the United States to disclose information about crime on and around their campuses. The law is tied to an institution's participation in federal student financial aid programs and it applies to most institutions of higher education both public and private. The Act is enforced by the United States Department of Education."
6. Jennifer Preston and Gardiner Harris, "Outcry Grows Fiercer After Funding Cut by Cancer Group," *New York Times*, February 2, 2012.
7. Ibid.
8. Ibid.
9. Jennifer Preston, "After Outcry, a Top Official Resigns at Komen," *New York Times*, February 7, 2012.
10. Ibid.
11. Jesse Bering, "The Prideful, Arrogant CEO of Chick-fil-A," *Slate*, August 6, 2012, http://www.slate.com/articles/health_and_science/science/2012/08/chick_fil_a_controversy_why_dan_cathy_s_statements_are_dangerous_.html.

CHAPTER 24

1. David Segal, "What They Don't Teach Law Students," *New York Times,* November 29, 2011.
2. See Steven Fink, *Sticky Fingers: Managing the Global Risk of Economic Espionage* (Dearborn, IL: Dearborn Press, 2002) for details about the case.

CHAPTER 27

1. Steven Fink, *Crisis Management: Planning for the Inevitable* (New York: AMACOM, 1986), p. 134.

2. Sian Beilock, *Choke: What the Secrets of the Brain Reveal About Getting It Right When You Have To* (New York: Free Press, 2010), p. 235.

CHAPTER 28

1. Remarks of Stephen W. Raudenbush, the Lewis-Sebring Distinguished Service Professor in Sociology and a professor at the Harris School of Public Policy Studies, at the University of Chicago's 511th convocation, June 9, 2012.

CHAPTER 29

1. Joe Sudbay, "Rupert and James Murdoch Testifying Before Parliament Face 'Uncertain Future,'" *Americablog*, July 19, 2011.

2. *Late Show with David Letterman*, October 9, 2009, copyright Worldwide Pants, Incorporated. And at: http://www.youtube.com/watch?v=BlBzi3GWWRg.

3. http://terribleapologies.com/.

CHAPTER 32

1. David Pogue, "The Year of C.E.O. Failures Explained," *New York Times,* December 15, 2011.

CHAPTER 34

1. William Shakespeare, *Julius Caesar*, Act IV, Scene 3.

2. William Shakespeare, *Henry V*, Act IV, Scene 3.

Acknowledgments

■　■　■

Many people across the country generously contributed valuable time, help, and insight to assist in the writing of this book, and some acted as sounding boards, early readers, and machete-wielding safari guides through some territory. I am grateful to all, but some deserve special recognition.

In particular, my sincere thanks to Will Bishop, Riane Kerwin, and Amanda Fink for their social media expertise, unique perspectives, and helpful suggestions contained herein. It was illuminating on many levels, and is much appreciated on all levels.

I am indebted to my good friend Steven Cohen, who provided helpful and timely sports research, perceptive analysis, and lively discussion pertaining to the Penn State crisis, and other weighty matters of the world—some of which we actually solved.

Also, special thanks to Stuart Fink, who weighed in with singular acute observational insight, which can be found in these pages. As always, he brings a unique and creative perspective to everything he does, and his contribution to this work is sincerely appreciated.

Matthew Clark Bures, of the Los Angeles law firm of Dongell, Lawrence, Finney, LLP, as well as a good friend, provided helpful research and analysis pertaining to Cumis counsel and other related subjects, and I thank him for his time and input. If these pages inadvertently mischaracterized any of his comments, the fault is mine alone.

John M. Penrose, Professor of Business Communication and Chair of the Information and Decision Systems Department in the College of Business Administration at San Diego State University, was most gracious in devoting time to track down an insightful and thought-provoking academic paper on crisis perceptions that contributed to this overall effort. I am grateful for his prompt and courteous assistance.

Two people at the University of Michigan's Stephen M. Ross School of Business also were very helpful and accommodating: Alison Davis-Blake, the Edward J. Frey Dean and Leon Festinger Collegiate Professor of Management at the school, took the time to introduce me to Corey Seeman, Director of the school's Kresge Business Administration Library, who promptly managed to track down a much-needed and hard-to-find research study. This humble Nittany Lion thanks these two stalwart Wolverines.

I am also grateful to Neda Salem of the Mark Twain Project, University of California, Berkeley, who was prompt and gracious in responding to my inquiries while I was on deadline, and then took the time to carefully proof, and correct, a quote of Mr. Clemens's so that I was true to the author's words and precise meaning.

Thanks, also, to my editor at McGraw-Hill, Knox Huston, for his guidance and continuing support of this project from its inception. I am exceedingly fortunate to have him as an ally. I am grateful, as well, for the talents and good humor of Patricia Wallenburg, my project manager on this work, who allowed nothing to stand in the way of an unrelenting deadline, except for dollar sushi night at her local eatery. Thanks, also, to my copyeditor, Alice Manning, whose assistance in turning the occasional manuscript copse into more lucid prose is much appreciated.

And finally, special and abiding thanks to my longtime agent, Alice Martell, who was an early champion of this book, and whose practiced hand, to say nothing of her patience, helped mold it in its infancy. Her wise counsel and unflagging encouragement over the years have meant so much to me and to my entire family, and it's high time she was told.

Index

About the Author

∎ ∎ ∎

Steven Fink is one of the world's foremost experts on crisis management and crisis communications, and the author of the seminal work on the subject, *Crisis Management: Planning for the Inevitable,* which remains to this day the most successful and widely-read book on the subject ever published.

As president and CEO of Lexicon Communications Corp., the nation's oldest and most experienced crisis management firm, he counsels companies and company boards in crisis management and crisis communications, strategic public relations, corporate communications, and economic espionage. In addition to working with a roster of distinguished clients over the years, he has been a strategic advisor and consultant to various branches of government, foreign and domestic, on highly sensitive crisis issues, some involving matters of national security and international diplomacy. A highly sought-after corporate speaker, he has lectured at major universities and leading business schools, and has conducted seminars, workshops and training programs for companies and industry groups throughout the world.

For more information:

StevenFink.com
CrisisManagement.com
Facebook.com/LexiconCommunications
TheCrisisBlog.tumblr.com

Printed in the USA
CPSIA information can be obtained
at www.ICGtesting.com
JSHW050220170824
68109JS00010B/132

9 781265 849696